D0699850

# Drama in Schools:
## its Theory and Practice

# Drama in Schools:
## its Theory and Practice

### JOHN ALLEN

HEINEMANN EDUCATIONAL BOOKS
LONDON

Heinemann Educational Books

LONDON EDINBURGH MELBOURNE AUCKLAND TORONTO
HONG KONG SINGAPORE KUALA LUMPUR IBADAN
NAIROBI JOHANNESBURG LUSAKA NEW DELHI
KINGSTON

**British Library Cataloguing in Publication Data**
Allen, John, b.1912
    Drama in Schools.
    1. Drama in education – England
    I. Title
    792'.07'1042          PN3171

    ISBN 0-435-18031-2

Published by
Heinemann Educational Books Ltd
48 Charles Street, London W1X 8AH
Printed and bound in Great Britain by
The Pitman Press, Bath

# Contents

# Acknowledgements

I would like to express my gratitude to Mr C. W. E. Peckett for permission to quote from his description of Dr Rouse and Cauldwell Cook at the Perse School, Cambridge; and to the director of Her Majesty's Stationery Office for permission to make extensive use of *Education Survey No. 2 – Drama* and to quote from *Music in Schools*.

My thanks also go to Longman for the extract from *Development Through Drama* by Brian Way; to Eyre Methuen Ltd for the chapter headings from *Improvisation* by John Hodgson and Ernest Richard; to Faber & Faber Ltd for the extract from *The ABC of Reading* by Ezra Pound, for two passages from *Reason and Emotion* by John Macmurray, and for the extract from David Margarshack's introduction to *On the Art of the Stage* by Constantin Stanislavsky; to Heinemann Educational Books Ltd for the extract from *The Intelligence of Feeling* by Robert Witkin; to Oxford University Press for the extract from *The Process of Education* by Jerome Bruner; to Macmillan for the extract from *The Educational Innovators* by W. A. C. Steward and W. P. McCann; to the Ontario Institute for Studies in Education for the extract from *Goals in Drama Teaching* by Richard Courtney; to Universal Edition (London) Ltd for the extract from *The Dance and the Drum* by John Paynter; to the Editor of 'Speech and Drama' for the review of Christopher Day's *Drama for Upper and Middle Schools* by P. Roberts.

# Introduction

This book is about the theory and practice of what is often called educational drama but which is more accurately termed drama in schools.

Most of us understand what is meant by practice. Theory is a more difficult word; but its derivation provides a very useful guide to its meaning. Theory is derived from the Greek word *theoria*, meaning a mental view, a contemplation, a conception of something to be done or the method of doing it. It has the same derivation as theatre, which comes from the word *theatron*, a seeing-place. The connection is a convenient one, for this book is a contemplation of the theatre, and of the drama which is the action, the *dromenon*, that takes place within a theatre, and it involves a concept of both something to be done, a dramatic action, and the method or practice of doing it, with particular relationship to the practice of drama with children and young people.

I conceived this book in the late 1960s. Drama, along with education in general, was on a rising tide. It so happened that when I came to set pen to paper, around 1975, the tide had turned, and I have written the book at a time when such drastic cuts and changes are being made to the whole structure of education that the qualified teacher of the future is likely to take up his post with a very different set of skills and attitudes than he exercises today. This state of affairs, far from being a deterrent, has spurred me on. When changes are forced upon a society, the dialectical processes are speeded up. War, drought, economic prosperity or slump will change the patterns of life and it is unlikely that things will 'ever be the same again'. Some of the changes have a kind of collective nature beyond our control; others will be the result of deliberate action. This process, in turn, will be a reflection of individual temperament. The conservative, the Virgilian mind, will lament 'the good old days'. The liberal Ovidian mind will enjoy and even encourage the metamorphosis of society. If, therefore, the not-always-very-well-informed members of the government, aided and abetted by the anonymous (and often courteous and usually much better informed) administrators in the Department of Education and Science find it necessary to impose considerable cuts in educational expenditure, not only intrinsically but by reorganizing the structure of the service, it is for the victims of the démarche to impose their own pressures on the dialectic of the situation and try to ensure that changes are for the better rather than for the worse. In short, let's make the best of a bad job.

But, there is more to this book than that. During the 1960s drama as an educational activity grew with extraordinary rapidity, and it is still, generally speaking, a good, if not a best-seller. At a time like the present, when many colleges and universities are hard put to it to recruit their numbers, drama schools still receive applications in their hundreds – and this for training in a profession which statistically offers minimal chances of artistic success or an economically stable career.[1] When I was myself surf-riding on this tide I gave a good deal of thought to explaining this strange popularity of a curious form of art; while now I feel that I must justify the survival of an educational activity that seems to have much to offer to young people while contributing only indirectly, as the pragmatists point out, to the gross national product.

I must ask to be forgiven a strain of autobiographical reference. This is not the result of an inflated ego but of a preference for discussion to dogma, for non-conformity to orthodoxy, for empiricism to absolute values. I have enjoyed a number of jobs and experiences that explain some of my attitudes or give authority to certain statements. This is particularly necessary in a book that contains some fairly forbidding chunks of theory.

I have passed my life in almost exactly equal proportions between the theatre and education. This was not the result of deliberate choice but simply the way things have gone. It is therefore the more fascinating to note the remarkable similarities between developments in education and the arts throughout the present century. I suppose that this is merely an example of the unity of culture; but the manner in which these similarities have expressed themselves is nevertheless a subject of considerable interest. Since my father was a dramatic critic, I have been accustomed to visiting the theatre from almost as far back as I can remember; and the first book on the theatre that I read, with trembling excitement, was Stanislavsky's *My Life in Art*.[2] This was my first peak in Darien when I saw opening before me a huge ocean of experience waiting to be navigated. The particular quality, I think, of Stanislavsky's great book lies in his vivid description of acting as a creative process that every actor must discover for himself. At school I had, like Polonius, been esteemed a good actor, and, as I say, I was a regular theatre-goer; but all such experiences suddenly faded in importance in the light of Stanislavsky's revelation of the theatre as what seemed then to offer a way of life. I have come across no single book on education that I have read with such a sense of revelation; but over the years I came to realize that what I have called the primary-school revolution was an attempt to realize in education what Stanislavsky had done for the theatre, to change an emphasis, to discover the very heart of the process, in one case the creative potential of the individual actor, in the other that of the learning child.

Later in life I emerged from what had been for many years almost total immersion in the theatre and modulated via the BBC into an almost completely educational environment. A close study of the twin processes of teaching and learning emphasized their close relation with the processes of artistic creation and it was not surprising that my bookshelves, already loaded with plays and books on the theatre, amplified with a small library on education, then had to accommodate everything I could find on Darwin, Marx, Freud, Jung, and their successors. An inclination to see a unity in human behaviour does, however, tend to blind one to the individual quality of the arts and sciences that compose that unity.

Psychology is a subject of perennial fascination. Does it not deal with the very substance of drama? At the same time it constitutes a threat. For over the world at large an immense amount of research is going forward and today's theory is tomorrow's heresy – or inaccuracy. The arts have an ambiguous relationship to psychology. They are said to be the expression of concepts and of emotions for which there is no adequate resolution in any other form. They are something to do with dreams and fantasy and the subconscious. If we can read the symbols perhaps we have a clue to the concepts that gave rise to the symbols. But we are defeated by the transformational quality of the artistic process. As with explanations of language itself we tend to revert to metaphor. Music pours out of Mozart, words out of Shakespeare, images out of Picasso, and we ask ourselves how we can structure education to ensure that the potential genius is not lost in the vast anonymity of a comprehensive school. I cannot wholly accept that it is a part of genius to force its way to the front willy-nilly. But herein lies the difference between education *for* art and education *through* art. I have not very much to say about the former and the little I have I shall confine to a later chapter. The rest of this book will be about the latter. For one of my convictions is that although the great creative artist is a rare and unpredictable bird, there is some kind of creative artistry in every single one of us. 'Oh I'm not musical, not imaginative, not artistic, not anything else,' says the teacher who is faced with the necessity of taking a class in music, or suggesting a subject for drama, or telling a story to young children. I do not believe a word of it. We are all creative, imaginative, artistic to a certain extent, but few of us have been given or have taken the opportunity to discover our talent. Yet of its existence I have no doubt for, as I shall try to show, artistic expression is built into our very nature.

I was fortunate in my parents. My mother was zealous for my cultural education and this enabled me to survive, only moderately scathed, an expensive and largely irrelevant education that lasted from the age of four until, at the age of nineteen, in a fit of independence, I quitted Cambridge in favour of the stage without a degree or a moment's disquiet.

In due course I became involved in education. Naturally I placed the arts, with drama as their centre, at the heart of the curriculum. And I was challenged on all sides. What is the purpose of education? What is the role of the arts in education? What is the value of educational drama? The questions came whizzing at my head. 'Stop,' I cried. 'Give me time to write a book. How do I know what I think until I've said it?' No one gave me time to write a book. I had to take the time. And here is the result, a hotch-potch of observation, theory, prejudice, and passion written in the conviction that the arts are as important as our daily bread and in the unconviction that the arts did not save a single Jew from a concentration camp. I differ from W. H. Auden, who made the comment at a time when theological attitudes were supplanting his former political attitudes and he was suppressing much of the poetry he wrote in the early 1930s. I cannot support the claims that some enthusiasts make for drama. It may not save Jews from concentration camps or reform delinquents; but I do believe that it helps the Jew to endure the concentration camp and the potential delinquent to come to terms with a society that he is rejecting because it seems to have rejected him.

It is customary in books of this kind to conclude the Introduction with a list of people who have helped the author, or contributed in some way to his text. In this case the list would be considerable and I shall pay my respects to many of my debtors as we proceed on our way. I court, however, the accusations of plagiarism; for through the very nature of my experience I have been involved with the work of a great many different people. I have neither hesitated to give them the benefit of my ideas, for what they may be worth, nor absented myself from discussion for fear of picking up theirs. There is no copyright in thought and the present premium on originality is the product of an acquisitive society that sets a price on everything. (Contrast our case with Shakespeare!) And value is a subject in which I have no interest. I was a young man when I read an essay by Emerson which included a splendid thought to the effect that we are reluctant to let our angels go, failing to realize that if we let them loose archangels may come in.[3]

Angels and archangels, the conversation is becoming very pretentious. I wish simply to make the point that I have had opportunity to follow the work of many distinguished teachers; I have sat on innumerable committees where ideas have been aired, discussed, developed, digested, disputed, rejected, ignored, defamed, delivered, and forgotten. I have had the privilege of discussion with innumerable teachers of drama; in seeking to understand their work it is impossible not to put something of oneself into it and to abstract something in return. 'I was first to' is a private arrogance that carries little weight in the market-place. The laws of copyright do not operate in a genuinely free society.

Thus there are many people with whom I worked closely throughout the 1960s and whose ideas have become so closely identified with my own that it is impossible to ascribe their provenance. Some were from the professional theatre; many more were from colleges of education. I am the more concerned to pay them the respect that is their due since much of what we created together has now been destroyed and the future position of drama in schools does not look like being anything like so extensive as it promised to be at the end of the decade.

On the theatre side I remember with gratitude Christopher Denys, who was then working at the Connaught Theatre, Worthing; Peter James of the Everyman Theatre, Liverpool; Colin George of Coventry; Keith Johnstone, one of the most gifted eccentrics I have ever known; William Gaskill whose name is still before the London public; John English of the Midlands Art Centre, Birmingham; and moving into the field of Children's theatre, Brian Way, the most resolute of champions; and Peter Slade who paved the way for so much subsequent work.

On the college side I remember gratefully Walter Ellis of Coventry, Brian Watkins of Birmingham, Michael Blake of Stockwell, Denis Dudley of Northern Counties, Winifred Hickson of Bristol . . . their names go on into the night. And I would add to them some of the County Drama Advisers for whose friendship and collaboration I shall always be grateful – Ronald James of Hampshire, Silas Harvey of Northumberland, Geoffrey Hodson of London, Hugh Lovegrove of Redbridge, Terry Jones of (then) Newham, Jack Mitchley of Essex, and one to whom I owe perhaps the biggest debt of all, Gavin Bolton of the University of Durham Institute of Education.

And finally, as many authors have done, I would like to express particular gratitude to my publisher, Edward Thompson. We have been friends for many years. He joined the firm of Heinemann at a time when I was trying to make a career in the theatre and raise a large family. His enthusiasm for books, pictures, theatres, music and the arts, education, Brighton, and good food has increased over the years. His tastes are catholic, his generosity unbounding, his judgement invaluable. He has given me the necessary incentive to write this book. He knows the kind of support, sympathy, and criticism on which an author thrives, and which is a necessary basis for all human relationships.

# 1 Children's Theatre

I first became aware of the theatre when I was very young, a result of my father's activities as a dramatic critic.

I first became aware of something specifically called children's theatre in the 1920s when my mother took me to a performance at Miss Joan Luxton's children's theatre in Endell Street. It was fresh, stylish, and colourful, rather like colour illustrations in a child's story book, and I was dimly aware that something was being undervalued and the children in the audience over-patronized.

I first became aware of a particular relationship between children's theatre and education when in the latter years of the war, as a long-suffering and intensely bored engineer-officer, I was taken by Jack Longland, then Chief Education Officer of Dorset, who lived beneath the splendid phallic giant of Cerne Abbas, to a performance of a dramatized Dr Doolittle story. It was given in a school hall in Weymouth by the West of England Children's Theatre, which was run by a gifted man of whom we should have heard more – John Morley. The performance was sensitive, a little rough in execution, and far from colourful – indeed it was singularly drab – and played on the floor of a large hall, in daylight. The actors, indicating character by the simplest sartorial means – a hat, scarf, jacket – established a close relationship with the children who were sitting on the floor in a large circle around the acting area. A member of the company was Brian Way who was subsequently to exploit that form of theatre with considerable success.

In some respects the performance was a revelation, not in the bare acting area and the absence of scenery, for I had met with plenty of that in the Group Theatre and at Unity, but in the children and their deep involvement in the performance.

On my demobilization I was invited to become responsible for a children's theatre administered by the Glyndebourne organization and found myself rubbing shoulders with Rudolf Bing, Carl Ebert, Casper Neher, John Christie, and a governing body that included the indestructible Sir Robert Mayer, Lady Violet

Bonham-Carter, and Jimmy Mallon, warden of Toynbee Hall, diminutive, white-haired, blue-eyed, and an incomparable raconteur.

There were six other children's theatres operating in the late 1940s—the Young Vic, Caryl Jenner's company at first based on the Amersham Repertory Theatre, Brian Way's Theatre Centre, Bertha Waddell's Scottish Children's Theatre, and the Osiris Players, a small group of indomitable ladies who toured Shakespeare manfully.

The progenitors of children's theatre had included the proselytizing Sir Frank Benson, though I cannot believe Tony Guthrie's story that he played Caliban on parallel bars to demonstrate his athleticism.[4] As a boy I had often met the strange stocky figure of Sir Philip Ben Greet with the mop of white hair falling on either side of his square, firm face, a man who had done much to bring Shakespeare to schools; there was Harcourt Williams's wife, Jean Stirling Mackinley; and, of course, Joan Luxton.

Of what was being done in schools by way of drama we none of us had very much idea. The evidence suggests a fair amount – but of that more anon. In the 1950s the foremost names associated with educational drama were those of Peter Slade and Brian Way; I shall have more to say about their work in the next chapter.

It is probably not unfair to claim that in the late 1940s the Young Vic and the Glyndebourne Company led the field so far as prestige was concerned. Both companies were fully professional and aimed at a high standard of performance. The Young Vic usually played commercially in theatres open to the public so that children could be accompanied by their parents. The advantages of this arrangement were somewhat offset by the financial risks involved, for unless there were large block-bookings from schools, which destroyed the spirit of parental participation, there tended to be empty seats and a shortage of children whose parents were not habitual theatre-goers.

The Glyndebourne Company usually played in school halls, giving ten performances a week at an overall fee arranged with the local education authority. In spite of the impoverishment of the country in the years immediately following the war, this fee of (usually) £450 was greatly in excess of anything that has since been paid for children's theatre. It was all part of a widespread attempt to realize certain social ideals that had been embodied in the Health and Education Acts of 1948 which helped to earn for the country the 'sobriquet' of 'the welfare state'.

All this is now the dry bones of history and one wonders what the condition of the arts would have been if a single authority had spent the 6d rate on cultural activities that it was empowered to do by the Act. I do not recall any having spent 1d: most settled for ½d which in a small borough was enough to raise £25,000.

To this practice of playing before captive audiences there was great opposition. It did not, does not seem appropriate that children should come to a theatrical performance in coach-loads and crocodiles, though in the circumstances it was difficult to suggest alternatives. School halls were usually quite unsatisfactory for our performances with their unraked floor, inadequate blackout, minute and inaccessible stage without space in the wings, and a lighting-set that involved putting a nail in the fuse – admirable for elevating a headmaster at morning assembly or governors on speech-day but useless for actors. In theatre or hall it was difficult to discourage teachers from pacing up and down the aisles before the performance telling children to behave themselves, not to rush for the lavatories in the interval, and once, before a morning performance of *She Stoops To Conquer*, not to laugh. It was this kind of episode that created a profound suspicion throughout the theatrical profession of all teachers. But this was before the days of T.I.E. (Theatre-in-Education).

Another problem lay in the nature of the Glyndebourne organization. The most enthusiastic member of the hierarchy was Audrey Christie (Mildmay) who died in 1950 at an unhappily early age. John Christie, an extraordinary eccentric living wholly out of his time, commented on our performances only when the scenery, which was always infernally heavy, since our designer saw fit to express his talent over areas of painted canvas, was not as substantial as that used on the stage of the Glyndebourne Opera House. Rudolf Bing, a professional iceberg but a warm and generous colleague, never gave the slightest indication that he might have been more interested in his many other responsibilities, the Edinburgh Festival; the Company-of-Four at the Lyric Theatre, Hammersmith; or the opera itself: but the absence of all reference to our work in his autobiography[5] suggests that his interest did not run deep. When in 1951 he left the Glyndebourne organization to become director of the Metropolitan Opera in New York I knew that the moment had come when I too must look for another job.

The lessons were clear:

It is a waste of effort to try to mount large sets of theatrically conceived scenery on the narrow platforms that go for stages in many schools, submitting the flats to Procrustean extensions and contractions and the lighting system to a load it was never designed to carry.

George Devine, then director of the Young Vic, used to question whether it was wise in any case to give theatrical performances anywhere but in theatres where they properly belong. I would not go as far as this; but I think that a theatrical performance requires its own and proper atmosphere which is compounded of a balance between an adequate playing-space, a good actor-audience relationship in physical terms with well-arranged seating and good site-lines, provision for the necessary lighting, reasonable acoustics, and a general atmosphere that does not wholly dispel the possibility of creating an atmosphere of recreated reality.

Most of all I was aware of the questionable policy of giving special productions for children and young people of such plays as Bernard Shaw's *Androcles and the Lion*, James Bridie's *Tobias and the Angel*, and John Drinkwater's *Abraham Lincoln*, which are distinguished examples of the adult repertory. When people asked me what was special about producing plays for children I used to rationalize vaguely about colour and clarity but I could never honestly claim that I produced them very differently for children than I would have done for adult audiences. The possibility of using far simpler methods of staging and a more physically expressive, even acrobatic style of acting was growing in my mind but this would have necessitated developing a wholly new concept of children's theatre. Although I respected, I had no wish to emulate the work of Brian Way, Caryl Jenner, and my other friends, while the demands of a growing family did not provide opportunity for much dreaming. Audrey Christie was dead; Rudolf Bing had gone to the Metropolitan Opera, I went to the BBC. The work of developing children's theatre was left to others.

During the 1950s the cause of children's theatre was sustained almost wholly by Brian Way and Caryl Jenner. There were other companies, mostly of a semi-amateur kind, and groups of teachers who took plays to schools; but most of this work was local and sporadic. Caryl Jenner must have been a thorn in the flesh of the administrators in the Department of Education and Science, for she continually boasted about making such a nuisance of herself, constantly writing to the Minister and insisting that public money should be given to children's theatre. She was undeniably a resolute, irrepressible, and highly determined lady who would not be fobbed off by bureaucratic discouragement. She had spent the 1950s touring the country with what she called a 'mobile theatre', giving performances mostly for younger children, and was now about to assume tenancy of the Arts Theatre, London.[6]

It was not only the Department of Education and Science which was harrassed by Miss Jenner's insistencies: the officers of the Arts Council of Great Britain were also fully apprised of Caryl's importunities and had themselves a large file of her letters. There was, however, a short period around 1964 when the cause of children's theatre was nearly espoused by the Gulbenkian Foundation, but after a period of negotiation, it was agreed that responsibility properly lay with the Arts Council who thereupon followed precedent by forming a Committee of Enquiry. This committee met monthly for the next two years and finally issued a report that included a number of recommendations. It was a long hard stint representing a splendid effort on the part of such distinguished actresses as Constance Cummings and Joan Plowright and a tribute to the dogged chairmanship of Hugh Willett.[7]

The recommendations resulted in the Arts Council assuming a wider interest in and responsibility for professional children's theatre, and including in its future budgets a sum of money for this purpose. This resulted in a number of regional theatres establishing small companies to play to children, often with additional support from the local authorities. The pattern of this work was established by Gordon Vallins who in 1965 was given a subsidy of £1,500 by the Coventry Education Authority, to establish a team of actors attached to the Belgrade Theatre to take theatrical performances to schools in the city. Gordon Vallins called his work Theatre-in-Education. The name has stuck.[8]

The other recommendations have not got us very far. A children's theatre has not been built in London: the Young Vic which was loosely conceived for this purpose has developed a different policy; nor has there taken place the expected proliferation of plays for children in spite of a competition run by the *Guardian* newspaper with generous prizes.

Nevertheless, the Enquiry, though failing to produce immediate or spectacular results, had longer-term effects of considerable significance and of an unexpected nature. For the availability of subsidy led to a rapid increase in the number of companies playing to children. A few were independent; most were related to a parent company, normally a subsidized regional theatre. Here arose an interesting difference in practice. Some groups were independent of, though administratively attached to the parent company while other artistic directors created the group that was to visit schools from the company itself. Colin George at Sheffield was so convinced of the value of his actors playing to children that he worked in this manner until the administrative problems became too great.

A slightly cynical attitude, however, arose in certain quarters. It was widely said that some directors expressed an interest in children's theatre because it increased their subsidy, put them in favour with the Arts Council, or simply went some way to increase future adult audiences. I used to react rather strongly to these suggestions, unnecessarily so perhaps; for the work of the best companies was so interesting that a bit of cynical tittle-tattle, whether founded on truth or not, was predictable and largely irrelevant. We do not live in a condition of cloistered virtue.

What was surprising was the nature of the work that developed. Gordon Vallins established the practice of taking his company into schools, even into classrooms, and working with the children. But he had been trained as a teacher and knew what he was about. Christopher Denys, then director of the Bristol Old Vic, wrote short plays on such subjects as the great train robbery and the Vietnam war and had them played in school halls by a small company wearing jerseys and jeans. Emphasis was placed as much on the discussions that followed the performance as on the performance itself. This tended to be retrogressive since the actors were much less good at discussing contemporary moral and political issues with children than at acting. There was one session when the boys at Westminster School were deeply resentful at being asked to join in a discussion after an admirable performance of *U.S.* by the touring group of the Royal Shakespeare Company.

Gradually it became evident that what was needed was a company of actors who had been trained as or had had experience as teachers. Some of the drama schools had been turning out teachers with the appropriate skills. At the Rose Bruford College, for instance, would-be actors and teachers took the same integrated three-year course; and a very large number of colleges of education were offering main courses in drama which gave students considerable experience of drama within their Certificate of Education course. Suddenly the expression 'actor-teacher' was in the air, and I remember the exasperation with which Caryl Jenner rejected this hybrid creature.

Yet they were not to be rejected so simply, for over the next few years – I am speaking of the early 1970s – students from the drama schools and the colleges of education increasingly constituted the personnel of these companies. But with greater confidence as teachers than as actors they brought a strong educational emphasis to all they did. As artists, and artists of the theatre, they were not on the whole significant, and their work tended increasingly to be of the kind that one can only describe as documentary. For they would take a subject, be it Women's Lib or the history of Trade Unionism in Coventry, and develop it with selected groups of children involving them most skilfully in the performance as actors. Fine, so far as it went; but the crucial questions were hard to answer. Were these actor-teachers doing anything that experienced teachers were incapable of doing themselves? Was payment for these companies the responsibility of the local education authorities or the Arts Council of Great Britain? Were the actor–teachers to be members of Equity or the N.U.T.? What was the proper relationship between a visiting company and the teachers in a school? Was the art of the theatre itself being undersold?

I will leave these questions as I asked them in the early 1970s and attempt an answer in the latter pages of this book. For the answers depend on what is happening in schools and the possible relationship between teachers and actors in an experience that will be more than just a diversion for the children. The matter is an important one; for Theatre-in-Education is now accepted as an independent genre, and the claims of some of its adherents that its main purpose is to act as a ginger-group to unenterprising teachers and to introduce children and young people to the theatre in a manner appropriate to their interests, is a somewhat patronizing attitude. The movement has developed in a way none of us foresaw ten years ago by identifying some of its activities with 'the fringe'.

Meanwhile former concepts of children's theatre have tended to go by the board. Some companies claim to do both T.I.E. and children's theatre. But there is a significant distinction. It is possibly quite easy to define T.I.E. or to describe what it is about. Less so children's theatre. For the moment we begin to use such unavoidable terms as 'theatre arts', the imagination, fantasy, we lose our sense of direction. Some people regret the need for this distinction. So do I. But when I go to a performance by a T.I.E. team I see a very different kind of work from when I go to the Unicorn Theatre in London. I do not press this distinction: it is there for all to see. And I think that an analysis of the situation requires what the American Joseph Jefferson said of the art of acting, a warm heart and a cool head.

Who is not ambivalent about administration? Committees are a necessary part of the structure of a complex democratic society. But who, having done his stint as a committee member, does not look back with a certain horror at the hours spent contributing by his very presence to the great grey Parkinsonian platitude of the 'Standing Committee'. I therefore record out of respect for those who served their turn that the Arts Council's committee which gave its attention to the problems of children's theatre was originally known as the Young People's Theatre Panel. In the years immediately following its report there were two other organizations significant in the field – the British Children's Theatre Association, run by the egregious and indefatigable Gerald Tyler, and the children's theatre section of the Conference of Regional Theatres in which the late-lamented Caryl Jenner played a leading role. These two organizations were eventually compounded into the National Council of Theatre for Young People which still exists. But the existence of the NCTYP has not deterred others from creating the Drama and Theatre Education Council, the Standing Conference of Young People's Theatre, the National Association for Teachers of Drama and several others of whose interrelationship not even their members are always clear. There is opportunity for ribaldry but necessity for discretion.

In many parts of Europe people are becoming aware that higher standards of living on the material level are not being matched by improvements in the basic quality of life. The arts are not supported as widely as they used to be and the level of culture, of which the arts are a part, is receding. Among those who have considered the situation there is some agreement that the answer is not simply to subsidize the arts to the limit of a country's capabilities, for that in fact is to subsidize an élite and augment existing cultural class distinctions. What is required, it is argued, is a vigorous programme of general cultural education that must begin in school and continue throughout adult life. In this respect the educational policies of the United Kingdom are something of a model to the rest of Europe. Theatre-in-Education companies and the new concepts of drama and theatre that find one form of expression in a sudden diversification of new organizations demonstrate the extent to which drama is shaking itself free of prejudices that have limited its practice to the production of three-act West End comedies in village halls. One can now expect to meet drama of a sort in the streets of our big cities, in the basements of big department stores, in most of the school halls of the country. And the same thing is happening throughout Europe. But we must beware; for as a result of typical Gallic imperialism this striking example of Anglo-Saxon individuality is referred to as 'animation culturelle' – and it is hardly necessary to emphasize that 'animation' must be pronounced in French for it signifies something quite different to the English animation. And what it signifies is that new kind of drama to which I have already referred and which is largely the subject of this book.

Nevertheless there is a very serious difficulty to be faced. Readers of this book who consider themselves to be progressive thinkers may detect a reactionary note in my description of certain current dramatic practices. This is because I believe that the theatre – and I include drama – is an art, and an art has certain laws and disciplines. Art is concerned with a certain area of human experience and sensibility. And however much the artist or the teacher of genius may seek to extend the expressive frontiers of that art it is necessary from time to time for him to remind himself of the basic nature of the art he is using. Quite simply: if I appear to undervalue the way in which drama is used to help personal development, to establish social attitudes, to provide experience in various democratic procedures such as decision-making it is not because I do not realize the importance of these educational experiences but simply because they become the less significant if, as so often happens, the nature of the expressive form that is being used to provide these experiences is itself minimized or devalued. I do not accept the dichotomy between drama and theatre that vexes so many people for I believe them to be aspects of the same experience and I shall have a good deal to say about the subject. Nor in fact is there a distinction of any more than degree between the process of acting, whether a text or an improvisation, and the giving of a performance in front of an audience. But if the theatre can play a useful part in the creation of a cultural democracy, and in so doing increase the perceptiveness and the numbers of its own audiences, what more can we want? Theatre-in-Education in the broadest sense of the term may be a useful form of 'animation culturelle' and help to develop a cultural democracy; but it is still a difficult and demanding art.

# 2 Drama in Schools: the Historical Background

Drama in schools is nothing new. Elizabethan grammar-school education involved a considerable amount of acting in Greek and Latin as well as in English, and we know that in the seventeenth and eighteenth centuries both the schools of Port Royal as well as those of the Jesuits used drama as a means of containing the spirit of humanism which could not be left to the laity and the devil. This has all been admirably chronicled by Philip Coggin[9] and other historians of the theatre.[10] There are records of a Miss Burrows having used dramatic methods in a small country school in Sussex in the early years of the century and there may have been others among the educational innovators of recent times. A Board of Education Report for 1898 speaks approvingly of the beneficial effect of practical drama on 'vitalizing language and quickening the perceptive and expressive faculties of boyhood', an encouragement that is repeated with greater emphasis in the Board's *Handbook for Teachers in Elementary Schools* (1929) and even more so in the report of an adult education committee on *Drama in Adult Education* (1934). But the immediate progenitor of the use of educational drama both for its own sake and as a method of teaching English was undoubtedly Cauldwell Cook whose work at the Perse School, Cambridge, he himself describes in his fascinating though rambling book, *The Play Way*.[11]

Recently I made some enquiries about the work of Mr Cook and was given a description of both him and his headmaster by Mr C. W. E. Peckett, then headmaster of a Shrewsbury School, who had been a pupil at the Perse.[12] I have abbreviated Mr Peckett's account.

'The appointment of Cook and the encouragement of his methods was the work of his Headmaster, Mr W. H. D. Rouse, who was appointed to the school in 1902. Dr Rouse was rather rotund and walked with a stiff-legged waddle, both his hands in his jacket pockets with the thumbs sticking out in front. He abominated motor-cars and rode to school on a bicycle, occasionally on a horse. His contribution to education was to adapt Latin and Greek to the direct method which two of his masters invented for teaching French. He had no study at the school. His office was his classroom where he had a writing desk at which he appeared to do the minimum amount of administration and which was lined with classical texts of all descriptions. He took all three years of the sixth together for reading. We read a vast quantity of Latin and Greek, all from plain texts, all unseen, and all without translating. Once we read the whole of the *Odyssey* one term and the *Aeneid* the next. The first book I ever read in Greek was *Agamemnon*. I understood about half of it but I have been haunted by its grandeur ever since!' Mr Peckett, who at one time while he was at the Perse acted Antony to Marius Goring's Cleopatra, says that he had no idea he was being taught in an unusual way. 'I thought that all boys wrote poetry as a matter of course. I supposed that in all schools, when you read Shakespeare, you went out on a stage and acted him. I thought all boys at Grammar Schools were taught to speak Latin and Greek and I was amazed when I entered the University to find that the professors of Latin and Greek could not speak half so much of the languages as I could.'

Cook joined the staff of the school in 1911. He was twenty-five and had just completed his B.A. He proceeded to develop the teaching of English in the manner that Rouse taught the classics. He wrote *The Play Way* in 1913 after only two years in the school which probably accounts for some of the naivety, dogmatism and repetitiousness of the book. Mr Peckett went to the school in 1920 by which time Cook had abandoned some of what Peckett calls 'his more fanciful practices', and Dr Rouse had abandoned the reformatory zeal with which he had propagated his methods in his early years. Nevertheless I think that his influence on the young Cook must have been considerable.

'Cook was a tall man and always dressed immaculately in a ginger or light-faun knicker-bocker suit. His wavy hair was well-brushed and there was a suspicion of perfume about him. He believed that children learn best when they are so deeply involved as to become creative and that, since all children are creative before shades of the prison-house begin to close in, it is best to make as much use as possible of this faculty while there is time. He had a tremendous power of invoking enthusiasm and frankly abandoned all traditional methods of instruction and discipline. He replaced conventional teaching with self-motivated activity. Instead of making boys acquainted with the masters of literature he got them to express whatever it was in literature that they themselves enjoyed. Visitors were surprised at the noise and the apparent disorder in the classroom and to find boys sitting on the desks and dangling their legs. But they were also astonished at the quality of the imaginative writing and of discussion on anything to do with English.

The Mummery, where Cook did most of his work, was made out of two rooms knocked into one in a large Victorian house next to the school. The floor of one room was higher than the other, thus making a stage with fitted curtains and an arras. There was simple but adequate lighting. The stage had a small apron with steps leading down into the auditorium which was the lower room and was equipped with benches . . . . 'When we read Shakespeare we used plain texts small enough not to cramp our actions. Cook did little by way of production. What is more important he never stopped us to explain a word or a phrase. Most problems of meaning were solved through our acting: the rest he explained to us in the discussion after each act.'[13]

When Dr Rouse retired in 1928 all these activities were ended by the new headmaster who told Cook to 'stop all this nonsense'. He resigned and soon after died 'of an excess of alcohol and a broken heart . . .' Cook was aware that what he was doing was new: Rouse that what he was doing was right.'

It was disappointing though perhaps not unexpected to find that subsequent visitors to the school, although they were highly appreciative of the original nature of Cook's methods, commented that they had had no effect whatsoever on other admirable teachers of English on the staff. Even in our own day I have heard headmasters complain that drama teachers talk a lot about integration and collaboration but do very little.

In 1949 the Ministry of Education, into which the Board of Education had been transformed, set up a small working party to consider all aspects of theatre and drama in education. This was the brain-child of Sir John Maud (now Lord Redcliffe-Maud), the permanent secretary of the Ministry, who was concerned about the possibility of professional children's theatre and drama in schools pulling in different directions. His fears were well founded. It was in 1951, I think, that a memorable conference on drama in education took place at the Bonnington Hotel, Southampton Row, London. Here, for the first time, I realized, with an alarm I can recall to this day, the depth of the split that was developing between concepts of drama in schools and the theatre arts. It is a distinction that I still am quite unable to accept, though it appears to exist wherever in the English-speaking world new attitudes to drama in schools have taken root. In those days the protagonist of the educational view of drama was the eloquent and articulate Peter Slade, whose book *Child Drama*[14] was largely responsible for rationalizing this unfortunate dichotomy. There is evidence that today a more synoptic attitude prevails.

The Ministry's working party met twenty-seven times over

the next two years and agreed upon a report that was never published despite the fact that it was a most interesting document and one that foreshadows many of the developments that have since taken place. The influence of Peter Slade is clear in its emphasis on the value of the whole concept of child drama as a kind of loosely organized dramatic play that children devise when left to themselves. A certain weakness lay in its failure adequately to define the role of the teacher though it does emphasize that he must have proper regard for the nature of the art he is handling and help the children to find expressive forms appropriate to their particular stage of development.

I have described how during the 1950s the role of children's theatre was sustained by Brian Way and Caryl Jenner. At the same time there was a good deal of activity among county drama advisers, many of whom had been appointed in the first instance as a result of grants from the Carnegie United Kingdom Trust. The local authorities were now in the process of appointing them to their advisory staff or Inspectorate. This in fact was a move of considerable significance since it meant that instead of being confined to working wholly in further and adult education, they could now assume responsibility for drama in schools, thereby helping the sequential importance of the subject over the whole of the curriculum.[15]

It is a little unfortunate that the administrative independence of local authorities has permitted a most patchwork development of local advisers and Inspectors. In some authorities drama and the arts are well served, in others poorly; but I think there can be no doubt that where drama advisers have been appointed the improvement in work has been notable.

During the 1960s, it was extremely encouraging to be able to follow the rapid growth in numbers and individual authority of the advisers and their professional organization, NADA, the National Association of Drama Advisers. Their role is likely to become increasingly important during the next few years, for with the far-reaching reorganization of teacher training and the changes in the nature of the qualification that will inevitably result, it will be for the drama advisers to provide continuity of teaching methods, stability of staff, and a developing theory. The B.Ed. degree, to which teachers are increasingly committed, may eventually produce a well-qualified profession but it does not provide for the flexibility of approach we enjoyed in the 1960s that led to some notable successes.

It was during the 1950s that the drama advisers established their authority, and during the 1960s that the colleges of

education came to the fore. Administratively their recent history
has been idiosyncratic. In the early years of the decade they
were bidden to extend their two-year training of teachers to
three years. Then in response to a sudden bulge in the birth-
rate, which I find hard to believe was as unpredictable as the
urgency of the operation suggested, they were required almost
overnight to double in size, and an enormous amount of new
building took place. They then faced the introduction of the
B.Ed. degree which necessitated in many cases the introduction
of a fourth year of training. In 1972 the James Report[16] proposed
a profound reorganization of the whole structure of teacher
training and this has become confused with a Draconian cut-
back in numbers following predictions of a considerable drop in
the birth-rate. Again I must express the view that although the
sexual mores of the British people are their own affair, the birth
of a child is recorded, and it is a mere five years later that he
goes to school. I have a feeling that the apparently erratic rise
and fall in the birth-rate is interpreted by politicians according to
their own Byzantine policies.

The colleges of education have plenty to bewail; but the
restructuring proposed by Lord James's Committee was a result
of apparent weaknesses in their professional responsibilities.
Great though in some ways yet another upheaval in teacher
training was to be regretted, there is little doubt that it was
necessary. When in 1961 I had occasion before visiting Australia
to examine the course-structure of the colleges in detail I was
astonished by what I found. This structure was of a tripartite
nature. The education departments were responsibile for teaching (or otherwise imparting) the theory, practice, history,
philosophy, and psychology of education. There were subject
departments responsible for main courses where students pursued various disciplines 'at their own level'; and the most
important area of all, that of curriculum study, which involved
the actual teaching of the various subjects, was usually a
twilight one in which responsibility was divided between the
education and the subject departments. Nothing was better
calculated to raise profound intellectual pother in the Principal's
study than the simple question – who teaches the students to
teach children to read and write, the English or education
lecturers? It may have needed the authority of Lord James's
Committee to suggest an alternative structure of teacher training, but the weaknesses of the system were apparent.

This lack of relationship between the study and teaching of a
subject was in many cases the direct result of university regula-

tions under which for curriculum purposes the colleges oper-
ated. And London University, to name an outstanding example
of obduracy, always refused to examine the professional or
curriculum aspect of any subject. The emphasis was upon
subject, not upon the process of education. Staff of colleges
were therefore not only encouraged but in many cases obliged
to teach subjects without any regard for the relevance of what
they taught in the classroom. Many colleges therefore offered
main courses in drama which included the study of drama for its
own sake; but many of these departments evolved into mini-
amateur dramatic societies in which the staff were jealous of
their independence and viewed possible collaboration with
other subjects, even where there was educational justification,
as a betrayal of their integrity.

Nevertheless in many cases the sheer professional honesty of
the lecturers prevailed and one could observe throughout the
decade how the more sensitive were becoming increasingly
aware of the need for a better understanding of the nature of
drama in schools both in its theory and practice. This was the
background to the Drama Survey for which I was responsible,[17]
to the Dartington Hall-Schools Council Research project into the
arts and the adolescent,[18] and even the recent Schools Council
Drama project.[19] All the parties concerned made increasing use
of their professional organizations, particularly the drama
advisers through NADA and the college of education lecturers
through the drama section of the Association of Teachers in
Colleges and Departments of Education (ATCDE).[20] There were
numerous courses and conferences and a rapidly growing
determination to improve the quality of the work.

It was quality and understanding that were needed. Over the
country a good deal of drama was taking place in schools, some
of it of an impressive kind. Malcolm Ross, who was responsible
for the Dartington project, painted a somewhat gloomier picture
and emphasized the enormous amount of uncertainty and
incompetence that was to be found. But we were none of us
complacent and drama advisers, college lecturers, teachers, and
local Inspectors were always ready to pool their prejudices. The
work had far to go but there were some distinguished teachers
coming to the fore and in many cases it is their contribution that
I am unable to separate from my own thinking. I have paid my
individual respects to them in the Introduction. Nevertheless I
hope that by the time this book appears in print the dust will
have settled.

With numbers of students in training being drastically

reduced and the whole structure of training reorganized, far too much thought and energy has been diverted away from the children in the classroom and concentrated on problems of administration.

Nevertheless advances have been made, and under certain circumstances all may be for the good if not the better or best. But I am not yet looking to the future. The past still occupies us, and I want now to consider the recent changes in the school curriculum that created a situation where drama could find living room. The drama advisers would not have been appointed, the number of main courses in drama would not have increased impressively during the 1960s if a congenial atmosphere had not existed in many schools and an attitude to curriculum innovation that permitted and in some cases encouraged the intrusion of what, until less than 100 years ago, was held to be the least reputable or respectable of the arts.

# 3 The Primary-School Revolution

The importance of what some people have called 'the primary-school revolution' first became apparent when as a parent I used to take my children daily to a nursery school in Harlesden. The classrooms were like artists' studios, not in there being works of art stacked round the walls, but in the evident preparations for extensive creative activity: boards of pastry, lumps of clay, pots of paint and piles of paper on the tables, buckets of water and tubs of sand on the floor. One's fingers itched to be doing as one stood in the doorway of these marvellous classrooms, so totally different from traditional ideas of what goes on in an infant school.

It was then that I realized fully that the names of the great educational reformers from Erasmus to A. S. Neil by way of Locke, Rousseau, Froebel, and Pestalozzi, stood not for abstract ideas but the kind of education that was conceived by the headmistress of this school in common with many other splendid heads scattered over the country, an education that was joyful, creative, and thoroughly practical.

The kind of education represented by this school was not wholly unique to this country; but it is largely true that educational innovation has always enjoyed a particularly congenial reception in England, owing to the decentralization of the system. Private and independent schools, the grammar and so-called public schools, and in particular the church schools boasted a long history before the government began to play a significant part in education. The legislative and executive roles of government have traditionally maintained a certain independence. The following injunction from the Preface to the Board of Education's *Handbook of Suggestions for the Consideration of Teachers and Others Concerned with the Work of Public Elementary Schools* (1905) is an example of the attitude to which I am referring. (I like particularly the expression 'suggestions for consideration' in the title. The author was no authoritarian.)

The only uniformity of practice that the Board of Education desires to see in the teaching of Public Elementary Schools is that each teacher shall think for himself, and work out for himself such methods of teaching as may use his powers to the best advantage and be best suited to the particular needs and conditions of the school. Uniformity in details of practice (except in the mere routine of schools management) is not desirable even if it were attainable.[21]

I do not want to drive a wedge between traditional and progressive educational practice any deeper than exists at the moment; but one can argue, I think, that John Locke would not have felt it necessary to urge with considerable eloquence the need for humane and tolerant attitudes to children if such values had prevailed in his time.[22] Rousseau's revolutionary ideas were clearly motivated by current practice; and the same can be said for all the ensuing educational thinkers and reformers up to and including the splendid A. S. Neil.

The term 'primary-school revolution' is not altogether a fair one. The educational practice which it implies has been growing for the last 150 years. For me, however, it has a precise meaning, that in the course of the present century the ideas of the innovators and of the so-called progressive schools have been largely taken over by the maintained schools. (By this phrase I mean generally the local authority schools that provide a bulk of the country's educational system.) This may seem to some people to be an extravagant claim. But I make it on the basis of personal experience. For a number of years I had a boy at a well-known progressive school. Although the education he was given was unexceptionable, the methods were no more 'progressive' than those I found habitually pertaining in the maintained schools of the area and these, compared with primary schools in other parts of the country, were not generally speaking of outstanding quality.

How did this revolution come about, this absorption of progressive ideas by the monolithic state system of education? It was the achievement, I think, of a group of HM Inspectors, supported by the relevant administrators in the Department. I met some of them when I ran a children's theatre; others in the course of the Ministry's drama working party. The success they achieved was evident to anyone who visited many of the remarkable primary schools in such Authorities as Bristol, Oxfordshire, and the West Riding of Yorkshire. Significant leadership came from Christian Schiller, a man to whom any idea of leadership was abhorrent but who saw clearly and steadfastly just what primary education could be. He was a thin, erect figure with wispy hair and long fingers and he was capable (like an Old Testament prophet) of thunderous rhetoric in support of the needs of children; yet conversely, when he took seminars, he could sit for an hour in silence forcing everyone else to reveal the disorder of their ideas, before modestly presenting the clarity of his own. The first indication of his far-reaching convictions is to be found in the primary-school section of the Hadow Report (1931), where it is stated that '(the school) lays special stress on individual discovery, on first-hand experience, and on opportunities for creative work. It insists that knowledge does not fall into neatly separate compartments and that work and play are not opposite but complementary.'[23]

The revolution was encouraged in the famous Plowden Report, properly described as *Children and their Primary Schools* (1963)[24] and if it makes a good deal more interesting reading than other important reports of the 1960s it is because the situation in primary schools was more encouraging than was to be found in secondary or tertiary education.

The Plowden Report in fact committed itself to support for the progressive movement in education. It includes an interesting and unexpected discussion on the implications for education of the genetic structure of the individual, of the interaction between a school and its environment, relationships between parents, teachers, and children; a qualitative survey establishing that about 1 per cent of the primary schools in the country were of outstanding quality and 9 per cent in a second category of high excellence. There was a useful analysis of streaming and close scrutiny of what came to be known as 'educational priority areas' to which Lady Plowden's name became attached.

What do we mean by the terms 'progressive' schools, 'good' schools, and the 'primary-school revolution'? What kind of education do they signify?

Let me begin by saying a few words about the kind of schools the educational reformers were opposing. What about this? The indefatigable James Boswell extorts the following proposal from the great Dr Johnson: '. . . children, being not reasonable, can be governed only by fear. To impress this fear, is therefore one of the first duties of those who have the care of children'. Elsewhere he speaks of the virtues of giving a child a 'cuff'.[25] John Wesley was of a similar persuasion. His reply to Rousseau's *Emile* was to urge an even stricter control of children. 'Break their wills that you may save their souls,' he wrote. Hannah More, writing in the same period, considered that the object of education was to counteract the innate depravity of children:

> Is it not a fundamental error to consider children as innocent beings, whose little weaknesses may perhaps want some education, rather than as beings who bring into the world a corrupt nature and evil disposition which it should be the great end of education to rectify?

The authors of the book from whom I have taken this quotation[26] continue:

> The whole approach to education as exemplified by these writers has been called the classical-Christian and it rests on four main propositions: that the child is evil by nature; that childhood is a preparation for adult life; that education must therefore consist of that which will be useful to the child when he becomes a man; and that the value of the subjects taught is not in their intrinsic interest but in the moral and intellectual training they give.

I would myself add another, which is the dependence of education on the acquisition of knowledge rather than the development of understanding, a value which has survived from Renaissance interpretations of the Greek philosophers insofar as they were thought to have laid emphasis on abstract knowledge as the highest attainment of a human being.

Some of these propositions, however wrong-headed many may believe them to be, are not to be brushed aside too readily. They still provide the ethos on which a large part of our secondary education is based. Progressive methods in primary-school education and modest reforms in secondary-school methods – and I am not referring to major administrative changes such as the movement towards total comprehensive secondary education – have been bitterly and consistently attacked in a series of Black Papers,[27] the most recent of which begins with the categorical pronouncement, 'Children are not naturally good', and includes the astonishing statement that 'The results of permissive education can be seen all round us, in the growth of anarchy.' The insidious aspect of this sentence lies, of course, in the implied identity of permissive with informal or progressive education. One is a social attitude, the other an educational technique.

This argument is a very dangerous one to have initiated in a context that does not permit more than a passing reference to the two points of view. But it is crucial for any teacher who is going to 'teach' drama or the arts to know where he stands with regards to the great educational issues. Mr Neville Bennett of

Lancaster University in his fascinating *Teaching Styles and Pupils Progress*,[28] reports the results of research into the success of formal and progressive methods of education. The book has drawn attention to the great number of variables involved in making a true assessment of educational success. The author emphasizes the extremely important point that it is a great deal more difficult to teach by progressive methods than by more formal ones and failures tend to be the more conspicuous. It is, nevertheless, depressing that with such names as Erasmus, Roger Ascham, John Locke, Jean-Jacques Rousseau, Johann Pestalozzi, Robert Owen, Friedrich Foebel, John Dewey, Maria Montessori, and A. S. Neil behind us, progressive education should still be on the defensive. Primary schools are for the most part a delight to visit. Indeed, many headteachers claim with pride, almost before all else, that theirs is a happy school. It was therefore with something of a shock that one read in the *Times Educational Supplement* (24 June 1977) in a comment on British schools by a student of comparative education in Europe that 'English primary-school headteachers speak unashamedly of their intention to create a happy school, a notion that would strike most of their continental counterparts as embarrassing, if not obscene: on the continent happiness is not an educational concept'. One might reply to Herr Gruber that no more it is in England, but many teachers consider it to be prerequisite to successful learning.

What other qualities does one detect in a successful school? There will be a kind of vitality in the atmosphere; and at the same time a sense of relaxation, even though all the children may appear to be extremely busy. The children will be polite and articulate when they speak to you, though by polite I do not refer so much to good manners in the formal sense as an attitude of respect which they show to visitors, the staff, and each other. You can sometimes tell quality of work by sound. There may be a lot of noise but there is a difference between the noise produced by children eagerly discussing their work and simply 'playing-up' or playing about. There may be laughter in the air which is much to be encouraged. And if there are sounds of music, real music, children singing, not piano-bashing, that is a bonus. You can tell a great deal about the quality of work from the visual appearance of the school. I am not referring to well-painted walls and reproductions of the masters in the corridors, but, displays of bric-a-brac, of a large variety of objects that are intended to evoke visual discrimination, excitement, and sensibility. I recall a marvellous display at Corsham

College of Art of hexagonal objects. Never have I seen nuts and bolts look more visually exciting; and at a school in Witney, Oxfordshire, there was a display of many objects and fabrics all in tones of white, cream, and light grey; and in another school a collection of all manner of natural objects the children had picked up on their way to school. In such places one is likely to see many pictures and models done by the children themselves. Each classroom will be 'exciting' in the arrangement of the desks or the manner in which the work of the children is displayed; and each will reflect the attitude of the teacher and the work she has elicited from the children.

I have put the word 'exciting' in inverted commas because although it is a word that is bleached from over-use it is one that describes the effect of a lively environment on a visitor. One is excited, as one is meant to be, by the stimuli provided by the school, as it is evident that the children have been excited to acts of creativity. I visited a school in Oxfordshire where a group of children spent three weeks working out the weight of the local church. What, as a result, they had not discovered about its design and construction was hardly worth knowing. There was a school near Kelmscott where the children were experts in the work of William Morris, where they gathered wool from hedges on their way to school, teased it, spun it, wove it, and fashioned it into fabric. One was surprised at nothing the children might achieve. And this was the result of inspired collaboration between the local HM Inspector, himself an artist of distinction, the local authority Inspector, and the teachers themselves who would come of an evening from all over the county to drink and talk in the Lamb Inn, Burford.[29]

In those days the primary schools of Bristol were much influenced by the work of Marion Parry, herself a member of the Plowden Committee. I have never seen more consistently lively, inventive, and imaginative play than went on in these schools. Hatshops, museums, bakeries, ships at sea – in every school one visited the children were extending the range of their experience by means of a kind of imaginative though structured play which was both an end in itself and the very basic material from which the experienced teacher draws educational experience, and encourages the growth of the intelligence. In all such schools it was hardly necessary to enquire about children's reading and writing. The latter was well advanced because they had something to write about; and suddenly I realized that whether or not the children would be artists when they grew up, this was the beginning of the creative process which is relevant to and a part of the growing process of every one of us.

This process was clearly exemplified in a school I visited in the borough of Newham. The drama adviser and I reached the school at about 9.00 a.m. The teachers were all busy in their classrooms, laying out empty cereal packets, balls of string, trusses of straw, scissors, paste, and such a collection of materials as made the fingers itch to be a child oneself. All very similar to the classrooms where my own children first went to school. The floor of the hall was covered with piles of sheets of paper with pots of paint and brushes placed beside them. At 9.15 the children burst into hall and classrooms – the verb is deliberate – they came running in with a kind of explosive enthusiasm to be doing, and in a few moments a scene of immense activity was taking place. At 10 o'clock things simmered down and it seemed to me that if the paintings, models, collages, sculptures, dances, and music-making that had taken place during that three-quarters of an hour had been assembled the whole philosophy of primary-school education would have been vindicated. Children are naturally evil? Creativity leading to anarchy . . .?

I have described general work in primary schools; I shall discuss drama in particular in a later chapter. But I should like at this point to say something about the atmosphere in which good creative work can take place; for a school does not exist to create beautiful works of child art: what matters is the growth of the child and his ability to express himself in a variety of media. I am emphasizing the point that has been made repeatedly by so many educational thinkers that the child must be helped to discover his potential by means of a varied process of exploration and discovery. I am expressing a vote of no-confidence in learning by rote and the memorizing of rules. I recall a class of eight-year-olds who could not understand the difference between × and +. The desperate young teacher set them a series of × sums (2×3, 4×4 etc.) and went round the class shrilling 'These are times sums, children, times sums'. (And that's about all the sign means to me and that's why I am disgusted at a lack of numeracy that I share with thousands of my fellows who have been similarly non-educated.) I am concerned with helping children to observe and respond to the environment and to develop in themselves the various skills and resources necessary for a human being to deal with those sometimes violent responses. It is a vote of no-confidence in the liturgical chanting of tables as a preliminary to the study of mathematics; in copying bowls of fruit on sheets of white paper with hard

pencils as an introduction to the world of art; in the association
of history with the dates of battles and the political results of the
ensuing treaties; in formal grammar and compositions with
margins to the left of the page an inch wide and the date in the
top right-hand corner as a contribution to the art of writing. It is
a protest against the imposition of discipline by use of the stick
instead of the cultivation of self-discipline by use of the arts. I
am concerned with the school where the children walk into
assembly individually, not in crocodiles, where on Speech Day
the children themselves report on the year's work to their
parents.

'Children are not naturally good.' I do not know the meaning
of this extraordinary statement, coming from a headteacher and
a Member of Parliament. I am tempted to pose against it a far
more encouraging proposition made by Sir Kenneth Clark
during a BBC brains trust in the course of the Second World War
– 'the left does not believe in original sin'. Nor do I. Nor in
original ignorance nor original ill-discipline, nor the original sins
that the children in our schools are heir to, whatever the first
chapter of Genesis may have said. The Jehovah of the Black
Papers sits in eternal judgement, a cane in his strong right hand,
a grammar book in his left. He is mounted on a dais and backed
by a blackboard and in front of him are the rows of young
people of whom society's greatest expectation is a contribution
to the gross national product. And I regret to say that he begins
the day with a so-called act of Christian worship, in the course
of which the pupils, in their serried ranks, are quite likely to sing
a hymn beginning, 'Onward Christian soldiers, marching as to
war . . . .' God has never been more mocked.

My years of school visiting depressed me to this extent, that I
felt the gifts required of a successful teacher to be almost beyond
human reach. He must be profoundly versed in the very nature
of the subject he is teaching; but he should be almost equally
aware of the nature of 'adjacent' and related subjects. He must
be profoundly versed in the nature of human nature. He must
know how we learn, not in a generalized way as a species, but
individually, idiosyncratically, indeterminately. He must be an
alert and rigorous member of society, for it is from his environment and his society that a child draws his interest, his
excitement, his motivation to thought and action. A teacher is
therefore involved in a constant subtly changing relationship
between the values he attaches to the subject he is teaching and
their relevance to the contemporary world. The pedagogic
methods of the medieval schoolmen, or the Elizabethan rhetori-

cians, or the eighteenth-century Jesuits, however admirable in themselves, might make less than sense in a London comprehensive school of the late twentieth century. Perhaps the greatest skill required of a teacher lies in realizing his opportunity for brain-washing his children, for influencing their attitudes, creating their prejudices. There is a celebrated American book that advocates the importance of teachers teaching children the art of 'crap-detecting'.[30] Fine – if you are sure of what is crap.

I have already drawn attention to Mr Neville Bennett's interesting *Teaching Styles and Pupil Progress*. The enormous interest that this modest piece of research has created is presumably due to its questioning of classroom methods. Mr Bennett makes a simple distinction between formal and informal teachers, and suggests that neither group can claim consistent educational success clearly attributable to his or her methods. One hardly needed research to establish so obvious a point. In the last few pages I have tended to relate formal methods of education with repression and informal methods with activity. Both attitudes are generally unrealistic. I do not care for traditional formal methods since I do not think they provide the opportunity for that individual creative response which is the very way in which a child sharpens awareness and develops intelligence. I do not care for over-formal methods of direction in the theatre because I think they tend to repress the creative contribution of the actor. But it is clear that the good formal teacher, like the good formal director, can produce excellent results under certain circumstances. I was once taught history by a most formal teacher who illuminated every subject he touched upon; but the great G. M. Trevelyan gave Cambridge history undergradutes the most intolerably boring lectures it has ever been my misfortune to attend. You know where you are with the formal teacher. The route is charted and if you follow it you arrive at a destination. The road may not have been very interesting, but it will not have landed you at midnight in a swamp.

So-called formal teachers must nevertheless carry a good deal of responsibility for the kiss of death they have imposed on many a subject that is a testament to life and beauty. Is it not still common to find young people for whom Shakespeare was 'killed' at school? We tend to shrug our shoulders and pass it off with 'Too bad, that is the way with schools'. But is it not quite intolerable that this should happen? That the dramatist most capable of eliciting pleasure, vitality, excitement, emotion, and an enormous range of responses, should have been made a dead letter by sheer bad teaching?

One might have expected things to be better in a university. But the other day I met a most able young music student whose study of *Dido and Aeneas*, in the course of taking a music degree at Oxford, had entirely destroyed her pleasure in this simple, fresh, and sublimely beautiful work. This will not do.

And, if one may revert to the other end of the teacher spectrum, what child can be interested in reading who is brought up on the exploits of Janet and John and their dog Fluff? No wonder that children of secondary-school age find it difficult to read the school text, but have no difficulty getting through the latest Harold Robbins in paperback. It was years ago that I read an admirable book by a New Zealand teacher[31] who begs for the use of realistic values in children's reading books. 'Does nobody ever say "don't",' she asks, 'do Janet and John never fall down and dirty their clothes and run crying to their mother?' Leila Berg carries on the campaign in England.[32]

The informal teacher, to be successful, must be a very good teacher. His task is a far harder one than that of the formal teacher. He or she is encouraging the children to work individually, at their own rate, even at their own subject. He encourages them to ask questions, to risk failure, to follow paths that are often wholly uncharted, certainly by himself. It is understandable, though nonetheless tragic, that low prevailing standards of literacy and numeracy should have been attributed to the maleficent results of informal methods of education. I fear that many teachers using such progressive methods must face the fact that their classrooms are sometimes chaotic and standards of achievement low. I remember once engaging an actor who turned out to have a voice that could not be heard beyond the sixth row of the stalls. When I tackled him about this he replied that I was not to worry since he worked psychologically. There is a curious and disturbing heresy around that psychological integrity can be accepted as an excuse for incompetent performance. This is really to cherish the soul at the community's expense.

Insofar as teachers of art and drama have recently tended to identify themselves with progressive rather than formal methods in the classroom, they must accept some of the prevailing criticism. The chaos that I have often seen in a drama class exasperates me quite as much as the boredom that so often prevails in the formal classroom. One of my purposes in writing this book is to discuss a problem of the greatest concern for all teachers and drama teachers in particular – how and why one should teach any art in a school and what is the relationship, in so doing, between educational and artistic considerations. For one can teach drama formally just as easily as mathematics and the results are no less disastrous. What we must ensure is that the process of learning is a personal and active process, not simply the absorption of an inherited body of knowledge.

I must, therefore, try to discuss the question of methods in greater detail and I think the best way of doing so is by considering the nature of children and the relevance of different educational methods to various stages of growth.

# 4 The Development of Children

New methods of teaching in primary schools have brought the arts into the centre of the curriculum and placed considerable emphasis on creativity. This view is very much in vogue at the present time, an ironical thought seeing that the 1970s are unlikely to go down in history as a creative decade. It is a word with no very precise meaning in psychology and one that in art we associate with self-expression. It has such personal connotations that before it can be fully discussed it must be placed in a proper relationship to the child and the individual to whom it applies. I hope that readers who are impatient to reach the subject of this book, drama in schools, will not skip this chapter, since it provides what in current jargon is called the conceptual framework for much of what I have to say later.

I would like, therefore, to consider some of the stages in a child's growth. If we breathe air that is as fresh as pollution permits and eat food that is not wholly drawn from the innards of a can, certain genetic, biological, and chemical activities will operate and we shall grow more or less 'all of a piece'. This organic growth will include that of the nervous and endocrine (glandular) systems and the functioning of a variety of structures and circuits that come into operation naturally and do not require education.

Nevertheless there are other essential aspects of growth that do not happen altogether naturally and depend on the child's first great teacher, his mother. Ernst Cassirer has written vividly of the chaos of sensory and retinal impressions with which a baby has to contend.[33] His education begins on the day of his birth, and although much of it is natural and organic, he will depend on his mother to create the environment and the relationships in which the processes of learning will function most readily. A child's preliminary investigations are of a world that is bounded by his mother's lap, his cot, his pram, his play-pen; and he carries out this exploration and discovery by means of touch and taste, as well as vision, using his finger-tips, toes and lips with almost equal frequency.

The Plowden Report includes a useful description of the growth of the brain and its developing responsibilities for control of the nervous system. Within the cerebral cortex there are primary areas of activity which mature in regular sequence; first the motor area, then the sensual, the visual, the auditory, while the areas of development spread out, as it were, from the primary areas into the surrounding areas of association. Within the motor and sensual areas there is strict localization of function to a certain part of the body and these areas of the brain develop in the same sequence as the part of the body to which they are related. This developing sensibility is of considerable importance in view of the emphasis that is placed in infant schools on offering children a wide range of sensory and motor experience.

While this complex neurological process is developing, the child's brain is acquiring the capacity to perceive and recognize his mother, food, toys, and to remember what he has seen and perceived, reconstructing in the brain what the various senses have perceived of the outside world. This capacity to achieve an inner construction of outer reality is what we know as intelligence and our capacity to handle this mass of impressions, perceptions, memories, and to make creative relationships between them is what we know as thinking.

We have noted that the neurologist speaks of the sequential maturation of primary areas of the brain – first the motor area, then the sensual (or sensory). A child will handle a biscuit (the motor process) and by means of various tactile tests he will realize what it is for (the sensory process) so that the next time he is offered one, instead of driving his mother frantic by experimenting with its tactile possibilities – it crumbles delightfully as we all know – he will recall its nature and eat it, and proud mother will rightly say how intelligent he is. The assimilation of experience is a never-ending process that continues throughout life adding constantly to our inner sense of reality, and a continually growing intelligence. Those who wish to study this important subject in detail will turn to the educational psychologists of whom Jean Piaget is perhaps the most penetrating.[34]

Very closely related to the sensory-motor process is the capacity for imitation. A child fairly early in life acquires the ability to imitate something that he has seen done in front of him. The imitation may at first be hesitant and unclear, for the process of associating what he sees with his own actions is not at first wholly confidential. But there comes a moment when he will imitate an action and laugh at his own skill; then, having imitated the action, he will remember it, and assimilate it into his own behavioural patterns. Piaget refers to this as 'deferred imitation' and it explains a large part of the educational process; for the action of deferred imitation is the assimilation of that action into a child's mental structure. One of my grandsons recently provided me with a very neat example of how a child uses the symbolic action. He was at an age when he could barely speak and was playing with plasticine. Suddenly he cupped a lump in his hands and put it to his lips as though he were drinking. Then he laughed. He was beginning to internalize, realize, and so to think; but with the aid of an additional developing faculty. The ability to remember an action (and to assimilate it) postulates a capacity to visualize that action. This visualization marks the ability of a child to internalize a vision and then, by natural extension, to project it. This is why drawing and painting are crucial activities for children and why they must be considered as part of the thinking process. Images enable us to think broadly, with free association, and less cognitively than language does.

I need hardly add that this development does not take place in isolation: the total growth of a child involves the constant enrichment of his mental structures, of his feelings about himself and his environment. And there are occasions when this environment impinges on him on a manner he finds difficult to accept. Then he is obliged to shift his mental attitudes to accommodate the new experience. Sometimes he cannot or will not do so and the result is frustration, tantrums, and the kind of behaviour we condemn as egocentric.

One of the extraordinary qualities of the mind lies in its ability not only to assimilate, reject, adjust, and remember, but to make meaningful cross-references, a process that is known as synaesthesia, and one that is very closely related to the faculty of imagination. It is our efficiency in these respects that dictates our intelligence or our capacity for creative thought.

Nevertheless there are parts of our nervous system which appear to be ineducable. Our instincts produce a more or less stereotyped response to stimulus, and these emotions, sometimes described as primary or primitive, are associated with the old brain. Among them are to be included fear, anger, hunger, joy, sex, and animosity. We share them with animals. When fully aroused they are very difficult to control and lead to stereotyped behaviour such as running away from things we are frightened of, clenching our fists when we are angry, going red in the face, and sweating. Charles Darwin wrote a fascinating book in which he describes many stereotyped forms in which emotion is expressed by man and animals.[35]

The old brain, which lies at the back of the head and at the top of the spine, is a survival of man in a primitive stage of evolution. The development of the brain is a product of a remarkable outburst of creative evolution when man's forbears descended from the trees, or came out of the water, and began to walk on two legs. They then proceeded to develop a brain of such extraordinary complexity that it turned man into a species wholly different from the animals yet subject to tensions and contradictions that he has not yet been able remotely to resolve. I mention this in passing not because I want to enter a world that is far outside my competence but in order to explain why the process of education is a good deal more complex than some of our administrators seem to suppose. We are even in some doubt as to the real nature of the creature we are educating.

There are, among the many contradictions to which man is heir, and which are built into his being, several of the greatest significance for education. One is the nature of his emotional or effective life; another is the control of, or relationships between his emotions and his cognitive faculties; yet another is the further relationship between his capacity for feeling and thought and the control of his body which provide the outward form of his behaviour. Teachers and educationalists, committed to responsibility for the development of young people but no more knowledgeable about the nature of the being they are educating than philosophers, psychologists, and the many who have no such commitment, have simply plunged in and taught where teaching seemed possible. What I have in mind is the concept of education which consists of cramming into a child's head a prescribed body of fact and fiction which he then has to regurgitate at various stages of his education in similarly pre-scribed and predictable forms. It has become the cry of more enlightened teachers that they must educate the whole man but this is just what they have discovered to be an exceedingly difficult thing to do. We are not even very clear what we mean by the phrase. Even the French have considered the advisability of setting fire to Descartes!

By the time a child is about two years old, sometimes a little earlier, sometimes a little later, the biological growth of the brain, and in particular the cerebral cortex, is on the way to full development and he is then ready to proceed with the acquisi-tion of language, a process I can only describe as miraculous. I

say 'proceed' rather than 'begin' out of respect for the theory
that there are certain genetic structures in the brain which
establish the possibility of speech in the new-born child.[36] It is
an astonishing process. One day a child may be hardly articulate, the next he will produce a stream of garbled chatter, then a
long and related sequence of words, structured in some way,
unintelligible perhaps to adults, but perfectly clear to any sibling
who will act as translator.

One must pause a moment to recognize the extraordinary
achievement of language. I have called it miraculous. Anyone
who wants to analyse the nature of this achievement should
turn to Professor Richard Wilson's penetrating but far too
little-known book *The Miraculous Birth of Language*.[37] Speech,
operating through a structure of sounds that constitute language, most of which have as few as 20 or 30 phonemes at their
disposal, can represent a series of actions far more quickly than
they can take place in reality. It enables thought to range over
limitless areas of time and place. It can analyse minutely and
generalize widely. It frees the human mind from the slow
experiential quality of the sensory-motor process and makes
possible the whole liberating quality of thought.

Differing aspects of a child's acquisition of language are to
be found in Jean Piaget's *Language and Thought of a Child*[38]
which discusses the egocentric nature of a child's speech, and
Vygotsky's *Language and Thought*,[39] which emphasizes the
importance of social relationships in the development of speech.
Although there is a certain divergence of opinion in these two
books, I do not think we need come down on either side. There
is a kind of organic individual growth, egocentric as Piaget calls
it, though even this is the product of interactions between a
child and his environment; and there is an even more obvious,
even if more significant, interaction between a child and those
immediately around him constituting the society in which he
must grow up. Vygotsky's view is predictably the more social
one of a Soviet citizen.

At the infant-school age, roughly four or five to six or seven,
children move to the stage at which, with a developing brain,
they are able to apprehend certain abstract concepts such as
space, time, movement, number, and measurement with visual
perception as usually the most dominant of his faculties, a
survival, presumably, of those days when man lived in trees
and depended on sight, more than his other faculties, for
survival. Piaget has conducted fascinating experiments with
children into conservation – the concept that a lump of clay can

take many different shapes and retain its original volume; seriation – the grouping of objects according to size or classification; space and measurement, time and speed, and even moral concepts.

Of extraordinary fascination is a child's capacity for fantasy, and how difficult to understand! Yet we all have this ability to dream; and for some curious reason we associate children with a dream life peopled with witches, ogres, and hobgoblins, when it is evident that it takes a child most of his time to deal with the world as it is, not as he has inherited it from adults. I am questioning not the existence of fantasy but the use we make of it in education.

How long does it take a child to know the world? Do we ever know it? I have a kind of rational grasp of evolution but to me it is really a mixture of miracle, myth, and metaphor. I accept the wind. But what gives it power? Is it surprising that the child sees natural phenomena in human terms? Until a certain stage of intellectual development a child has neither the will nor the capacity to apply to 'natural' phenomena that rationalizing process that pretends we understand them. It is far more natural that he should seem to humanize them, giving the sun a face, explaining the wind as a giant who blows great blasts of breath, or frost as the demonic work of an icy figure who roams the land on winter nights. These anthropomorphic concepts fit snugly into our still basically anthropomorphic minds. And in educating our children we indulge them with these fantasies one minute and send them to encyclopaedias the next.

Yet how understandable the attitude of children towards natural phenomena when we read of people who believed that the throwing of various parts of a sacrificial victim into the sky led to the creation of the sun, the moon, and even to creation itself. A child's fantasy has much in common with the mythopoeic thinking of primitive peoples and that is why he enjoys myth, legend, and fairy stories as well as stories about the real world. Science and fiction are not wholly in opposition.

I emphasize the point because it is widely claimed that children are imaginative. Either this is a misconception or we are misusing the word imagination. My own inclination is to follow Coleridge.[40] 'Repeated meditations led me first to suspect . . . that fancy and imagination were two distinct and widely different faculties. . . . Fancy is indeed no other than a mode of memory emancipated from the order of time and space'; whereas imagination is 'the living power and prime agent of all human perception and a repetition in the human mind of the eternal act of creation'. Childish fantasy is therefore a product of his capacity for image-making (image-ining), confused with his inability to distinguish conceptually between dream and reality or one aspect of reality and another.

We live within a natural environment that we can do little about and a society that is of our own contriving. We oscillate between these two opposing influences, the one shaping the other. This is a process that many psychologists have emphasized, especially in the Soviet Union. In so far as it is a problem of assimilation, this relation is formative of the individual; but when the whole mental structure of the mind has to be shifted to accommodate a new view of society we are involved in the formulation of those social attitudes that dictate whether an adult is going to be a conforming member of society, a social misfit, a rebel, or a mixture of them all. One of the recent Messiahs of educational theory is the American professor Jerome Bruner. It is interesting to find that in his five articles of faith[41] he lays particular emphasis on the child's relationship to society:

> All education proceeds by the participation of the child in the social consciousness of the race, a process that begins at birth and includes every aspect of his consciousness and his behaviour. The school is a form of community in which is concentrated everything that helps a child to share in the inherited resources of the race. Education, therefore, is a process of living and not a preparation for future living. The centre of a child's education is not any single subject but the child's own social activities. Consciousness is essentially motor and tends to project itself in action.

And as we grow our consciousness becomes enriched, and as it becomes enriched, we grow.

By the age of about eleven a normal child has achieved a certain freedom of thought by means of a complex symbolic code that is expressed in terms of speech (language) and visual symbols (the written word and mathematics). He has learnt to differentiate between the apparent chaos of his private images and the world of natural reality. He is becoming increasingly aware of his own identity and is able to differentiate one aspect of the environment from another, apprehending certain principles of cause and effect in natural phenomena. Thus he is master of a certain kind of intellectual freedom which provides him with the ability to abstract ideas from any immediate, subjective or sensory-motor experience and to become articulate through the ability to use appropriate symbolic forms. In current jargon he is literate, numerate, and orate. His education in the formal sense is complete.

I have spoken of a young person's increasing ability to handle various symbols or symbolic forms. The concept of the symbol is so widely discussed and has become so popular a piece of educational apparatus that I must say a word on the subject. The concept of the symbol was not discovered by Susanne Langer although it was certainly she who popularized it. Ernest Cassirer's majestic but rather inscrutable three volumes, *The Philosophy of Symbolic Form*[42] was the source of Miss Langer's extremely readable *Philosophy in a New Key*,[43] and a number of other distinguished books have been written on the subject in recent years. The process of symbolization begins with the child's capacity for internalized vision which we discussed earlier in this chapter. But in the very process of internalization the vision is transformed into our own expressive forms. The face, the house, the scene the child paints has little relationship to external reality; but it has a great deal to do with his own internal sense of reality. This is why we say that the externalized expression is symbolic because it is the person's own statement of how he has transformed a response to reality into his own conceptual form. Symbolic action is not only a basic and crucial aspect of the whole growing and educational process but it is particularly relevant to the use of artistic forms and so to the whole nature of education itself.

The crucial part of the process is the transforming of reality into the appropriate symbol that both embodies and expresses the initial concept or image, and this process, so simple to describe and so difficult to achieve, accounts for every example of creative work from a child's simplest scribbles to the Choral Symphony or the ceiling of the Sistine Chapel; and much of the sweat and the agony of artistic creation, and of much classroom work as well, derives from the difficulty of creating a satisfactory symbol, an acceptable artistic form.

One of the many marginal notes I made on my first reading of Susanne Langer's book was 'How do we teach the use of symbols to children?' I think the answer is very simple: we don't. What we do teach them, if teaching is a permissible word, are the arts of painting, writing, sculpture, music, drama, and, before all else, the art of speech. We provide them with opportunities to carry out these activities and help them to acquire the appropriate skills and techniques so that they learn to embody their feelings and thoughts in a satisfying form of expression. To a large extent the symbolic element looks after itself. It was the evolutionary creation of our forebears. Though we no longer need to create symbolic forms we must learn how to use them.

In terms of personal development this ability to handle the symbol is an aspect of human behaviour, of our capacity to think. It is the means of transforming an intensely complex neuro-electrical process that is largely centred in the cerebral cortex into forms of action. Therefore the responsibility of the teacher, if I may be allowed to repeat myself, is to provide his young people with opportunities for a wide range of behavioural forms and activities. It is indeed the responsibility of teachers to educate the whole child, but this cannot be done by any single specialist, however liberal his view of the art, discipline or subject he is teaching. But to establish a relationship between thought and feeling, with every kind of priority given to the former, to the virtual exclusion of the child's affective life, seems to me to ask for the very aggressive and illiberal behaviour that the traditionalists associate with progressive and affective methods. It is not without significance that one finds that the Drama Survey quotes a notable variety of headteachers, who, although they did not claim to be specialists in the arts, were quick to attribute freedom from disciplinary troubles in their school to the attention they gave to the arts. If we began to look on the arts more as a form of behaviour and less as an unapproachable domain for genius, we should resolve a large number of seemingly inexplicable problems.

Discipline is so often equated with methods of education I discussed in the last chapter and concepts of emotion I am discussing in this, that I would like to quote what the philosopher John Macmurray has to say on the subject.[44]

> The idea (of discipline) has come to be associated with punishment so that when we want to talk big about punishment we call it disciplinary action. Originally the word simply means 'training', and the fact that through the development of history it has come to stand for the use of force and fear and severity is surely a symptom of a sinister degradation in our concept of education. There is something far wrong when the normal association of discipline in our minds is with efforts of repression and chastisement . . . It is the desire for power itself that we have to get rid of . . . The discipline of the mind takes the form of forcing or persuading other people to believe what we think they ought to believe. It is a denial of freedom of thought . . . The other side of this tendency is the suppression of the emotional life. The discipline of the emotions is still thought of as a necessary repression of spontaneity in order to secure conformity to established habits of feeling . . . The very idea of a training in

freedom of feeling and the expression of feeling has hardly begun to find a place in our ideals. Consequently the relation between mind and body is broken and we have to have a separate discipline of the body to supplement the discipline of the mind . . . The result is that the divorce of mind and body reveals itself in a system of education which seeks to discipline the mind and the body separately and not together in the natural intimacy of their relations.

Feeling is the motivation of all gesture. If we are hungry, circumstances permitting, we get something to eat. If we are uncomfortable in our chair we shift our position. If we are hot we remove a jacket or open a window. These are stereotyped responses to instinctual or sensory stimuli requiring more or less unreflective action. I say unreflective because there will be individual mannerisms in the way we carry out these actions; but they are not what we might call primarily creative. These are actions that require some considered behaviour, that we perform in order to manipulate, in however trivial a manner, some aspect of the environment. The motivation for such actions is affective. We are stimulated to take action by an emotion. But human nature, over the tens of thousands of years of its more recent development, has discovered that in all its vast complexity it has had to create a variety of behavioural forms to satisfy its infinite affective needs, and many of these emotional forms are what we know as art.

One of the most irritating and unhelpful distinctions that has recently been made in art criticism, and one that educationists have been quick to accept, is that between the so-called fine arts – the abstract arts of music, painting, and sculpture – and the useful arts. It was a distinction first made in the eighteenth century when canons af art criticism were being laid down on classical models. A painting is held to be an expression of feeling and so as an academic discipline it is rejected by supporters of the thought-and-knowledge schools of educationalists, while for the very same reason it is accepted by critics as an example of fine art. A table, however, is rejected on both counts. It is useful and so basically devoid of feeling and therefore unacceptable as an example of fine art; and being devoid of cognitive content it is unacceptable academically. One group of teachers in a school will therefore encourage the young people to carve wood into 'interesting' shapes, responsive to feelings about the wood; another will teach them to make joints and mouldings. And it is usually the 'bright' who are thought to have sensibilities and so are encouraged as artists and the duds who are confined to the carpenter's bench making bookcases. But both lots are vulnerable to rejection by the academics. There is no valid distinction between useful and fine art; only between sensually living work and dead, repetitive reproduction.

In his adolescence a young person is able to think in an abstract and conceptual manner; but he is also subject to considerable emotional stress. It is not that he begins to feel for the first time, since we have seen that human behaviour from birth is motivated by a series of sensory-affective stimuli. What genetic and biological changes do occur in adolescence to make his capacity to feel as strong as his capacity to think is very difficult to say since psychologists are reticent and uncertain in their analysis of emotion. I suggest that the development of sexuality has something to do with it; his increasingly complex relations with society are another. But perhaps the explanation lies in the simple fact that a young person has acquired the capacity to think. I do not find it possible to accept the Platonic view that man is capable of a kind of pure or abstract thought, for thinking is not a pure, isolated activity of the cerebral cortex but a complex process of symbolization and association by means of which we try to give meaning to otherwise meaningless experience or visceral upheavals. But these upheavals, these endless and related moments of perceptual excitement are themselves emotional. Thinking gives rise to feeling and feeling to thought. Neither thinking nor emotion are 'states' or 'conditions' of experience, but aspects of a continuing process. Coleridge says that deep thinking is attainable only by a man of deep feeling.

Nothing is more obstructive to a proper concept of education than the Platonic idea of pure knowledge and the fear of emotion. We teach children to think not by giving them lessons in thinking – though even this has been attempted by certain rash psychologists – but by giving them experiences in which thought is required. We do not need to teach children to feel since they have vigorous emotional lives whatever we may do about it; but we do need to give them opportunities to express their feelings. *Dido and Aeneas* was killed for the Oxford undergraduate, as so much Shakespeare is killed for others, by an exaggerated emphasis on a cognitive and analytical approach to the work at the expense of its 'feeling-form'. This is not to say that critical analysis is to be abhorred. No one needs to understand the meaning of *Hamlet*, and every detail of the text, more than the actor. But the meaning is not merely cognitive: it is also expressed in the actor's emotional, physical, and vocal projection of the role.

I am, of course, aware that all this is to sail in deep waters. But

I take encouragement from a writer of distinction like John Macmurray from whom I have quoted generously. We are dealing with a subject that perplexed the Greeks and has tormented philosophers and psychologists ever since. Are we right in giving such priority to the senses? Plato seems to agree. In *Phaedo* he says, 'The simple sensations which reach the mind through the body are given to men at birth but the reaction of these sensations to behaviour is acquired slowly and with difficulty by education and long experience.' This line of thought relates the growth of knowledge to social education and does little to support romantic concepts of the eternal verities. It is an emphatic statement in support of empirical knowledge.

But in the same work there is a statement that has dominated European philosophy and the philosophy of education ever since. Plato says, 'I decided to take refuge from the confusion of the senses in argument and by argument to determine the truth of reality.[45] By argument, by means of 'pure thought' says Bertrand Russell in a rubric on Plato.[46] But I wonder whether there is such a thing as 'pure thought' and, if there is, whether it has not been to the detriment of education below university level. Sensory stimulation involves the re-ordering of experience in a way that lies at the heart of both art and learning. It is the process that Piaget analyses in many of his books.

It is in adolescence, even late adolescence, that a young person is most susceptible to emotional experience. He falls in love, turns against society, develops passions and prejudices. It seems to me almost incredible that we should have dismissed the 'education' of our emotions as irrelevant to the education of our brains. Young people are aggressive and destructive *because*, say the Black Papers, they have had an education of a progressive kind. Because they haven't is the likelier answer.

# 5 Creativity

This is a now fashionable word, coined by teachers and educationalists to mark a new and positive approach to the arts in education. Writing can consist of exercises in composing letters applying for jobs, dictation to test spelling, or any application of pen to paper that has a practical purpose. Creative writing is an exercise of the imagination. To act Hamlet is assuredly a creative process; but creative drama is usually thought to consist of writing one's own play, or improvising a situation. It is not a term I find particularly acceptable, but it is a useful one and helps to point the relationship of the arts to traditional form (which tends to be considered uncreative). There is no need to speak of creative art since art teachers have long since freed visual expression from the tyranny of the 2H pencil, the study of perspective, and the collection of still life; but music education suffers from an excessive preoccupation with notation and the five-line stave, and dancing with despotic techniques.

So where do we begin? With the sources of action, of behaviour, I think, with motivation. We are in an area of conflicting theories. I would like to think we can agree that action begins with some kind of reflex–stimulus. That at least is how I shall refer to it. A sensory response to a stimulus. A message is flashed to the brain. It is decoded and transmitted back in the form of action or activity. Sometimes it may be to settle more comfortably in our chair. Sometimes it may be a stimulus that sets in motion a long and curious process that ends in the composition of *War and Peace*. But it is consciousness projected into action. This is why sense–perception is something very much more profound than sensation.

Creativity has nothing to do with making artefacts. A creative housewife will arrange some flowers in a vase and so place that vase in a room that flowers, vase, and room are all enhanced. Creativity can transform the trivial into the significant, the commonplace into something unique. One is always interested to know what the creative person is thinking or doing with his life. It is stimulating to be in his company. I do not mean by this

40

that he is necessarily extroverted in his behaviour: he may achieve his transformations in an introverted manner. He may be a poor conversationalist, hesitant in society, unable to express himself clearly on paper. But he will find a way of exteriorizing his inner life. He will be alive, not dead.

We saw in the previous chapter how a nervous (mental) adjustment to external stimuli constitutes a part of the learning process. This constant adjustment, building up an inner reality which we project in expressive or symbolic form, is also part of the process of creativity. In the more or less normal child the processes of assimilation and adjustment are constant and serve to build up within him a vigorous inner life which is identifiable with what we mean by the learning process. We have seen how this involves an element of imitation. Sometimes we behave as we have seen others behave, according to the norms of society; sometimes, when these imitations are inadequate for our needs, we act independently, individually, and create our own patterns of behaviour. This is to act or behave creatively; and it often requires considerable force of character.

When in a subsequent chapter I shall discuss the nature of characterization in acting, I shall have something to say about the relationship between our behaviour, the role we are playing, and our personality. We are not yet playing a role. We are with my grandson who picked up a lump of plasticine and by means of an imitative action transformed it symbolically into a cup. Thus, by means of what Piaget calls a 'deferred imitation', an act of transformation took place that we can call creative.

Professor Gombrich has discussed this process of transformation in his admirable *Meditations on a Hobby-Horse*.[47] He was skilful in his choice of metaphor; for a hobby-horse is not only a kind of representation of a real horse, but an archetypal symbol of all that is most fascinating in the play of a child and the transforming process that is found in all creative work.

We can no longer avoid the word 'play'. I had a rather starchy childhood myself so far as play is concerned with a mother who was too busy with intelligent activities to play and a nanny who did not understand these things. My only clear recollection of play is of hunting-games played with my father behind the armchair in the darkest corner of the sitting-room where I begged him in terror to hunt rabbits and not bears. I realize in retrospect that what frightened me was not the fiction of the savage animals but my father's ferocity when pouncing on the offending beast.

One of my daughters was particularly inventive in what I

might call 'dramatic play', casting herself in the role of a rather
repressive teacher and playing out all her impressions of the
adult world. It was a most vivid example of a child using a form
of 'let's pretend' to make her own social adjustments.

Educational thinkers of the past have not been slow to realize
the importance of play, but the literature on the subject has
swelled as the respect accorded to play and the opportunities
created for it in schools have increased.[48] This has been all a part
of the primary-school revolution, one of the basic educational
results of which has been an insistence on the importance of
play. This is no new concept. One finds Erasmus making the
point five hundred years ago. But it has been a matter of
increasing emphasis in the theories of Froebel and Maria Montessori and of increasing attack in the Black Papers (see note 26).
Parents who are concerned for their children's success in the
world visit classrooms and wince at the amount of what seems
to them to be purposeless activity. 'They spend all day playing,'
I have heard them say of their children.

Play is a profoundly important activity in the process of
personal development, and one that we share with higher
species such as apes. Jerome Bruner, in an impressive collection
of papers on the subject, establishes a wide variety of justifica-
tions and explanations.[49] Play is clearly seen to be one of the
crucial activities for adaptation and learning both among
humans and what are called the higher primates, while some of
the most interesting contributions show the way in which a
child can project in play some of his profoundest experiences
and most personal fantasies. One of the aspects of play that I
find most fascinating is the readiness of a child to establish rules
for his games. Indeed in watching a group of children at play
one is aware that there are accepted rules that have not even
been discussed. There is a kind of implicit acceptance that
constraints are necessary to make the winning harder. This in
fact is probably the distinction between play and a game,
though the vernacular allows us to speak of 'playing a game'.
The Russian language, for example, does not make this distinction and uses one word for both activities. When playing takes
on rules, constraints or a form – a word that in this context I am
reluctant to use – it changes its nature and becomes a game or a
play.

Iona and Peter Opie, in their remarkable book on children's
games,[50] describe games which take the form of rituals, tests of
skills, and trials of strength. There are games that depend on the
possession of a certain space, chasing games that end in

capture, searching games and hunting games, games played in teams, contests requiring skill or strength or stamina, games involving the guessing of a riddle; all these seem to suggest a remote ancestry and a great variety of biological needs that propose the necessity of games for adaptive purposes. Some of them remind me of the grim ritual that is described on the first page of *The Golden Bough*; some, of the scapegoat who bears the sins of the tribe; of the Sphinx and its riddles; of the ritual death of the tribal leader, and the 'he' and the 'it' from who knows what kind of ancient mystery.

I have emphasized the importance of rules in games because 'progressive' teachers of the arts have developed a critical attitude to rules, laws, forms, and all manner of constraints which they consider to be inimical to the creative arts. I shall discuss in due course why various kinds of constraints are crucial for creativity; but we can see in the way that children not only accept rules for their games but invent them themselves an indication of their basic necessity. Two of the most fascinating contributions to the anthology on play I referred to above are Jean Piaget's analysis of the manner in which children develop their own rules for a game of marbles and Balinese have established the most sophisticated rules to govern their love of cock-fighting.

The psycho-analytical approach to play has been fully though rather untidily discussed by D. W. Winnicott.[51] The substance of his arguments is that creativity, which is the mark of a healthy, balanced, and contented person, stems from the ability to take a positive and adaptive role towards human activity. Children, says Dr Winnicott, manipulate external phenomena in the service of their inner needs. This rather rebarbative expression suggests that there is a creative aspect to the assimilation of experience; that a human being is constantly faced with the necessity not only of absorbing experience, which may involve a considerable and even painful process of adjustment, but of transforming it for his own personal and social needs in his activities and in his behaviour, transforming aspects of reality that have impinged on his senses into gesture and activity. My daughter with her dolls was a good example of this.

Play for a young child is an egocentric activity, like his speech, but as he grows older he learns to communicate and to form relationships, so that play is frequently a shared or social experience, the process of transformation being carried out in a social context, and so, to press the implications even further, bringing him into contact with the culture of his society.

In writing rather blandly about the process of play, I do not want to minimize its difficulties and dangers especially for parent or teacher; if play is to mean anything at all the child must be left free; and when he is left free he will make his own associations; and when he makes his own associations he must make his own transformations. We shall see the particular difficulties of this when we consider the role of the drama teacher. But the fact is that if play is to have the free adaptive value we are claiming for it, we must allow children opportunities for the expression of their fantasies however awkward or even antisocial these may appear to be. What as adults we must not do, which in fact we do constantly, is to encourage our children to feel and think and play and fantasize as long as they are busy and absorbed and behaving in a generally socially acceptable manner, but when their individuality brings them into conflict with authority or society, to say that this must stop. We impose constraints. And the child becomes 'difficult' or shrugs his shoulders and goes into a shell and accepts a penitential role for the rest of his life. 'These flowers are not for you to pick' is writ large over a city child's sensibilities.

Yet I must come back to the child's own acceptance of rules. For children are not basically the destructive libertarians that progressive educationists have sometimes encouraged them to be and formal teachers are convinced they are. The natural anxiety and motivation of a child, of any of us, is to employ the capacities with which we have been born to master the environment, not to kick it over, and these natural capacities involve the transformation of chaotic and uncomprehended experiences into forms of expression that satisfy the child's internal schema. And the uncomprehended experiences that disturb a child far more than anything he is likely to meet in the outside world is unquestionably his own life of fantasy. Freud, who was not on the whole very complimentary about artists, says somewhere that a creative writer is going through the same process as a child at play. Each is creating his own world of fantasy; recording it in outward forms, and investing it with emotion; and thereby extracting the reality from the fantasy. What the author does in writing, the child does in play. Thus the child moves from egocentred to conceptual thinking, and as the egocentred and conceptual elements in his play decline, his play becomes less spontaneous and more self-conscious. As he learns to think in abstract terms, he will learn to free himself from limited and constricting relationships with his environment. He will be able to handle symbolic form adroitly, expressively, and to satisfy his own needs. He is moving from playing to the play, from creativity as a growing process to the act of creation.

Nevertheless the passage is by no means always as smooth as I might have made it sound. Psychologists in fact tend to emphasize the importance of a chaotic subconscious, of opportunity for free association. Professor Rogers writes of the importance of adding to sensory and visceral experiences a free and undistracted awareness or consciousness[52] and elsewhere, in arguing the importance of play in creativity, he discusses the need for opportunities to play around spontaneously with ideas, colours, shapes, relationships, 'to juggle elements into impossible juxtapositions, to shape wild hypotheses . . .' Others have gone so far as to suggest that the whole creative process depends on the production of abundant associative ideas as well as on the existence of a playful, permissive attitude. One thinks of the movements in theatrical production when the work will not move and the actors do not know where to turn. Sometimes one works with increasing discipline and regard for the words, the characters, the situations; but sometimes one asks the actors to play around with the scene, do it at double speed, at half speed, very loud, very soft, in cockney, in a tragic manner; and as like as not the jam is broken, for no very profound reason, I think, but that there has been opportunity for juxtapositions, and associations, and a freer flow of those strange inner forces that provide our capacity to imagine.

Up to this point I have been describing what amounts to the beginning of the creative process. It so happens that it is also the beginning of the manner in which we all function as human beings. There is no dissimilarity between natural growth and normal behaviour and the development of those faculties which make artists of us all. In its early stages creativity is little more than the expression of a lively intelligence.

We have seen that one of the main purposes of primary-school education is to provide children with a wide range of opportunities for the projection of this intelligence in various forms of behaviour and activity to some of which we have attached the word symbolic. Much of this activity can be described as play and the skilful teacher can help a child to relate his natural projections, games, play, and activities to conceptual understanding so that his intelligence and creativity are increased and so in turn are the quality and variety of his play.

Many teachers describe a child's early creative activities as self-expression. It is an accurate description. The child in his play is expressing something of himself. But the term 'free-expression' has taken on a broader connotation and is often used to describe and justify a wide range of activities, largely of a playful or moderately creative kind, as ends in themselves. A child, it is argued, must have plenty of opportunity for free self-expression. It is a concept that has brought progressive educational methods into a great deal of trouble by implying that play and creative activities are fully justified as long as the child is busy and active, even though the activity is chaotic and undirected. I have already spoken of children's ready acceptance of rules in their games. The role of the teacher is to help them find clarity of expression in all their creative activities. This is a stage beyond self-expression and it is a natural stage. Inarticulateness in any activity is not natural to anyone.

It is the responsibility of both home and school to provide constant opportunities for a child to follow his impulses in discovering the nature of a certain medium, material, or activity before he can, or should, be helped to project the activity into external shape or form. But this is in fact an incorrect analysis of the problem, for it is not in the nature of a normal child to be persistently destructive or to enjoy uncreative activities; not because children are goodies in the Victorian sense, at their most acceptable when seen and not heard, but because they want to come to terms with the world. Their play is not chaotic self-expression but a very remarkable manifestation of the need to form relationships between inner and outer reality, to project their disturbing fantasies, to test their developing strength and skills, to live with their peers. The term 'self-expression' is therefore of limited meaning and dangerous application. It should not be expunged from our phrase book but used with greater precision than is customary.

Perhaps in emphasizing the natural creativity of children I have underestimated the destructive element in our nature. Disintegration and collapse are the corollary of integration and construction. There is much that one has to destroy in oneself and often in one's medium or surroundings before one can create; but there is a difference between wanton destruction for its own sake and destruction that is a part of the creative process.

There is, however, a time when creativity breaks away from its common stock with intelligence and behavioural activities, and sets in motion a process that develops its own momentum. Self-expression and general creativity move towards the next phase of development. If we look on the infant school as the home of play, we must look to the junior school as the place to study the next phase of child development. In the first, the sensory-motor stage, the organic structure of the body has developed sufficiently for the child to be able to exercise his faculties in a natural manner. Jerome Bruner calls this second stage that of 'concrete operations' for it is the period when the child internalizes his personal reactions, his thoughts, his emotions, his response to the environment, and reconstructs them with a higher degree of clarity, with less egocentricity and more communicative awareness, with clearer differentiation and more confident use of symbolic meaning. But the child cannot operate outside the immediate present, the here and now, the objects he encounters. He is unable to speculate, to envisage a range of alternatives. He is circumscribed, but it is creative activities that develop his ability for internal representation and so in turn enable him to break out of his circumscription. While it is not true to say that a child between the ages of six and eleven is creating or even beginning to create works of art, he is capable of using artistic form to create artefacts of great significance. I have discussed the danger of using such terms as child art, child music, and child drama, but I entirely subscribe to Peter Slade's insistent claim that the drama of children can be something expressive, creative, and moving in its own right, and I shall give a number of examples of this. I do not like giving titles to these phases, however convenient they may be, but if I refer to the infant-school phase, or the junior-school phase, I do so only to give an indication of the area to which I am referring, intensely conscious of the fact that all such phases overlap and apply only in the most general way to that unpredictable creature, the growing child.

# 6 Drama in Junior Schools

Primary schools generally devote a considerable amount of time and effort to teaching reading, writing, and arithmetic. If they fail in this, and standards are seen to be falling, there is a rumpus. If they succeed they are accelerating the process of creating structures in the child's mind that enable him to think and to discuss subjects outside his immediate experience.

In his first stage of development a child can investigate only what he is seeing or experiencing at the moment. In the third or pre-adolescent phase, he can discuss or write about experiences remote from the present. In the second stage, which is the subject of this chapter, he is moving from one to the other. This is why one does not see so many displays and exhibitions in junior schools as one does in infant – and none at all in secondary, unless they are formal displays of the pupils' work. The infant school is concerned with helping a child to discover his own faculties; a junior school with helping him to discover his relationship to others. This is why school journeys and visits are an important aspect of work in a junior school and provide an extension of the time devoted to environmental studies. A child of five will weigh a lump of stone: a child of ten will work out the weight of the local church.[53]

Here we have an additional reason for the importance of the arts in junior schools: they are concerned with the here and now. When a child paints a picture he is projecting an image or an aspect of his visual fantasies or simply encouraging the natural patterns of the paint as it runs across the paper and changes its colour as it mixes and flows. This is why it is useless to ask a child what he is painting because what he is usually painting is painting. One can ask him to tell you about his painting and one can get an answer as once I did, from a very young child, 'The dragon is chasing the shadows of the birds and the road is deserted,' which seemed to have little to do with the picture on the easel. On another occasion a boy was showing me a picture of some sea-monsters. 'And that,' he said, with evident seriousness, 'is an octopus, but you needn't be frightened because it's only a lump of paint', and in his West Riding brogue he drew out the vowel sounds of 'lump' and 'paint' to embody all the irony of his thought. I am sure that if one had questioned the great J. W. M. Turner in the act of creating one of his gigantic fantasies he would not have reduced his vision to a literary concept, it was the transformation of nature into paint that excited him.

There is a similar immediacy when children are making music, their instruments in front of them, and that best of all instruments, their voice within them, and there is nothing but the present and the problem of creating a pattern of sound. Past experiences and remote fantasies may play their part but the act of making music is immediate. Sound is creative of more sound.

And also with dancing. Why are teachers so reluctant to ask children to examine their bodies? What a marvellous piece of construction is the hand! Why is it the way it is, with all the work being done by thumb and forefinger? What happens to our body when we run? Does running make us feel any different? If we feel low in spirits do we move differently? And what happens when we hear a lively piece of music? Does this make us feel any different? And then want to move or use our bodies differently? It's important that children should learn who the Vikings were, and who the Romans, and who discovered America, but few teachers seem to think it important that they should know anything about their own bodies, which is surely the beginning of the answer to the vexed and eternal question, who am I? I hope I am not right in suspecting that there may be a deep puritanical fear of encouraging narcissism or even masturbation. But I think the question is an important one, for I suspect that the present widespread interest in acting may be due to uncertainties about the personality. But of that more anon.

The first infants that ever I saw dancing were doing so because they were interested in their toes. The teacher had asked them to discover how much they could keep their toes off the ground, how fast they could move their toes, what patterns on the floor they could make with their toes. And the result was that having begun to move their toes, and so their feet, they began to move the rest of their bodies and so to dance with all the joy and spontaneity and physical energy of which children are capable. That school was in Manchester.

Now what about drama? First let us note the importance of dramatic play. It is in play that children can begin to move out of what one teacher called 'their small individual world' into the more challenging scene of social relationships and creative activities. What enchanting play I have seen! I think of a school in Bristol where the boys in a certain classroom had built a boat out of packing cases and boxes, and from their experiences and adventures on this boat the teacher had led them towards a host of educational experiences. The only trouble was what to do with the girls in the class, for men don't have women on their ships. They were under-employed; and took a rather poor view of the boys' insistence that they should get their tea ready on their return to port. Recruits for women's lib, no doubt.

I think of a school in the North of England where the children had elaborated a crude but lively wedding in which the bride was a big boy of six and the bridegroom a rather wispy girl somewhat younger. The boy, dressed as a girl, though true to his sex and strength, pushed his bridegroom to church all round the classroom in a little trolley muttering as he passed the visitors, 'Ain't it a bugger when a bride has to push her bloke to church for his own wedding!'

This episode took place while the children were playing. All the teacher had contributed was a suggestion that the boys and girls should find ways of playing together. For although it might seem a natural thing for them to do, this is not in fact the case, and the teacher, in common with many others, was worried at constant sexual segregation. Nevertheless her suggestion had had its effect. The boys and girls were marrying each other.

This episode also showed that children can be aware of the different levels on which they can operate. The boy who had painted the fish was convinced of the reality of the transformation from paint into sea-monster. The bride was aware that in his assumed role he was behaving improperly while conscious of his responsibility as a boy and anxious not to let the role-play spoil his fun in pushing the trolley.

When I look back over all the dramatic play and drama that I have seen I am conscious of an absence of fantasy. Children, contrary to supposition, do not act witches and warlocks, fairies and fays, talking animals and the repertoire of roles thought to constitute the imaginative world of children. This, already, is rather the world of adults writing for children. If children have a fantasy life that demands expression, they will find ways of absorbing it into the existing structures of their play and these structures are usually drawn from real life. The assimilative and imitative instincts are understandably powerful. Children of course do 'act' or improvise plays on themes involving fantasy but these themes often seem to have been supplied by the teacher. The child's natural interest is in the life around him and I am inclined to think that the daydreams and fantasies of a young child are on the whole too undifferentiated for him to be able to project them. He suppresses them, or lives with them, or transforms them in the course of various activities, but he only projects them when he moves into the phase of creative or artistic activity.

I can recall one class in a school in Northumberland where the children were making up a play that involved witchcraft and magic. There were two elements of this that clearly fascinated them. One was the composition of spells since this gave them an opportunity to create a new language without regard for meaning; the other was the concept of transformation. But they kept getting into difficulties, for their lively imaginations threw up a mass of material that they found great difficulty in organizing into a coherent story. This of itself was a valuable educational experience. But their experiments with spells provided a fascinating example of one of the liveliest and most creative forms of play, that with words. The vivid images and the insistent rhythms of the Macbeth witches appeal to children while the rest of the play may be a closed book.

The dividing line between dramatic play and play that is not dramatic, and drama that is not play – if it ever isn't – is a fine one and not to be pressed. Play can be free of drama: it often is. But by its very nature drama usually includes play. Play can be a test of skill or strength. A child can play with a ball or a toy for its own sake or some private and personal reasons. But drama nearly always involves play because it offers children opportunities to assimilate, transform, and project aspects of real life in personal and subjective terms.

In a previous chapter I quoted a passage from the Plowden Report, describing the manner in which the developing brain of a child matures in a regular sequence involving sensual, visual, auditory sensations, along with areas of association. The teacher in the infant school cannot teach these faculties but he can provide children with opportunities to exercise them. What more fascinating experience than to help children to feel by touch, to hear, to see, to smell and to watch what happens when these natural faculties are aroused, and to transform these sensations into concepts that help develop that inner structure of the mind on which both activity and intelligence depend?

It is the transformation of dramatic play into embryonic drama that we must now consider, and I shall say a good deal about the physical conditions and the personal resources necessary for children to express themselves in this form. Let me therefore begin by describing the plays I saw in a small Fenland school where each of the four classes made its contribution.

The bottom juniors (seven to eight) acted Goldilocks and the Three Bears. This is a well-known and for children an intensely exciting story as I can vividly recall. A little girl is alone in a strange house. She breaks a chair, eats a bowl of porridge and goes to sleep in a strange bed. The whole story is beautifully shaped in units of three – three chairs, three bowls of porridge, three beds, and three bears. There's the ritualistic repetition of 'Who's been sitting in my chair? Who's been eating my porridge? Who's been sleeping in my bed?' And there's a dénouement in the return of the three bears that increases in tension with constant retelling.

The problem encountered by these children was that a precise and formal structure which is highly comprehensible in narrative terms is intensely constricting in dramatic. At an age when they had not learnt in any way to discipline their speech or their use of speech to the formal requirements of so tightly structured a story they had to act in a most constrained manner even though the material was well within their comprehension. The teacher did not realize that the dimensions of narrative and dramatic form are totally different. She had not read her Aristotle.

The children of eight to nine fared little better with Red Riding Hood. It is another dramatic story but it is not at all of the stuff of drama. The story centres on four characters, mother, Red Riding Hood, grandma, and the wolf, and the opportunities for that open-ended free-flowing use of the imagination that is characteristic of children of this age did not exist. The children had to act within the limits imposed by the story. Moreover in both these cases only a small number of children from each class were involved, and I suspect the parts went to the children who were the best 'actors'. The rest had to watch. It is always a problem in a drama class to involve all the children but at seven to nine they are a little young to be subject to extreme selectivity and the impositions of an undramatic narrative.

The nine to tens did very much better with Hansel and Gretel which provides opportunities for a rich deployment of animals and birds who pick up the crumbs dropped by the children on their way through the forest. Moreoever an imaginative teacher had provided an admirably anthropomorphic forest. The trees were not merely a group of children with their arms stuck out but a rather impressive concatenation of limbs and torsos that reacted to the lost children in a natural manner, assuming attitudes of hositility and friendliness, while making forest murmurs of an inventive and un-Wagnerian nature. There was also an interesting relationship between the forest, with its whispering undergrowth and rustling branches and the creatures who lived within it, with a rather observant distinction between those that come out by day and those that venture forth at night. Here was something of the scope one looks for in child drama.

The top juniors chose *Childe Rowland*, a brave and interesting choice. This is a story that has always exercised over me a particularly powerful spell. 'Childe Rowland to the dark tower came'. Why was Rowland, who was clearly a heroic figure, called a childe? Why did the word have an 'e' on the end? What was this dark tower and why did he come there? And what a terrifying thought that if one circumambulated the tower three times widdershins, anti-clockwise, one was carried off to Elfinland. Which, of course, Rowland proceeded to do in order to rescue his sister Bird Ellen. The power of these images was such that Elfinland began to assume a powerful but mysterious reality. The whole legend is steeped in those emotional and visionary undertones which I think children who are moving towards adolescence are old enough to comprehend. What is the significance of moving anti-clockwise to a child who is not even aware of the meaning of clockwise direction? What is the significance of an eccentric spelling of child to someone who can barely spell the word normally? The full significance of the great myths and legends depends as much on a structure of inner reality as does the comprehension of other great mysteries, many of a more scientific kind; and more so perhaps because myth is a projection of those profound apprehensions which are expressed in rich, vague, symbolic and imaginative terms just because they are not susceptible to expression in more precise and comprehensible ones. A child may be quick to appreciate the significance of myth intuitively since he still sees the world anthropomorphically, undifferentiated; but I do not think it can be assumed that he will understand its significance until he has acquired the intellectual detachment of adolescence.

This picture of the progression of drama in a junior school suggests that the teachers of the younger children were trying to impose a sense of form upon the children before they had worked through the stage of applying their creativity specifically to drama; for this is the next stage and it is suggested by the kind of drama that seems to be particularly appropriate for children between the ages of about seven and eleven. Young children play; older children act plays. Children of junior school age are moving from one to the other.

I take as a typical example of drama in the junior school a version of the Nativity that I saw in Bristol. The boys, who in this particular class seemed to be more enterprising than the girls, cast themselves as shepherds and the girls as sheep whom they drove into a stockade made of chairs. They then mounted guard and took advantage of the situation, very much like the shepherds in the *Second Wakefield Play of the Shepherds*, to indulge in a lengthy gossip. This was brought to an end by a brilliant piece of invention. The sheep were attacked by a pack of wolves. This provided a justifiable opportunity for a fight. Eventually the shepherds killed the wolves and then applied themselves to digging a trench in which to bury them. When the corpses had been lowered in and the ground filled up, the girls who had escaped being cast as sheep appeared with great effect, standing on desks, as Gabriel and the angels.

This was an interesting example of a story adapted by the children to comprise their own interests. There was opportunity for physical action and a good gossip. And I need hardly add that the gossip went on for a very long time. The whole improvisation lasted for some three-quarters of an hour; and I think that the teacher was entirely right in only suggesting from time to time, in the most sensitive manner, that a certain episode had perhaps gone on long enough. The fact was that the children were playing within a richly imaginative situation and projecting their feelings about the story into a dramatic, that is a physical and linguistic, form. The adult concept of an episode having its own proper length in relation to its content and the structure of the whole story, is a further stage in the mastery of artistic form, of which more later.

I have in fact seen very little drama in junior schools that is not based on an existing story or material. I once visited a school in Devon where the headteacher encouraged the children to read Enid Blyton because it gave them material for drama. In a London school I once found the children taking their stories from X certificate horror films they had seen on television to provide opportunities for extremes of blood and slaughter. Most teachers are probably happier with more wholesome material and one sees plenty of Greek mythology used as material for drama. Yet in primary schools, just as much as in secondary, in the context of which the subject will have to be fully discussed, the whole question of choice of material is of the greatest importance; for a good teacher will push or bend the class in a certain direction with various educational experiences in mind and his choice of material must have, to use a fashionable word, some relevance to something he wants to clarify or that in his mind makes sense for the children, and that they may wish to investigate.

Yet at the risk of begging the whole question I would suggest that children are not very old before they enjoy doing all kinds of things for their own sake, because they take pleasure in doing them, not because they are good for them. This is not to say that children are necessarily aware of the educational advantages of a certain activity, or, for that matter, that the teachers are. But to enjoy an activity for its own sake has both advantages and drawbacks. For example, much of the pleasant, innocuous but not very telling drama that goes on constantly is a kind of reinforcement of an experience that has been enjoyed and is a pleasure to recall. I believe it to be the reinforcement of existing social norms that accounts for the large number of disturbingly innocuous plays produced by the contemporary theatre.

The constant reversion to myth and legend is understandable. The Greeks particularly produced a large body of enchanting stories which we are tempted to use at their face value. Yet their attractiveness and ultimately their power derive from their being myths and not fairy stories. That is why the great myths like the story of Theseus, the Biblical Nativity, or Beowulf, exercise so powerful a hold on the imagination of us all and lend themselves to re-expression on innumerable different levels of reality.

The 'good' teacher will get indications from the children of their interests by watching closely their spontaneous dramatic play, particularly, perhaps, in the playground at break, by listening to their conversation, and in fact by talking to them in a properly communicative manner. I use this latter rather tiresome expression because it is not all teachers who are able to talk to a child directly and unpatronizingly and listen to what he has to say, even though it is the relationship that lies at the heart of all teaching and learning. But children do indicate at least some of their needs, interests, and even inadequacies to the teacher who is sensitive enough to read the signs.

Many teachers experience difficulty taking drama owing to a basic uncertainty about their professional role. 'I could never do drama,' I hear them say, 'because I am not imaginative enough –

or do music because I am not musical, or art because I am not artistic.' This is to reveal the insecurity of their position which is the result of false standards of professionalism that have grown up in the adult world. While it is true that a certain level of commitment and sensitivity to an art is necessary for the attainment of high professional standards, such dedication is not needed to enjoy the arts either in an active or passive role at a lower level of sensibility. But in the context of this book I would go much farther than this and say that experience suggests that all children are artistic. Indeed it is a basic part of my argument that artistic expression is in the first instance what may be called a form of behaviour and acquires the nature of art only when the reflex-stimulus and the reproductory and representational process demand a form of presentation. Hence the need to insist upon the distinction between social and artistic behaviour, between the process of ordinary living and the creation of artistic artefacts and activities.

But much of the process is the same and that is why it is necessary to emphasize its biological and neurological nature. It is the responsibility of classroom teachers to reveal in children the whole creative process at a level of which they are capable, and of headteachers and educationalists in general to ensure that schools are organized and teachers trained to make this possible; and in urging this I do not exclude Bruner's ideas about school as a social experience or the need to provide parallel experiences in mathematics and science.

One of the greatest dangers besetting the teaching of any subject in a school is to see that subject in isolation. This is particularly true of the arts. Drama teachers are fond of asserting that drama is about life; then let it be about life and let us help children to see life and learning in their totality. Most primary schools try to give some kind of breadth to the education they offer by providing a wide range of subjects, scientific, environmental, mathematical, musical, artistic, linguistic, literary, historical, geographical, and so on. Where their relationship is left to the discretion of the teacher the school uses the rather malodorous expression, 'the integrated day'. But such an organization of the curriculum does make possible a concept of totality and allows for the extraordinary transformational quality of creative expression, which explains why a stimulus of one kind, visual perhaps, may take substance as a piece of writing. Michael Tippet has described how he conceived his second symphony while gazing at the waters of Lake Geneva.[54]

A good school builds up the resources of its children. It

introduces them to stories, to music, to pictures, to number and geometry, to the environment itself, less productive perhaps in King's Cross than in the middle of Oxfordshire. (A friend of mine once visited a school in Islington when a teacher in planting some geraniums in a tub found a worm. The excitement among 300 children was immense.) So the teacher who wants to give the children an experience in drama should find in every child resources on which to draw, or, expressed more realistically, a variety of forms through which to express themselves, remembering the particular connotation we have given to the term 'self-expression'. Drama may therefore provide an original imaginative experience, a reinforcement or extension of an existing experience, depending on the resources of the children and the skill of the teacher. Many children express themselves more readily in one form than another. It is for the teacher to develop special talent but not at the expense of other forms of expression.

This is one of the reasons why I think it quite unnecessary for a teacher to be defensive about his inadequacies. In a good school the children will be equipped with a rich variety of expressive resources. They will not be taught to be creative but given opportunities to be so. No teacher is required to exercise the hand of God; but he is required to touch the creativity that God has already placed within his pupils.

The material thrown up by other subjects often provides the material for the drama lesson. This has given rise to the widely held belief that drama is a tool for teaching other subjects. It is indeed very understandable that teachers should invite children to try to experience by means of imaginative projections a variety of terrains, of climates, of conditions of life. I have seen Red Indian villages and Aboriginal settlements, Nigerian markets and Kenyan compounds. I have seen children climbing mountain heights, crossing scorched deserts, battling with fierce winds, drenched with heavy rain. They can begin to experience what life can be like under conditions they have not experienced themselves and the nature of some of the problems that have to be solved to live at all.

An aspect of such improvisations that requires examination is this. Does the quality of understanding depend on performance? Has the child who can 'act' climbing up a mountain convincingly a greater understanding of the climatic conditions involved than the child who cannot act what he feels? Or has he failed in feeling because he cannot act? I believe that this is the case. The ability to express a feeling is closely related to having a feeling to express. Moreover the feeling of being cold and tired is not a separate experience from its expression. We do not therefore teach children to act but to express, to embody, to project. Acting comes later. This also explains why the more able child is often the best actor; because intelligence is not a separate concept from that of expression but a part of the same internal mental structure expressing itself in action.

Drama is sometimes popular with the history teacher who has to deal with the dimension of time. I have myself been a Celt subjected to the Roman power; I have held a spear in the court of Cleopatra and crawled on my stomach as we simulated life in the trenches during the Great War. I have been more impressed, however, by what I have seen than what I have done. How vividly I remember a Viking ship in the middle of a junior-school classroom. There were the shields along either side of the hull, each emblazoned with the arms of its owner, and the beaked monster at the prow. Vigorously the Vikings rowed until they made a landfall in the Thames at London. There the object was to carry off female prisoners. The cautious teacher suggested that treasure, in which London was rich, would be more appropriate and cause less trouble.

I recall a splendid lesson on the battle of Crécy. The teacher had explained some of the principles of medieval warfare and the particular problems facing the army of Edward III as he tramped the plains of northern France in search of the enemy; how he found the French army and chose his position on a ridge of high ground with a windmill at one end. The feature of the lesson was the way in which the teacher told the children about the Welsh archers, how they drove their stakes into the ground and then made ready their bows. The children had to work out how to hold a bow to get their strength behind it, a very different matter from playing with twigs and string in the back-garden. When the French cavalry appeared at the bottom of the hill I could almost see the individual horses and the ensuing attack which did not need accompanying music by William Walton to make it convincing; for the eye and the mind were engaged and the tension was created physically, by that row of immovable children, their bodies lined up behind their straight left arms holding the great bows at the ready and the string drawn back with the arrows in place. One would not claim this to have been a drama lesson but it was drama used in the service of history, and very successfully used. In order to understand exactly what took place I think one must see it from the point of view of history rather than drama. The problem of teaching history and geography in the junior school is that of enabling children to comprehend the great abstractions of time and space. This must begin as a sensory-motor experience in children's earliest years but it is impossible to enlarge that experience outside the immediate present by those means. Yesterday and tomorrow, let alone last year and next year, are concepts that a child will grasp gradually and as a result of his growing intelligence, the maturing capacity of his brain to create representations or schemes of the outside world that comprehend such abstractions as time and space. Indeed some primitive languages do not even have words that distinguish concepts of space more complex than here and there or of time beyond now and not now. At this stage intelligence is extended by the great creative and transforming power of the imagination which I have had described to me as the faculty of putting known factors together to get the unknown, a definition of which Coleridge would have approved. What were the known factors in this case that did not require abstract concepts? Most children of nine and ten will have formed an idea of what a soldier is and what it means to fight in a gang or in that marshalled and highly disciplined gang we call an army. The teacher was able to suggest the kind of uniform the archers wore and he was certainly able to convince them of the reality of the bow by the sheer disposition of their bodies. By means of the association of these known factors each child, according to the creative capacity of his imagination, would have been able to construct his own view of the reality of the scene. But the teacher can only test this reality by the ability of the child to project it in terms of acting, painting, writing, or even talking about it.

When we say that children are acting out a situation we mean that they are involved with their muscles, their senses, their imagination, and their feelings. In these terms they are assimilating a concept, and making the necessary mental adjustments. In the mind of a child there is an interdependence between intellectual and imaginative powers just as there is between intellectual and creative. But at an older age these qualities and capacities tend to separate under the pressure of divisive educational practices.

I remember an episode of a far more superficial kind but one that nonetheless provided an opportunity for the children to grasp various geographic and linguistic realities. For reasons I cannot recall the teacher had set up in the classroom an improvisation on the subject of a cross-channel swim with the usual bland but observant radio commentators. There were five

English supporters and fifteen French for the interesting reason that the children found it much more fun to shout 'magnifique', 'bravo', and 'encore' than the plain 'hurrah'. I do not think that any children were left in doubt as to the reality of England and France and the dividing channel.

Something more about resources; and first of all I would like to consider music even though musical talent is not crucial for work in drama. I have already apologized for the need to use the term 'creative music' but music education has been so dominated by the work of the classical masters, by insistence on learning notation, by the singing of part-songs in diatonic mode, and by the piano as the principle instrument for music-making, and rendered so bleached in the process, that that over-used word 'creative' is justified (for other kinds of music-making). What a different and refreshing picture of the possibilities of musical education is provided by John Paynter in his splendid book *Sound and Silence*.[55]

Music is very closely related to drama in two ways. Drama itself is dependent on physical movement which is a rhythmical form of physical expression and so closely related to the basic rhythmic qualities of music. Drama is also closely related to language which involves pitch, tempo and volume as its principal expressive ingredients. And as rhythm (tempo), pitch, and volume are the principal ingredients of music it follows that the relationship between music and drama is or should be a close one.

Can we not therefore suggest that creative music begins with a sense of rhythm for the expression of which children do not need an instrument. They can tap rhythms with their hands on the floor or on any hard surface, and they can sing rhythms with their voices. What an enchanting exercise it is to make rhythmical sequences out of Christian names, or the names of flowers, to vary their pitch, volume, and dynamics and in fact 'to play around with them'. When instruments are required there is now available a range of percussive and pitch-percussive instruments that lend themselves to the simple forms of music-making with a minimum of skill. But even more fascinating is the interest of music teachers in other ways of making sound and of notating sounds that lie outside the limited scope of the five-barred stave. For much of this we have to thank the innovatory work of Carl Orff.

And what has this to do with drama? First, I think, it is important to establish the point that many of the sensibilities aroused by music are highly relevant to drama. For it is not only part of a child's education that he should be given a rich vocabulary of words but a sensibility in uttering them, that is to say – expressive speech. I do not think that this is best taught directly, as it was in the days of elocution, for to make the ear sensitive and the voice expressive requires a deeper sensibility to sound of a kind that can only be fostered by musical experience. French teachers of English, faced with a pupil who cannot master the rhythms of our language, send him to the music teacher, often with admirable results. And I recently met a voice teacher who had invited a student to discuss the extent to which a reader is dependent on his own phonetic awareness for understanding a text. Stylistics indeed!

I have not seen a great deal of the kind of relationship between drama and music which, in view of developments in both arts, I would have anticipated. I shall say more about this relationship in due course. But it is clear that part of the trouble is that music is traditionally associated with a kind of mystery and very complex techniques. If music education could be approached afresh as the organization of sound, with emphasis on rhythm, tempo, volume, and dynamics, whatever means are used to create the sound, primary-school teachers would feel very much more confident in tackling an area dominated by a 'holier-than-thou' attitude on the part of the specialists.

Nothing, however, has ever delighted me more than a performance I once saw in an infant school in Manchester. It was not a performance in the usual sense. I happened to be in the school to look at some dancing and the headteacher asked me rather hesitatingly whether I would be interested to see something that a certain class had done but which she did not even know how to describe. (German composers of the 1920s would have called it a 'vocal fugue' but the term is not in general use.) I quote from the Drama Survey:

> The children were sitting on the floor of their classroom. They began by repeating the word 'Bethlehem' lightly and rhythmically. Then a group of them changed to 'Mary on a donkey' which they repeated a number of times while the rest provided a ground-base of 'clippety-clop, clippety-clop'. Some then took up the refrain of 'Baby Jesus sleeping in a manger' and others 'Shepherds in the fields watching their flocks'; and in this way the whole story of the nativity was developed to a climax of 'Good Tidings' loudly repeated several times and the singing of a carol.

The sensitivity and the vitality with which these young children handled this basic traditional material was very moving indeed and I attributed this to the prevalence of dancing throughout the school.

One of the main resources in our approach to drama is movement. This is a subject which until recently has caused a good many hackles to rise; but the determination of Peter Brinson to bring the whole study of dance education into question has cleared the air.[56] The study of the art of movement, which in the educational context is closely associated with the work of Rudolf Laban, has had an unchallenged monopoly in primary schools, while in secondary it has not produced the results which its dominating position might have led one to expect. But in junior schools teachers have been provided with a means of analysing movement and making a start with movement education. Silly though some of Herr Laban's basic exercises, such as dabbing and flicking, may be, his analysis of qualities of movement, closely related to the movement of the body in terms of time and space, has put the whole theory and practice of movement education on a new basis. The art of movement allows for qualities of creativity and natural spontaneous free expression; but it has bred in countless teachers a terror of skills, techniques, shape, form or the very art which in its title it claims to be. Quality of movement is all and this is at least a fair start, for quality must be the result of a feeling and feeling relates to the sensory-motor experience, and self-expression as opposed to self-indulgence.

We are not, however, concerned with functional movement, the purpose of which is to strengthen, relax and co-ordinate the body, but expressive movement, movement that is expressive, through its various qualities, of certain emotions. It is clear, therefore, that if a child can move freely and expressively with a sense of time and space, he possesses qualities that will help him to develop in two directions, those of dancing and acting. Let us look for a moment at the former.

Most teachers of dance seem to have found it very difficult to define the art.[57] I do not propose to do their work for them. Indeed I cannot. But it is clear that dancing is a basic form for the expression of emotion; for if we feel deeply about something, we express our emotions more clearly and immediately in physical terms than in any other. If we are particularly elated we have wings on our feet and we walk lightly down the road; if we are dejected we drag our feet and slouch at the shoulders. And the reverse is also true: we can induce a feeling of joy by skipping and of dejection by moving slowly and heavily.

But there is more to dance than this. When we speak we

express ourselves in at least two different ways, through the meaning of the words we utter and the emotional quality we give to their utterance. When we dance we are embodying emotions in gesture. R. G. Collingwood has described dancing as 'total bodily gesture'.[58] Maybe an acrobat or a boxer would make a similar claim; and I have heard a pianist explain that to play a single note with a single finger involves the proper disposition of every muscle in the body. An acrobat may also use every muscle but his task is not to express emotion. If he does, he is lost. He may create emotion in the spectators, but that is something different. And while it may be emotion that drives an athlete to exert himself to the utmost, he is not running to express emotion but to win. Whereas if the dancer does not express emotion he is accused of being a mere athlete.

Drama is different from dance because it involves a linguistic element, and the physical expression of emotion is less powerful. But it is the linguistic content of drama that makes it apparently easier to teach than dance; for the words enable the actor to say who and where he is. Teachers get lost in dance because they look for a content; a subject; and the content of dance is dance.

Now dancing and to a lesser extent drama have a very curious quality in common. They alert all the other faculties to a very high degree of sensitivity; and I have often wondered why this should be so. I think the answer is a biological one in that movement tones up the muscles, ensures the full arterial circulation of the blood, alerts the mind, and gives a kind of physical tone to the whole body. This quality it shares with other athletic activities. The difference of the art of movement lies in its additional expressive and affective qualities. The purpose of movement and dance is to express an idea or an emotion or to respond to a reflex-stimulus of perhaps uncertain origin. An idea is a moment of perception, of understanding, of sudden cross-reference. The particular quality of expressive movement or dance lies in a combination of intense physical experience with an accompanying and closely related sensory-emotional one.

These observations are based on my impression that in many outstanding primary schools the movement is of a very high order. It might well be asked whether the schools are good because of the movement or the movement good because of the schools but this is to fail in appreciation of that kind of dialectical interrelationship that is necessary for any successful collaborative activity. This was very much the case in what was then the West

Riding of Yorkshire where a particularly high regard for the needs of children as well as for their teachers was fostered by Sir Alec Clegg. This attitude of general 'caring' and in particular of concern for the arts was common throughout the County Inspectorate and to be found in many schools.

The children moved, acted, danced, improvised with the most outstanding sensitivity and invention. Many of them came from mining families with fathers 'down t'pit'. In school they spoke with a broad but comprehensible Yorkshire accent; in the playground with a formidable dialect of which I could hardly understand a word. They were no angels, but tough 'kids' from working-class families.

The children moved with considerable athletic prowess particularly those from the oldest class, and could manage most of the gymnastic feats one expects of children of that age with outstanding skill. They knew the difference between functional and expressive movement. If you gave them a football they could throw it about among themselves in a manner appropriate for the training of the Castleford Football Club. If the teacher said, 'See what you can do with the ball' or 'Turn it into something else', their invention would be outstanding. I have seen them improvise plays galore, or simply improvise, using such subjects as the Pied Piper, the Gunpowder Plot, the Jabberwocky. They would begin to work on a subject, the teacher would throw in a suggestion and they would develop their theme with almost incredible inventiveness. One day a group of them carried out a brilliant parody of an interview with Cassius Clay, as he then was. A visiting Inspector once asked them to get out of their skins. Once in the middle of a class a boy suddenly slewed down the middle of the hall clinging to the tail of a runaway bull. It was a moment of spontaneous creativity and quite electrifying.

But this was not a school where everything was subjected to movement and drama. The classrooms were models of their kind. The children could write and draw and do their academic work at a high level of sensitivity. What impressed me most of all and convinced me of this inner discipline which seems to be one of the most lasting results of the creative process was the behaviour of the children at Wheldon Lane when a team from the BBC descended upon the school to make a TV film. On the second morning a series of disasters such as fused circuits, late arrivals, acoustic inadequacies, and domestic resistance to the whole invasion threw the school into the chaos one associates with these occasions. Suddenly I heard some children singing in clear sweet voices. I went to the classroom from which the music was emanating and found the children, ready dressed for television, and in the absence of the teacher, passing the time by singing, telling each other stories, and each in turn 'taking the class' in some purposeful activity.

Miss Bessie Bullough must be accounted, from her results, the best primary-school drama teacher I ever encountered. When I first met her she was the leading lady of the Castleford Amateur Dramatic Society and a teacher using formal methods in the classroom. She met a West Riding Inspector, who had done much to establish movement in the Authority's schools,[59] and went to some classes in modern educational movement. She applied what she had learnt to her teaching with astonishing results. In working with the children she stood at one end of a long narrow hall communicating with them in some extra-sensory manner since the abominable acoustics made her speech-sounds incomprehensible. But the children understood all right. At one end was an open stage she never used and at the other a large window outside of which trains puffed and shunted persistently. She used gramophone records of incredibly poor quality, to which the children responded with extraordinary musicality. When I once asked her headteacher what he thought was the advantage of all this movement, he replied in his dry Yorkshire manner – 'When I go into the streets of Castleford and I see all the mothers with their prams and one of them is moving decently I say – that's one of mine.' An Inspector who gave very considerable help to the school[60] said that she thought the children reached an altogether higher level of experience than most people ever attain.

A curious situation arose in the late 1960s, when a number of teachers became so concerned about resources for dramatic work that Gavin Bolton pointed out most shrewdly that drama seemed to be all preparation and no performance. Most courageously he would take a class of children and lead them firmly into some dramatic situation, relying on the creative power of their imagination rather than their expressive resources in speech and movement. This approach, however, can be dangerous in the hands of an unperceptive teacher. For drama will almost inevitably lack truth and substance if it is neither the outcome of a stimulus nor the stirring of the creative imagination. Drama cannot exist outside the elements of which it is compounded: thought, feeling, imagination, vocal and physical expressiveness.

In case I should be thought to have made excessive claims for drama, I have left what I have to say about speech till last. The development of speech is clearly one of the most trenchant examples of symbolic form relating closely to the growth of the intelligence and general cognitive powers. Psychologists argue vigorously about the relationship between speech and thought. Vygotsky's book on the subject has become top of the trendy charts; but the question remains – is there a capacity for thinking apart from the capacity to speak? My own observation of the schools where a rigorous policy of encouraging speech has been carried out is that speech and thought are most closely related. Before I prescribe, let me describe.

The most extraordinary use of language by young children I ever heard was in Tom Stabler's school in West Hartlepool, situated in an impoverished area and drawing on children of no great natural ability.[61] Mr Stabler had recently attended Mrs Heathcote's course and was at the time particularly interested in the acquisition of language by young children. I was familiar with his work from a television film in which a class of children involved themselves in the surprising subject of King Ahab and his mistress Jezebel. It was clear that the children could talk with remarkable fluency and argue with considerable powers of reasoning. But I was not really prepared for what I found. One of the younger classes was working on the story of *Beowulf*. The part of the hero was being enacted by a boy of eight and the whole of the class was involved. When I entered the hall an argument was in progress centering round the chieftain's exasperation at the inefficiency of the guards who had twice allowed the monster Grendel to invade the castle of Hrothgar by night and carry off some of its inmates. There was a fine moment when the young chieftain threw his sword to the ground in exasperation and the defending guards stamped in reciprocal anger. The level of discussion coming from children who were of an age at which in many schools they would have been ploughing through the trivia of Janet and John was quite astonishing.

This, however, was outshone by what took place in the top class. The children had been working for some weeks on the story of the plague in the Derbyshire village of Eyam. The time was the seventeenth century. The story concerns the identity of a thief, a woman accused of being a witch, the death of her son, and the poisoning of the water in the village well. After a short talk with the head on what they had done hitherto, the children launched into an extraordinary improvisation, playing on these interrelated themes continuously for the next forty minutes.

They showed an extraordinary ability to grasp all the elements of a most complex situation and to develop the interrelationship of a great variety of characters. They picked up the lead from each other and advanced the action, not by inventing new episodes but by developing the relationships of the various characters with each other and to the central situation with increasingly greater depth of understanding. Their language was rich and fluent though the drive and speed with which they spoke in a lilting, to me near-Geordie accent, made it impossible to record. They used with complete assurance the space of a large hall, avoiding either bunching or straggling, established clearly the relationships between the characters in the various groups as well as of the groups to each other. Mr Stabler claimed that the purpose of all this was to make the children think. I cannot question the validity of his claim.

As there was nothing particular about the children in the school, so there was nothing particular about the school itself. Except this devotion to linguistic thought. The staff consisted of good average teachers who respected what Mr Stabler was doing and used his work in drama as a basis for classroom writing. There are examples of their written work in the Drama Survey.

Another example of a similar kind comes from a school in the London Borough of Redbridge where the staff were particularly interested in Shakespeare. The children of nine and ten had been studying *Richard III*. On this occasion they were working on the last act. They put balaclavas on their heads, grasped wooden swords in their right hands and equipped themselves with saucepan lids for shields. The battlefield of Bosworth gave rise to some lusty language in the course of which Bolingbroke's followers heaped a torrent of imprecations on the unhappy king with the climatic words, 'May you have his liver for breakfast!' How easy to jeer! But how difficult to think where else on the curriculum such imaginative panache could be achieved!

The top class was working on *Macbeth*. The teacher had had to leave to supervise a hockey match so the children pushed back the desks and said they would act the play for the visitors. Thereupon they proceeded to give a forty-minute improvised version of *Macbeth* that kept extraordinarily close to the spirit of the original and included a number of splendid lines, such as, 'Send the men to the jousting!', and 'I often wonder what's inside those rebel heads.' The scenes between Macbeth and his wife had something of the same close reasoning that I had noted in Hartlepool; and the great witch scene that opens Act IV

ended with the memorable line spoken by the first of eight
witches – for all the girls had to be found parts – 'Ladies, let us
return to our stew.'

I am not at all convinced that these exercises lead to much of
an appreciation of Shakespeare, for what of Shakespeare
remains when you remove the language? The question is not
rhetorical. The situations he poses amount to very little when
you remove the material with which he develops those situations. Can one think of a way of simplifying a picture by
Constable? By copying it in water colours? And what would that
amount to? But I am sure that they are of immense value as
improvisations and I do not think it matters whether the subject
is taken from Shakespeare, Tolstoy, or European history, provided it offers opportunities for the projection of a kind of
reality. That is why Enid Blyton stories do not qualify. They are
projections of a sentimental view of life which does not provide
opportunity for the enlargement of experience that was a feature
of the examples I have given.

People argue that one learns to write by writing, to paint by
painting, to dance by dancing. This, of course, is true. What I
am suggesting is that drama provides an imaginative context for
speech that enlarges the situation and calls on a greater affective
motivation. Although this has often been suggested, it is
nevertheless a considerable claim because it suggests that a child
will learn to acquire a richer vocabulary and a greater facility by
expressing himself orally in an imaginative dramatic situation
than ever he is likely to do in real life. And this is exactly the
issue. I am surprised that the Bullock Report[62] does not discuss
the issue more fully.

It so happens that I once visited a school in the West Riding of
Yorkshire where one particular teacher was giving great attention to quality of speech without involving drama. When I
entered the classroom the children were painting. Every time
they spoke the teacher required them to express themselves
fully and as accurately as possible. 'Hold up your picture, Mary,
for the class to see. What have you to say about it?' No
stammering chorus of 'Not bads'. 'Well, Mary,' said one girl, 'I
think you have painted a lovely picture, but I don't care very
much for the way you have used colour. The blue you have used
for the sea seems to me not consistent with the blue you have
used for the sky,' etc. I am hesitant to quote more, although I
wrote a great deal down, because to read the way these children
conversed is to give the impression that they spoke pedanti-
cally. To a certain extent this is true; but there was so very much

more to their speech than an over-exact use of words. It was meaningful and full of feeling. There was a very relaxed atmosphere in the room and the children spoke to one another with absolute ease and confidence. I did not think to ask whether they were ever accused by other children of 'talking posh' because the quality of their conversation left one astonished. The fact was that they could think. I have instanced the way in which one of them began to discuss Mary's painting. In conversation I found that they had recently visited Coventry Cathedral and were able to converse fluently and easily on the architecture and the stained glass windows. They had read widely – most of them had read something in the region of a hundred books – and they were able to discuss their favourite authors with enthusiasm. I could only conclude that the relationship between speech and thought was virtually proven, and I turned again to the Plowden Report, which was very much in mind at the time, where I found it said, 'The evidence of research increasingly suggests that linguistic inadequacy, disadvantages in social and physical background, and poor attainments in schools are closely associated.' Here the positive reverse was proven.

What advantages then has drama over straightforward experience in speech such as this teacher was developing? My answer would be – variety and flexibility, the ability to handle a variety of registers of speech, and a conceptual and imaginative quality to extend the cognitive.

I would ask my readers to consider the examples I have quoted in the last few pages. Obviously the most developed work usually comes from the so-called top juniors, children of about ten and eleven. This in fact is the age that is covered by Piaget's third main stage of development, that of formal or symbolic operations. Is not this exactly what the children I am thinking of are beginning to do, to handle symbolic form in a complex manner in order to project some area of experience, to direct their creative impulses into some kind of articulate form? to use developed play in the adaptive process? to represent aspects of reality by re-expressing them in symbolic form?

I would like to press the matter further by suggesting that there is a relationship between the symbol and this sense of form. Children have shown themselves to be capable of handling symbolic ideas competently. But I have pointed out that improvisation tends to run on, almost interminably, only to be interrupted by the end of the lesson or the discretion of the teacher. Here we shall find the difference between this particular stage – may we use Piaget's term and call it the stage of symbolic operations? – and the fourth stage when the children begin to work towards the creation of a work of art. The work I have been describing contains elements of art; but it is not yet fully art because children are only in the process of learning how to handle the symbolic form and have not yet realized the need for selectivity and that shaping of the form which embodies whatever of the initial stimulus or concept remains. Process still dominates the creation of an artefact even if we accept, what is today severely challenged, that that is the proper outcome of the artistic process. Words and actions are now seen as a representation of reality rather than, as in the undifferentiated world of the child, reality itself.

We are dealing, though in embryonic stage, with art, a proposal that some teachers will view with horror. But I am proposing that there are few differences between artistic and educational values. I am also proposing that there is a precise equivalent between art and symbolic form, which is an important concept since it establishes the equilibrium between creativity and artistic discipline. Creativity is free-flowing, open-ended, transformational. Artistic discipline is a constraint – but here lies the paradox – only until the discipline has forced the creative material into its appropriate pattern; then there follows a sense of freedom and exaltation that is the ultimate reward of all artistic creation.

# 7 Drama in Secondary Schools: Aspects of Organization

The fact that I cannot in this chapter discuss continuity of drama training from primary to secondary school is a serious criticism of our system. I would defend against all comers the right of a headmaster to run his own curriculum; but throughout my eleven years in the Inspectorate and other periods when I have been working close to education, I have not come across or even heard tell of a single case of continuity between a primary and secondary school in any vital aspect of the curriculum, let alone in attitude to the arts. It was lamentable that the children from the West Riding primary schools should have moved on to schools that offered the most formal of approaches to education. We simply do not know what children might achieve if offered the continuity that every kind of common sense suggests. There is a certain provision for continuity in music and dancing since musical talent often reveals itself at a very early age and in the case of dancing the body has to be trained at least from the age of about ten. But in terms of general education the lack of continuity is a mark of confused and intractable educational thinking on the part of many secondary heads and administrators.

Nor do I think that the recent creation of middle schools has done very much to improve the situation. They have only served to create a further hazard in the continuity of development; and faced with uncertainty whether they are extensions of primary schools or preparatory schools for the secondaries, they have established no clear identity of objective.

In the whole field of drama in schools it is work in the first three years of secondary that is most open to criticism. Standards are often a good deal lower than one finds in the top classes of the better primary schools and this is largely the result of considerable uncertainty about the nature of the work and methods of teaching. This in turn is the product of an over-simplification of certain basic tenets of education. It has been

71

held for some little time that primary education is child-centred and secondary education is subject-based. However greatly teachers may want to question the terms, we all know the kind of methods and organization to which they refer and I have given plenty of examples of current primary-school practice. In secondary schools we have teachers who are specialists in teaching certain subjects. They may be good teachers but the traditional emphasis rests on their knowledge of the subject they are teaching. So we have not just teachers as in primary schools, but teachers of the various subjects – English, mathematics, history, music, art, drama, and so on.

Drama, then, is supposedly a subject, and we have specially qualified teachers to teach it. Among all the subjects on the curriculum, with the possible exception of the social sciences, it is probably the newest, having reached some kind of respectability during the 1960s. I said something about this phenomenon in an earlier chapter. A large number of main courses in drama were established in colleges of education and a very large number of teachers began to take up posts in secondary schools to teach drama. Heads were interested and often sympathetic. 'What is this subject you want to teach?' they asked. 'Tell us about it. If you want a place in the curriculum you must justify your claim against a great many competitors.'

The result was something of a panic among teachers of drama. They had to define their subject. Immediately they found themselves in conflict with teachers of English who said, 'What's all the flap about? We've been teaching Shakespeare for years, yes, and we teach Shaw and any other dramatist worth his salt. And as for the so-called practical aspects of the subject, we have always been responsible for the school play and we have no objection to some of our teachers indulging in exercises in improvisation, if you consider them to be so important, especially with the more backward children who have got to be kept occupied.'

This attitude divided the drama teachers irrevocably. Some accepted the olive branch from the English department; others felt that the integrity of their subject demanded independence. But this increased the need for definition. Under English, they had little to worry about: on their own they needed a rationale. There was little joy to be had from the Newsom Report[63] which appeared in 1963 to consider, according to its brief, 'the education of pupils aged 13 to 16 of average and less than average ability'. It is not in its references to drama a particularly impressive document lacking altogether those pretensions to vision that make the Plowden Report most worthily open to attack and the triteness of its comments on the arts is quite unacceptable. The Robbins Report is now something of a bad joke, but in any case it was concerned with administrative provision, not educational theory. The Drama Survey appeared in 1968 and served to give teachers of drama a boost even if it did not solve any of their problems. It is in most respects a descriptive survey, which, having weathered the disgruntlement of the educational press for not having been helpfully prescriptive, throws the ball back to the teachers saying it is for them to define the subject they want to teach.

A number of attempts at definition then began to appear. Here is part of one composed by members of a local branch of the National Association of Teachers of English.

> . . . the study of drama is, in essence, the study of personal relationships through *all* the possible media, and the artificial recreation of such relationships in order to explore and demonstrate. It is essentially a practical subject needing considerable space and the liberating effect of informal clothing. It follows that all possible media must be used, dance, movement, speech, improvisation, playmaking and production – although all worth-while means to an end cannot by themselves constitute a complete drama course which is much more concerned with what is implicit rather than explicit in expression.

This will hardly cause masters of either philosophy or English prose to turn excitedly in their graves; but I quote it to show how extraordinarily difficult many teachers found it to define a subject they were prepared to teach. I was also rather horrified to discover how difficult it was to define any other subject on the curriculum and how easily such bastions as English and history distintegrate when analysed as a so-called subject. One can teach a skill, but a subject is something different. And if teaching is not a skill how do you teach teaching? One should not jeer at the difficulties of definition.

A rather more encouraging definition of drama came from a group of drama teachers meeting one weekend at their residential centre.

> Drama in education is a form of creative expression. As the basis of drama is no more than being able to speak and to move it is thus accessible as a means of expression to all children. In the very young child it takes the form of self-centred and instinctive imaginative play. As the child develops it becomes a unique form of creative contact between individuals using physical, vocal and emotional

resources. Such natural abilities can rarely be related and used constructively at one and the same time except in drama, which can also incorporate a number of skills in other subjects. This fusion of natural abilities and acquired skills makes dramatic work with its immediacy of presentation, a vivid, direct and unique experience. As the active explanation of human relationships is essential to drama, it can be claimed to make an individual contribution to the full education of a human being.

Teachers are now rather better organized but, as this was typical of the kind of thinking that was current at the time (1966), it is worth looking at the statement in a little more detail.

Drama is described as 'a form of creative expression', not as an art. This is to sidestep most of the problems. 'Its main ingredients are the ability to speak and move.' I think one would wish to go a little further than what amounts to no more than a definition of behaviour. Drama involves behaviour; but much besides.

'Among young children it is egocentric' – only in some respects – and 'related to play'. Accepted. 'But among the older children its main justification is in terms of personal and social contact'. This concept of the social aspects of drama is one that has been frequently expressed. I suppose it owes something to Jerome Bruner's concept of the school as a community, and also to the widespread interest in social values that are a more or less inevitable product of a society that is politically dishonest and materialistically corrupt; but the attitude goes even further than this and I will return to it in the next chapter.

Drama is based on 'a fusion of natural ability and acquired skills'. While this may well be true it is a suggestion that reveals the basic difficulty of defining drama as a subject. For if one removes the acquired skills as properly germane to other disciplines, what is drama left with? Something that one calls natural ability. Ability for what? Acting? Where's the argument?

Drama is unique for two reasons – 'its immediacy of experience and its synthesis of a number of other skills'. With the concept of its immediacy I am wholly in agreement; but not that drama is unique in this. What about music? The author would claim that music-making does not involve so many skills all being used at the same time and with so common a purpose as drama. I find that this *gesamtkunstwerk* concept of drama a dangerous and not altogether valid one. For while it is true that drama can involve many other skills and disciplines, it is dangerous to suggest that these can all be involved at the same time. The *gesamtkunstwerk* under a lesser than Wagner is an inscrutable mush; and even Wagner does not always avoid creating an artistic casserole.

Are those, in short, the kind of arguments that would impress a headmaster under pressure from every subject specialist on his staff and many outside it? Can we not sympathize with his difficulty in accommodating a subject that can be no more sharply defined than by such pieces as this, limp with platitude and heavy with pretentions? In scores of meetings, conferences, and courses I have heard teachers of drama repeat the claim that 'Drama is Life' – a point that will be readily conceded by anyone who is not a practising necrophiliac. The trouble about such generalized claims for any one of the arts is that the others claim to be similarly concerned with the human predicament. Drama cannot lay claim to a unique prescription in personal therapy.

Attempting then to establish unassailable credentials, drama teachers went off on a new tack, claiming that drama was a tool for teaching other subjects. This view has wide support. It was being propounded all over Australia when I visited the continent in 1959. Now there is absolutely no doubt, as a number of examples I gave in the previous chapter testify, that personal involvement can often transform an overtly cerebral concept. But to claim that drama generally is a tool for teaching other subjects is an offence to Shakespeare and a disservice to the very specialists who are making the claim. Drama may be of some help at various times to the English, language, history, and geography teachers but it is they who will be the first to realize its limitations. The drama specialist must look elsewhere for disciplinary salvation.

A further argument that has been widely propounded by drama teachers is that their subject is of particular value in the personal development of the child. This seems to constitute a claim on those neurological and biological activities that I discussed in an earlier chapter. The claim can virtually include the whole educational and developmental process, and once again I must express my concern at the readiness of drama teachers to make claims for territory that has already been staked out by other specialists. The difficulty besetting these claims is that they are all justified. Of course drama is an essential ingredient in human development; of course it can be a useful aid for teaching other subjects; of course it can be a socializing influence and a valuable adjunct in developing human relationships. But the other arts can make similar claims, and if they are not so justified in one respect, they are more so in another. The arts are not the product of human ingenuity but of human necessity and evolved as a part of the biological need for adaptability in expressive, communicative, and behavioural forms of action.

The object of every teacher in school is to get as many little rectangles as possible on the timetable, and he will be quite unscrupulous in the claims he makes for his subject. An education officer once told me that when he asked his subject specialists to pool their minimum requirements for a small comprehensive school, the sum of their proposals would have covered eighteen acres. A headmaster will justifiably wish to know the content and justification of every subject he includes. 'Life?' he will reply to the drama teacher, 'but my whole school is concerned with helping young people to live. A tool for teaching other subjects? Then its place should be in teacher training establishments. You can hardly expect me to timetable a subject whose nature is the embodiment of emotion and whose content is form. I wonder why you do not claim that drama is an art?'

I wonder too.

But let us leave this now and look for a moment at a more urgent matter, the implications for drama of that prodigious grid known as the timetable on which the life of staff and pupils depends. Whatever the importunities of his staff, a headmaster cannot go far in the composition of his timetable without a fairly clear idea of his educational priorities and principles. The problem arises largely from the vast number of subjects that press for inclusion on the timetable. It is very easy to tot up some forty subjects with valid claims for consideration. What is a beleaguered head to do?

Curriculum development requires a headmaster to consider whether there is any way in which the forty competitors can be grouped in subject-areas. Are there various headings beneath which they can be grouped, headings that represent basic concepts of curriculum development? What are the basic areas of the curriculum – the arts, sciences, environmental studies, social studies? Where do languages fit in? Someone suggested a heading that involved something to do with symbolism which made a tidy marriage between the arts and mathematics. Where do games fit in? Is movement to be included under physical education? And dancing under movement? Endless trouble has resulted from this assumption. Should we not include drama with the arts, since many are ready to claim it is an art; or with languages, when many identify it with English; or the humanities, when others claim that its main purpose is problem-solving? And what about religion and the whole question of moral values, when drama is said to be largely a matter of exploring human relations? And if you increase your headings, your subject-areas, you are destroying the whole purpose of your simplification.

Yet I believe that this is the only valid way of tackling the problem. I would be horrified to think that young people in their first year were being offered, say, three hours drama a week and no music. Yet if I heard that a certain class was enjoying plenty of music of a lively kind and that their English lessons included the discussion of important issues, I would not worry greatly if they were not doing much drama. I believe it to be necessary for a headmaster to work out what experiences he thinks it necessary for his young people of different ages, aptitudes, and abilities, to have at any one moment – ensuring that they are always receiving a balance of subjects from the four or five main subject-areas. This is why it is of crucial importance for all teachers to be sufficiently interested in education as a whole to see their own subject in the context of the complete curriculum. A spell of teaching in primary schools might not be bad for some of our over-specializing specialists.

A subject-based curriculum and hence a timetable has got to make sense vertically, in terms of sequential development, and horizontally, so that there is coherence in everything the pupils are doing at any one moment.

A headmaster will therefore need to know the attitude of his specialist teachers towards their subject. There are certain language teachers who would rather meet a class for twenty minutes a day than two or three forty-minute periods a week. Art and drama teachers are often appreciative of long if infrequent periods. Dancers need shorter but more regular classes. One of the best drama teachers known to me worked in a school at Coalbrookdale with a most sympathetic head. He took every class in the school for three complete days, but only about once a year. In those three days he gave his young people an unforgettable experience. This disposition of time suited his method of working which was to improvise with the class, on the spot, a complete story. This would have been quite impossible in the twice-weekly forty-minute periods that are usually allocated to all teachers, and that many drama teachers are content to accept because it suits their own way of working, and, frankly, their limited resources.

Another method of applying the subject-area concept of the curriculum is by timetabling a group of teachers, classes, and children to work together for a number of periods. This may be called Integrated Studies, Humanities, Combined Arts, or what you will. I once asked a small boy at a school in Market Drayton what the first of these expressions meant. 'Lumpin' everything together', he said laconically. I wonder whether the system really works. It depends again on the real professionalism of the teachers as educators, their ability to see their own subjects in relation to others, to be able to be modest, flexible, inventive, and thoroughly collaborative. Quite a tall order.[64]

A further comment on the timetabling of drama. There is usually generous provision in the first year, lessening progressively until the fourth year when there may well be none. The reason for this is that as young people move up the school they must devote an increasing amount of time to preparation for exams. Now if one accepts that exams are in themselves a Good Thing, there is a certain justification for this policy. If one thinks that they are an unnecessary thing, there is still a certain amount of justification. But there is increasing support for the view, enshrined in the general principles of the Certificate of Secondary Education, that if one is to organize the whole of the school's curriculum round the concept of one external examination for all fourth-year pupils, let it at least be as good an exam as possible, encapsulating the work of the school, and not a kind of lottery that some teachers are very skilful at helping pupils to win but which nevertheless involves unacceptable elements of chance. It has been properly said that many exams prove nothing but that the pupil is good at passing them, and various devices have shown the derisory difference in standards between the various Boards.

Drama teachers, quick to see the force of the argument, have not only preferred their own CSE exams but even pressed the main examination Boards to offer General Certificate of Education exams in drama and even dance. This at least ensures for their subject a place on the timetable right up till the fourth year and I hope they are successful in proposing examination structures that do not involve unacceptable compromises for the sake of respectability, and remain in the best interests of the children. One must be clear what one means by drama if one is to offer an exam in it.

If, however, we revert to the first-year timetable, we find a tendency, in a streamed school, to give far more drama to the academically weaker children than to the more able. Now even if we accept this distinction between the bright and the less bright, which I am extremely hesitant to do by ordinary standards of assessment, the suggestion that the former 'need' less art than the latter is a quite intolerable misreading of the nature of children and their education. If the arguments in favour of drama that I have advanced in the previous chapters mean anything at all, they apply to growing children as a whole, though in different ways according to their different needs, a distribution I will analyse in a subsequent chapter. I quote from the Drama Survey:

> 'Our bright children do very little better at drama than our lower streams', it is often said. 'They can throw up more material, but they seem to be inhibited from making use of it.' 'The bright children have been trained to think in abstractions and this seems to inhibit the artistic process of expressing thought and feeling in symbolic form.' 'Weaker children need help in the use of words to clarify their concepts, and brighter children need drama to help them use words in concrete fashion.' And as one headmaster expressed it, 'Remedial children fight: 'A' stream children fight with a purpose.'

We will consider the inconsistencies in these comments in a later chapter.

With the departure from school of a certain number of adolescents at the age of sixteen, drama tends to become an option in the upper school and is all the better for that. Young people have caught up on themselves after the disastrous results of the break between primary and secondary schools and take up work in drama, if at all, with conviction and enthusiasm. As adolescents, they can now think and handle abstract problems and select their hobbies, preferences, and specialisms according to their tastes, needs, and natural gifts. They begin to see the future a little more clearly and to understand what the different arts and disciplines have to offer.

Even the teacher can worry less about personal development and give unrestricted attention to the mastery or understanding of an art, its relationship to society, the inheritance of the masters, traditional forms, and the creation of new ones. And if this renaissance of study is to be encapsulated in 'A' level examinations, let it be ordered in the light of an honest attempt to define the nature of the art. If 'A' level exams in drama continue to be a reflection of English literature papers with an emphasis on plays rather than poetry and fiction, we shall make no further progress.

The report of the Schools Council's enquiry into drama courageously attempts definition; it is an impartial survey of the subject with many examples of work in schools – carefully and constructively analysed. If it is weak on aesthetics, it is notably strong in pedagogy, almost to the extent of limiting the concept of learning; and if there are those who do not think that it goes far enough into the complexities of the subject, they must agree that it leaves the field open for the more adventurous. But certain basic principles about the educational function of drama have now been established and future investigators can begin where the Schools Council team have left off.

# 8 The Drama Teacher

In this chapter I will suggest some of the responsibilities of a drama teacher; but before going into detail I would like to quote from a pamphlet published by the Department of Education and Science called *Music in Schools*. [65]

> . . . the two factors common to all (music) teachers and without which no teacher can excel are delight in music and a sense of style . . .
> The sense of style that enables an infant teacher to vitalize a nursery song and a great conductor to reveal a symphony is essentially the same and it differs not in kind but only in degree.

I suggest that for 'music' the word 'drama' be inserted and my first point will be made. The universality of dramatic experience is for me not in question. Enjoyment is (nearly) all.

By the time the drama teacher applies for a job he will presumably have decided what is the distinctive nature of teaching drama in contrast to teaching other subjects, and what particular contribution it can make to the education of children.

I think that the particular distinction he has to make is in his relationship to English. Does he want to be a member of an English department? Is he able, equipped, or qualified to teach English? And to what level? This will depend on his training as much as his inclinations, upon the extent to which the English department is concerned about speech; not received pronunciation in an elocutionary sense, but speech that is used for the expression of thoughts and feelings. This is a far sharper issue than might be at first suspected; for if there is genuine discussion in a secondary school some awkward questions will be asked. Heresies will be aired. The editors of the Black Papers will be horrified. But one cannot have it both ways. If you encourage your pupils to speak their thoughts, to reveal their attitudes and their individuality, you cannot place a ban on what is said. You do not know what is going to be said until it is said; and if you stipulate in advance no heresies, no criticisms, no sex, politics or religion, you might as well pack up. That is not the way drama lies – nor education. If members of the English department combine a willingness to listen to anything their young people have to say with a respect for the traditions of English literature, there is basis for a common course between English and drama. But if the English department is mostly concerned with syntax, spelling, presentation, critical analysis, and textual sophistries, the drama teacher had better make common cause with his own shadow.

The next question: What is the relationship between improvised drama, scripted drama, and theatre? He must have his answers pat because it is a question that he will assuredly be asked. The drama–theatre controversy shows little signs of abating; but I have absolutely no fear for the teacher who has a synoptic view of the whole process. Some years ago I suggested that this could be summed up in the phrase 'from play to the play', although this is perhaps a little glib and over-simplified. But the issues are in no way mutually contradictory: they are aspects of one complex developing process.

The young teacher will recognize, nevertheless, that techniques in improvisation, of which so much has been made in recent years, do constitute a challenge to accepted dramatic forms. For again it is not an either/or. A young person of secondary-school age must be helped to keep open the sources of his creativity; but as we saw at the end of the last chapter, he is approaching the age when he will acquire increasing skill in handling symbolic form for the manipulation of abstract ideas and this will lead him inevitably towards a sense of constraint, of selection, of the shaping of a concept into a projected form; and this is a lesson that he will learn in all the subjects he studies, in mathematics as well as in English. There is no particular libertarianism in or freedom about drama.

I would hope that every teacher of drama has worked out some kind of criteria for the assessment of a lesson. This is very difficult – as with every subject that does not involve the creation of an artefact or a correct answer to a puzzle, but depends on qualitative judgement. He will tend to give high marks to the extrovert and mark down the contemplative. But if it is the latter who scores in the poetry test, is not this a fair exchange? I do not know. The contemplative must expect poor marks for gymnastics. Does he complain about this? I never felt unduly humiliated at school for my inability to climb a rope or turn a cartwheel, although I would have enjoyed this kind of prowess; but I got better marks in English than some of my more athletic friends. The danger is not so much in overmarking the extrovert as in undermarking the introvert. But even the young person who is hesitant in the expression of ideas and limited in his capacity to project them dramatically should be assessable for the quality of his ideas, his participation in class activities, his judgement and criticisms, his understanding of the medium. We are not speaking of someone who is wholly dumb.

Nevertheless assessment is not easy and the teacher will have to decide whether he is assessing quality of performance. The crucial distinction is not between the extrovert and the introvert but between the show-off and the creative 'actor'. There is a wide spectrum of ability, and he will have to help each of his pupils to find his own level, form, and style of expression. If he can release this in each individual pupil he should have no great difficulty in assessing achievement.

Drama teachers will need to make up their own minds about some of the questions I raised in the previous chapter – how is drama organized within the school? is it a subject in its own right? or is it attached to English? or any other subject or art? is it used by any of the other subject teachers? as a tool? do the language teachers, for example, ever invite their pupils to do a scene from a play in the language they are studying? do they use the direct method of teaching? do the ghosts of W. H. D. Rouse and Cauldwell Cook still walk? I have seen some splendid classroom drama in French and Spanish but never unhappily in Latin or Greek.

A drama teacher will need to find out as best he can by what methods and with what success other subjects are taught in the school, English and the other arts in particular. He might even ask not how, but what other subjects are taught, bearing in mind the constant extension of the curriculum to include social sciences, psychology, ecology, and who knows how many other -ologies and -isms. Drama can draw material from almost any subject and perhaps offer something in return.

In this connection I am not referring to integration, but simply to the fact that if English is well taught in the school the drama teacher can count on the children being articulate and well read. They will be familiar with a variety of literary forms and registers and styles of the spoken as well as the written language. If dance is well taught they will know how to express themselves physically and if there is no dance but some success-ful athletics he can look to find some physical altertness. And so with music and other subjects. And there are plenty of young people who contribute little to drama but write good stories.

Why should this be? What is the reason for success or failure in a subject? What do we mean by natural talent?

Other questions – what is the attitude of the headmaster/mistress to the school play? (I shall make my own contributions to this controversy in Chapter 10.) And what facilities for drama exist within the school? (This I shall discuss in Chapter 12.)

There is a further set of questions to be answered by a teacher who is already a member of a school staff and is preparing his lesson.

Where is the lesson timetabled to take place – in classroom, hall, studio, workshop, theatre, open-air? This will considerably affect his approach to the lesson and what he plans to do. It is not simply a matter of convenience. The venue, the environment, the size and nature of the available space can affect profoundly the nature of the work that can be undertaken. I recall the day I first realized that the biggest space available is not necessarily the most suitable. The class was one of backward boys at a school, now closed, in Islington, and a fine young teacher had been given the hall out of respect for my visit. But the boys went mad, tore around, lost in space, and over-stimulated. They had no concept of creating their own area – a difficult undertaking at the best of times, and the teacher could find no way of holding them together.

At what time of day and on what day of the week is the class taking place, and how might this affect the pupils? In some schools Monday can be a particularly difficult day if a majority of the young people come from poor homes. They arrive at school frustrated and disturbed. Friday afternoons with the promise of two days of so-called freedom can also be an unsatisfactory time for concentrated work.

What has the class been doing previously? What is their next lesson? Have they arrived exhausted from games? or exhilarated? or bored? or unduly suppressed? He will have to cope accordingly. Similarly if he is sensitive he will not send them on to their next lesson in a state of high excitement – or late. Primary-school children react very strongly to the weather. Teachers dread a windy day more than a cold one.

The next group of questions involves the teacher's knowledge of his children: how well does he know them as individuals? Can he identify their individual needs, interests, prejudices?

Any teacher who claims to provide opportunities for individual expression must be at pains to know his class as a group of individuals. Although he may often decide to encourage them to work as a group, he will soon spot those who are able to work collectively, and those who cannot. So he must be ready to find ways of controlling the exhibitionist, holding back without snubbing or frustrating the natural leader, encouraging the backward, the shy, the less articulate; of accepting a contribution from those who are ready to give it and drawing one from those less ready. I remember being deeply puzzled when having watched a drama class at a school in Seton Delaval, Northumberland, I commented to the headmaster on how talented Johnny appeared to be. 'Johnny's a damn nuisance,' he replied, 'we must keep him under.' Johnny had in fact been kept under with such success that he was a nobody, a nothing, until it came to drama. And I wish we could have analysed the nature of those qualities which Johnny expressed in drama to impress a hard-bitten inspector and exasperate a headmaster.

There has been, I think, far too much emphasis throughout education on class-teaching and the group response. One of the most significant reforms of recent years has been the emphasis placed on individual work. I used to be appalled when as a writer and producer of BBC school programmes I visited schools to listen to a production at the receiving end, to hear a teacher say at the conclusion of the broadcast, 'Now take out your crayons and draw an episode from the story,' or 'Take out your pencils and write the story you have just heard.' Is not our response to something we have enjoyed a moment of recollection? And if there is to be gestation is it not likely to take one of many different forms? Do we not introduce children to artistic activities in schools in order that they should become familiar with the relationships between the initial reflex-stimulus and its projection in symbolic or artistic form? The period of gestation, of emotion recollected in tranquillity is as valid for a child as for Wordsworth himself.

Another question: what role does the teacher intend to play in the class? More in drama perhaps, where everyone is playing a role, than in any other subject the teacher has the opportunity to play a variety of roles. I have described Bessie Bullough, a hypnotic figure crouching in the corner of a long hall throwing in suggestions and leaving the children for long periods on their own. At the other extreme is Dorothy Heathcote who places herself in the midst of her class and assumes a role that challenges the people she is working with to answer the questions she throws at them. Some teachers assume the role of chairman, some dress up themselves. Some become autocratic, some self-effacing. One is what one is, but there remains a considerable area of choice.

Again: what work has the teacher done previously with the class he is to take? Is continuity essential? or planned? or to be disregarded?

The forty-minute drama lesson once or even twice a week presents almost insuperable problems of continuity. By the time the young people are ready to work, have decided on the nature of their work, and leaving time for cooling-off or discussion at the end of the class, how much time is left for the slow gathering process of creation that does not respond to clock or bells or a recalcitrant timetable? Lessons tend to be isolated one-off affairs. No wonder teachers turn to books of exercises and tips. Lessons in drama should be self-germinating, transformational; but for this one needs conditions different from those pertaining in many secondary schools. This is one of the reasons why it is so important for the drama teacher to have established relationships with the children outside the drama lesson. Teachers assert that they get very much further in drama with pupils they take also for other subjects than with those they meet only in those isolated and infrequent classes.

Another set of questions more closely related to his teaching: what does he intend to do in the lesson he is about to take? What are his aims, if any, and how does he intend to carry them out? How is he going to decide on the theme, subject, or content of his lesson?

Everything is brought to a head in his answer to these questions. Perhaps the core of the matter lies in the generative element of the experience. A drama lesson depends for any kind of success on the willing collaboration of the participants. Agreement or concurrence on choice of subject is therefore crucial.

Drama, even in its most formal sense – and I mean by this a production of a full-length play – is still a kind of adventure of discovery in which teacher–director and pupil–actors go hand in hand. There is a type of director who works out all movements in advance and imposes them willy-nilly on the actors, just as there are teachers who spout at the children whatever they have in mind to spout without fear or favour or any sensitivity towards the nature of the teaching-learning process. But that is not the way that artistic truth or any kind of reality in oneself or the outside world is discovered.

Lynn McGregor and her Schools Council team have attached considerable importance to this question. They have described it as 'the negotiation of meaning'. It is a bravely used expression for it defies all those who will question the meaning of meaning and supports some of the fundamental concepts that Robert Witkin has discussed in his important book *The Intelligence of Feeling*.[66] It means that the teacher must come to terms with the class about what they are going to do and why; for a drama teacher cannot hope to win whole-hearted collaboration from his class if he has told them in authoritarian terms to improvise on a certain subject that stimulates no visceral response in those depths of the being where creativity has its fount and origin.

Nevertheless the phrase 'the negotiation of meaning' is not to be taken too blandly; for there will be many children in the lower forms of a secondary school unable to accept the responsibility of discussing the subject of their lesson in the somewhat abstract manner in which the expression is used. If they cannot, they must learn. This is then another problem the drama teacher must be prepared to face – how to help children to perceive the relationship between what they want to say and their means of saying it. The only thing worse than being misunderstood is not to be understood at all.

The next question follows from the last. How does the teacher propose to organize his lesson? Are the young people to work as a group? or in small groups? If so, of what size? or individually? This will depend on the content of the lesson as decided between teacher and class.

And the next follows on again: how is the teacher going to ensure the active participation/collaboration of all the children? A general question, this, and one that is related to the means of control he is going to use. Anything, for my money, but the drum or the whistle. We are dealing with delicate sensibilities, not a game of football.

More practically: to what extent is he going to use rostra, lights, sound, music, properties, etc.? These are not arbitrary decisions but closely bound up with choice of material and methods of work. They are elements that can themselves spark off or extend creative work. Their use can be the subject for a lesson. I shall say more about them in Chapter 12.

And finally there are questions related to his actual method or manner of handling a class. He will remember that even though his method is to share responsibility with his pupils and to discuss with them the work to be undertaken, he is still their teacher, and ultimately responsible for the lesson. And above all he is responsible for atmosphere. How far has he succeeded in creating an atmosphere in which the young people want to work creatively? The atmosphere must be such that the young people will be ready to reveal something of themselves, something personal, possibly profound. They will only do this, it is only fitting that they should do this, when the atmosphere is one of trust and confidence. The key word these days is vulnerability. One is intensely vulnerable when one is creating and it is for the teacher to do what he can to ensure that the young people are protected. 'I will tell you what I think, I will show you what I feel, if you promise not to laugh at my disingenuousness.' This unspoken promise must have the force of a solemn vow. We are never more vulnerable than in adolescence.

Nothing is more difficult than to get an improvisation off the ground, persuading someone to speak first, deciding on the actual point of departure. The teacher may have to exercise consummate skill and tact in these difficult first moments. And then at last the improvisation is under way, and he must face the problem of what in the professional theatre would be called 'directing the production'. There are many different methods of doing this. He can stand back and do as little as possible. He can direct like an autocrat in the theatre. He has chosen his role: now he must see it through. But the role of a teacher in a drama class is wholly different from the role of a director in the professional theatre for all the evident similarities. The teacher in the classroom, even more than the director in the theatre, assumes the responsibility of assisting the creative process. For without this the drama lesson is meaningless. And for this reason he must cherish some kind of an idea of what the creative process involves and how it seems to operate in every one of his pupils.                        .

People talk today about 'working in depth'. 'We are going to do an improvisation in depth', says the enthusiastic teacher. But if the class is working superficially, if they are extracting no great reality from the situation, or if their work lacks concentration, what is he going to do about it? How do you make a young person who is improvising superficially, improvise deeply? What do we mean by depth? The first problem to decide is what has gone wrong. Has he assessed the quality of work? Why are the children working inadequately? Does he take them into his confidence and ask them directly? At all events he interferes. He stops the scene and discusses what has been happening. He may ask them questions to help them focus on aspects of the situation that will increase their sense of reality, or recall them to the agreed purpose or theme of the improvisation. There are many alternatives open to him. But they cannot always be readily applied because his purpose is not as clear as that of a director in a theatre who has a text to work from. It is not sheer quality of performance that he is seeking, but understanding. In a curious way it is something less than quality of performance, something a little earlier in the developmental process that culminates in a work of art. It is the selection of a symbol he is after, and the shaping of the symbol in a preliminary and rudimentary way to express a meaning, the meaning of which may only become clear in the course of the improvisation. The means are more important than the end, the journey is more important than arrival. For the final form of the improvisation is not predictable, nor is it anything separate from the process of creation in which teacher and pupils in a curiously intimate relationship investigate or seek to embody a certain area of human experience. The end is dependent on the means because it is not anything separate. That is why the metaphor of the journey is inappropriate. In art we are not travelling from London to Athens, but to Shangri-la, a place whose identity is shaped by the nature of the journey we undertake to get there.[67]

This is the appropriate moment for the teacher, according to Lynn MacGregor and her colleagues, to discuss with the pupils the experience or the subject they are investigating and which they are going to 'act'. For this will establish the meaning of the symbolic projection with which they are involved, and so define clearly the area of learning.

So the questions are these: how does the teacher develop the work? How often, in what manner, and with what objectives does he intervene? And the only answer that can validly be given is that this depends on the purpose of the lesson and the 'meaning' that he has negotiated with the pupils before it began.

And finally he must decide how to end the lesson. With criticisms? with a discussion? or simply by stopping the work five minutes before the bell? This will of course depend on what has happened during the lesson; he should have regard for what the class is going to do next. If they are going to some kind of athletics a certain amount of excitement might not matter greatly. But I think that as a general principle it is not right to end the class and send the young people away in a state of excitement. This is because excitement is a stimulus for action. Excitement that is not canalized into action leads to frustration and even acts of aggression, certainly to irritability. The excitement that is chorused in a drama lesson should be canalized into action; but if time is running out the teacher must find other ways of cooling everyone off.

I make a particular point of this because drama teachers have commonly associated drama with emotion and emotion of an excitable kind, often induced by dark lights and pop music. Whether this is a satisfactory form of drama is his own concern, but it is clearly wrong that other teachers should suffer because of it.

There is some doubt as to whether a class should end with a discussion of the work that has taken place. 'The words of Mercury are harsh after the songs of Apollo.' But I am inclined to think that a moment of tranquil recollection of what may have been achieved will serve to reinforce the experience and provide a forward look to the next meeting. I think, moreover, that it is not just a question for the teacher of coping with excitement, but of providing a modulation between the imaginative world of projected reality in which the class may have been living and the reality they are going to face in the corridors and as they take their seats in the next lesson. If the one experience has been intense the change of key must be managed as skilfully as if it had been composed by Mozart.

In my own contemplative moments I envisage a school where the staff will not all be out for themselves but interested in the totality of education they offer collectively. At the end of a drama class the teacher would say – 'So you are going on to mathematics. You will study a way of analysing and defining the environment. You will learn about certain laws that are important for survival. Have you ever considered the mathematical precision with which leaves on trees are shaped? Have you ever compared this with the precision of shape and pattern that is required of you by your drama teacher? And how this precision of pattern and shape affects your work in drama? Why did you arrange those rostra in the way you did? Because you felt that that was right? Let us discuss at our next meeting whether anything you have done in drama can help your work in maths – and the other way round. See what your mathematics teacher might have to say.'

Then might we see the Muse of drama in all her splendour.

# 9 Further Observations of Drama in Schools

Aristotle in his celebrated sixth chapter of *The Poetics*[68] says that tragedy, which began with improvisation, is composed, in order of importance, of plot, character, diction, thought, song, and spectacle. In this chapter I propose to discuss some of these subjects as applied to drama in general. (The extraordinary quality of Aristotle's thinking becomes clear in the impossibility of operating outside his analyses.) And I propose to begin with improvisation, about which, by implication, I have said a good deal already.

The practice of improvisation as a valid form of artistic expression is one of the most interesting of recent developments in the arts. Improvisation itself is nothing new. Italian improvised comedy dates back to the early sixteenth century and I suspect that talented performers have improvised ever since human beings first began to entertain each other. They have continued to do so because it is the most natural form of acting and also because, as I have argued, it is a basic part of the creative process.

The musicians seem to be a good deal ahead of the theatre world in this respect. Composers like Bach and Mozart did not need to improvise because their music seems to have sprung up in their minds complete and whole and they had to do little more than write it down. But Beethoven brewed over a musical idea for many years while it matured in his mind, and I suspect that his well-known skill in improvisation may have helped to establish a rapport between his sensory and his motor faculties. It is in the world of jazz that prodigious feats of improvisation are achieved and I attribute this not to any particular quality of music that differentiates it from drama, but the sheer professional skill of the musicians.

I believe that improvising is a basic part of the creative process. I have implied it in all that I have said about drama in primary schools. The child improvises in the sense that he plays, because he is still at the stage of development when he is unfamiliar with created forms. Everything is process, associa- tion, discovery. Since he has not yet learnt to think in abstract terms he has not yet learnt to think, as we might say, conceptu- ally, which is to select with great care the words in which his thought is to be expressed or the lines and colours that are to embody his vision. He is playing about with symbolic and expressive forms but he does not see the need, nor is he ready, to attempt the creation of a work of art. But the adolescent in the secondary school is moving in that direction, and his improvisa- tions might develop to the stage when selection and shaping take place and a work of art begins to emerge. At the stage of which I am writing, it is not a matter of either/or, either improvisation or the play. The former is necessary to keep all the options open as long as possible; the latter, because this is the final outcome of the process. Psychologists writing about creativity in general refer to the importance of association, of a free trade in ideas. While we improvise we are uncommitted. We can stand ideas on their head and stand on our head ourselves. We are fools if we surrender this privilege too readily for the sake of some false ideal of art.

Improvisation lies at the very heart of theatrical art by virtue of the fact that it allows the actor, be he child or adult, to stand in his own space, his 'green', and perform an action in the reality and truth of which he, as well as anyone watching, will believe. It is quite remarkable and very simply done. He holds out his hand and we all look eagerly to see what is in it. He may not even need to say what is in it: it may be enough that he shows us by his movements, by his whole attitude. Or he may simply be sitting. Why? Is he tired? Is he waiting for someone? Is he thinking? He is not anyone doing any of these things: he is someone. And our interest is very easily aroused. He may be joined by someone else. Do they look at each other? If not, why not? Do they know each other? Are they communicating, though not looking? And if they look at each other, how do they do so? And the transformation of reality begins, for it is far more interesting to watch an actor improvise someone who is waiting for something than a person in real life, than a real person on Waterloo station. Such exercises are examples of non-verbal communication, an experience of which there is growing inter- est among people in many artistic and para-medical disciplines. Even the popular game of role-playing is not far removed.

The person who has not seen the intensely interesting rela- tionships that can emerge between two people working simply but sensitively together does not know what improvisation, or for that matter theatrical art, is all about. It is not to do with the Russian Revolution and the end of the world: it is to do with the words and actions of a human being who feels very strongly about something. At the same time by action one does not mean furious activity. Maurice Maeterlink has a splendid passage in an essay called 'The tragical in daily life',[69] in which he says:

> There is a tragic element in the life of everyone of us that is far more real, far more penetrating, far more akin to the true self that is in us than the tragedy that lies in great adventure. Must we indeed roar like the Atrides before the Eternal God will reveal himself? And is He never by our side at times when the air is calm and the lamp burns on unflickering . . .

While you have every right to improvise on the subject of the Russian Revolution and the end of the world if that is what excites you, you will have to come to terms with the fact that although the intellectual and imaginative scope of improvisation is limitless, its constraints are imposed by its qualities and those are the expressive abilities of a human being. These abilities are both physical and oral. A synthesis of the two enables us to express ourselves in a wide range of levels at the same time. We can say far more at any one moment than is expressed in the literal meaning of the words we are using. Shakespeare is the supreme master of creating a realistic foreground against a landscape of almost infinite metaphysical complexity. But then he was a poet. The value of dramatic improvisation in education lies in the opportunity it provides the young person to project the realities of revolution in terms of the violence of human feelings that can lead to such enormities of behaviour.[70] This is play-adaptation on a high level of reality. Art is a projection of our love–hate relationship with society in all its variety and uncertainty.

Three important books have appeared in recent years on the subject of improvisation. One is Violet Spolin's *Improvisation in the Theatre*.[71] It made something of a stir on its first appearance in this country for it propounded a new concept of dramatic games. Miss Spolin has selected some basic elements of the actor's art – concentration, relaxation, ensemble playing, quick imagination, verbal agility, physical accuracy of expression, and group sensibility, and proposed a variety of exercises by which they can be developed. She presents these exercises as games that enjoy the additional advantage of being fun. She includes a useful chapter on how these games can be related to work on texts and the more complex techniques of performance.

The interesting aspect of these exercises for a drama teacher is that they suggest methods of balancing the acquisition of technical skills with the freeing of the imagination which excessive technique is often thought to destroy. But their limitation is that they are self-contained, one-off exercises, almost wholly lacking that exploratory, transforming, and creative quality that makes improvisation a crucial part of the artistic process. They provide so accessible a collection of activities, roughly related to the practice of drama, that teachers tend to employ them in the place of drama itself. In fact they represent little more than the limbering that a dancer will undertake before a class: they do not constitute a drama class in themselves. I am reminded of Gavin Bolton's strictures on the dangers of mistaking a preparation for drama for drama itself.

Another book to which I should like to draw attention is Clive Barker's *Theatre Games*,[72] in which the author proposes a fairly complex rationale for the use of games in the training of an actor and includes an interesting discussion on the complex mind-body relationship that is found in Gestalt psychology. He covers a good deal more ground than Miss Spolin and in this respect his book is both more and less helpful for teachers, more thorough in analysis, more complex in application.

The third book is the work of two college of education lecturers, John Hodgson and Ernest Richards. They have called their book quite simply *Improvisation*[73] This is an immensely thorough and painstaking book in which the authors discuss many aspects of drama, including an approach to work on texts, and analyse qualities of dramatic work such as sensitivity and freedom. This they do by referring constantly to play which they see as that activity which most fully and satisfactorily embodies these qualities. Here are some of the chapter headings which indicate the range of the book and the variety of approaches to drama that have to be encompassed if it is to be thoroughly understood as an art: developing concentration and spontaneity; stimulating the imagination; building characterization; explaining mood and feeling; understanding the nature of a dramatic text; seeing the play as a living whole; understanding the kind of play; sensing the shape and rhythm; meeting and knowing the characters.

Yet one may question the capacity of any book that claims to be a practical manual to provide those aids to imaginative vitality which this book sets out to do. A lifelong resistance to tips and aids is based on an apprehension that a book about the imagination and creativity must be as imaginative and creative as the very experiences it is describing. The problem is to get to the root of the process so that the teacher will not follow a set of rules, which will be inhibiting, or of exercises, which can be unproductive, or prescriptions, which are daunting, but find a clear point of departure from which, with guides to prevent him wandering too far afield, he will map out his own route and make his own landfall.

A corollary to the well-structured exercises to be found in Miss Spolin's book is to be found in Brian Way's *Development Through Drama*.[74] I find it difficult to accept the general premise of a book which equates drama with life. 'The intention of this book' says the author, 'is to suggest ways of providing practice at this particular skill (skill at living).' In this sense a basic definition of drama might be simply 'to practice living'. Fond though I am of Brian Way, and respectful of all that he has done for children's theatre, I am bound to say that I find this attitude questionable. I do not think that I need here reiterate what I have emphasized constantly, namely that innumerable activities we do, either as children or as adults, in the various arts, are of very great remedial and therapeutic value even to the most apparently normal of human beings; but to suggest that the basic purpose of drama is to provide skills in living is wholly gainsaid by many practitioners and teachers of drama who are often delightful people but no more proficient in whatever Brian Way means by the skills of living than anyone else. And I would not by any means exclude myself.

Nevertheless the book contains passages of great perception: I was particularly interested in Brian Way's description of the preliminary stages of improvisation as 'scribbling':

> There are few activities undertaken by human beings that do not contain a 'scribble' stage when there is little mastery in skill, no sense of form, no beginning, middle or end, speech is faltering – but the group often knows what is happening and needs to go through this play-stage. What will happen now depends on the decision of the group or the teacher about their purpose or intention.

And that is really the stage that we have reached in our discussion. The teacher and the class have to decide on their area of work. I have said a good deal about this already, but there are various points on which I would like to be a little more specific. And the first is what I can only call the search for truth.

The difference between improvising and acting a play is that in the former the actor begins with his own conception and develops it to whatever degree of formality he wishes, even, in some cases, to writing down the improvised text; in the latter he has to move backwards from the formality of the text to the truth that lies behind it, a most difficult process and one with which all actors will be familiar. Perhaps I should add in passing that there is no definition of what constitutes an improvisation; it may be a single exercise, done once and forgotten; but it may equally well be an episode that is built up over days and weeks to the formality of a full-length play. Nevertheless, improvisation begins with an idea which is developed and dropped at the will of the participants.

Choice of subject and methods of working on it reveal almost limitless examples of the phoney and the unreal. Let us consider choice of subject first. As we saw when we were discussing primary-school drama, it is very much easier to take an existing story and improvise it than to invent one's own. This is because a story provides a structure, a setting, a projected reality, and the players can concentrate on making their own 'version'. An archetypal story of a general kind obviously presents very much more suitable material for this than a story by, say, George Eliot. For example, the Nativity story, like Greek myths, is of general application and can be individualized in innumerable different ways; but a story by a novelist is already so individualized that nothing can be done but an attempt at recreation. This is far more the function of the scripted play than of improvisation. Tom Stabler, who, it will be remembered, used drama largely to develop in children the capacity to think, used almost entirely the great epics of the Bible and ancient civilizations. Myths carry their own potent associations which are far too often smothered through their being treated as fairy stories.

The present age has set a premium on originality. This is because there is a very considerable demand for good quality original material by the voracious broadcasting organizations. But I think that educationally there are more important reasons. The reflex-stimulus produces its most vigorous response from immediate experience. We may be stimulated to improvise on the subject of the Nativity or the Circe story. Through these stories we may make a profound comment on contemporary society, or we may enjoy the stories for their own sake. But the activity that really interests us and that seems to lie at the real heart of artistic creation is that which derives directly from a view of society or humanity which is developed in terms of an attempt to reconstruct an outer reality with absolute integrity towards the original stimulus and the original vision of that society.

On the whole, drama teachers have been enterprising in this respect. One of the results of their slightly brutal rejection of inherited form and the repertoire of classical drama has been an emphasis on young people's own material, even if this has tended to involve a rather superficial and limited view of reality. A good deal of drama in secondary schools is only an extension of the kind of dramatic play which we saw in primary schools. Innumerable improvisations on spacemen are only an extension of the cowboy and Indian prototype; and I have seen youth groups improvise on the most extraordinary subjects which can only be explained as a development of their early dramatic play using rather more sophisticated material. But there is a good deal of drama, which may amount to little more than role-playing, which does nevertheless attempt to tackle reality, or, in more practical terms, contemporary issues and social problems.

I do not want to overemphasize this point of view and suggest that the only valid drama is of a social kind. I am trying to emphasize that the impetus for creative activity must be a response to contemporary reality and an attempt to recreate this reality in as honest a manner as possible. An over-rigid application of this view excludes an element which I emphasized in discussing primary-school drama – and that is fantasy. Fantasy is not just an element of which one takes a dollop to add colour to one's improvisation: it is a very part of the creative transformational process itself, which differentiates perhaps more clearly than anything else the work of one individual, whatever his age, from another.

People frequently speculate on the extent to which an artist is aware of exactly what he has created. I believe that when an artist is working at the full stretch of his creative power he uses material which is not the outcome of deliberate invention but thrown up by the force of his creative psyche from the depth of his subconsciousness. It is presumably what E. M. Forster was getting at when he spoke of the artistic process as consisting of a bucket that the artist drops into his subconscious 'drawing up something which is usually beyond his reach'.[75] This is why much creativity is self-generative. And it is why a dramatist is unwise to direct his own play: he is not always aware of exactly what he has written, because some of his material is the inexplicable product of his subconscious.

I have said that the creative process is an attempt to reconstruct reality in as convincing a manner as possible. I do not think that convincing is altogether the right word, but the only other I can use is the word which we hold, since Pilate's unfortunate question, in the greatest distrust – truthful. What does it mean to be artistically truthful? It is much easier to say what is artistically false or phoney. This is not the place to become involved in a discussion that has vexed the critics and exasperated the artists over the centuries; but one can argue, I think, that by proceeding from a central idea that is a response to existing reality, by way of the kind of accretions that are thrown up by Stanislavsky's 'if', with the kind of associations that are the product of a lively imagination, we can construct a theatrical or artistic reality, which is a kind of symbolic form, and acceptable as artistically truthful. What would I do if a certain circumstance arose; and what would be the consequences? And the consequences of the consequences? And so on. The initial action is the stone thrown into the water. The ripples at first are close, rapid, and indistinguishable from each other; the outer ripples have a slower rhythm. The metaphor does not altogether hold, for in reality the outer and more delayed ripples may be deeper than the initial ones. One thinks of that delightful fantasy *Clochemerle* where the building of a public lavatory in the square of a small town almost brings Europe to a state of war.

There is yet another word to describe the quality I am discussing and that is sincerity. It is one that many people claim they can discern and which they value highly. Yet it was borne in on me many years ago that sincerity is not a matter of feeling. A feeling is a feeling and cannot be an insincere feeling. What it can be is a feeling inappropriate for a certain situation. If an actor cannot find the voice or the gestures for a certain character in a certain scene, we say that he is unconvincing or insincere. Sincerity is thus a matter of finding the right expression for a certain feeling; or the right feeling for a certain scene. An actor is almost bound to be insincere in a role that lies outside his technical competence, for he will not have the range of vocal and physical expression to match the emotional demands of the part. When we praise an actor for his sincerity we recognize an appropriate feeling adequately embodied in his acting. Sincerity is thus closely related to skill and the whole manner in which a concept is projected. Insincerity, like sentimentality, is a corruption of feeling and it is used by autocrats for political and entrepreneurs for commercial purposes.

I will give a very simple example of what I mean. I recently set up an improvisation for some third-year students by asking one of them to lie on the floor in the middle of the studio. I did not say anything about the body, whether the person was alive or dead, asleep or resting, ill or gazing at the sky, hoping that the group would make their own decision. Slowly one of the students began to approach the body. He knelt down beside it. A moving reality was growing. Suddenly a member of the group shouted out from the side of the studio, 'Don't touch it.' Immediately the growing reality was destroyed and gave place to a kind of theatrical excitement. In a moment we had moved from the transformation of a genuine reality to an imposed fictional reality, a kind of short-cut to an exciting but not necessarily very convincing theatrical situation.

An acute sensibility to theatrical truth was fostered in me during the late 1930s when I worked for Michel St Denis at the London Theatre Studio. One of my first assignments was a group improvisation on the subject of the impact of a storm on a seaside town where there was a beach for tourists and a small port of fishing vessels. I saw no way of introducing a dramatic element but with the aid of smugglers and pirates, and such highly theatrical stereotypes. St Denis, however, was insistent that I let the drama grow out of the reality of the situation: the effect of the storm on the holiday-makers on the one hand and on the fishermen on the other. It was a hard but salutary lesson.

The same law of truth and sincerity must operate when one's medium is the highly formalized one of dance or music – formalized because the form is remote from ordinary reality. There is nothing 'real' about someone blowing down a brass tube except that he is doing just that. There is nothing 'real' about someone pirouetting round the stage thirty-two times consecutively. Yet the blowing of the trumpets, the twisting and turning of the dancer can excite in us a powerful emotion which we recognize as having something truthful about it. Although it is often difficult for anyone but the expert to say much about music except whether it pleases us or not, we can usually tell whether it is sentimental or pompous or theatrical, all terms indicating some falsity in the feeling of the music. And we can also tell whether it moves us. I suppose the most complex and complicated form of art ever created is an opera by Wagner. Yet the paradoxical fact is that the prodigious extravagances of *The Twilight of the Gods* can fill us with such an overwhelming sense of reality and tragedy that when we come out into the street at the end of the performance, the reality of real life seems paltry and unreal. What is important is what has just happened in the opera house – Siegfried is dead, Brünhilde is immolated, the Rhine has overflowed its banks, and Valhalla is in flames. It is nonsense – but of a transcendent reality. When Aristotle refers to music as the most mimetic of the arts, I think he has the same phenomenon in mind.

Some of the most moving moments I have had in schools have been confrontations with young people struggling to express the reality of a situation. I gave a number of examples in the Drama Survey. I think particularly of three boys of about fourteen who were working on the Crucifixion. As Roman soldiers they were nailing Jesus to a large cross they had established on the floor of the hall. Suddenly they paused and the conversation went like this –

> 'What soft feet he's got!' (*Pause.*)
> 'Yes, like a dancer's.' (*Another pause.*)
> 'Well, let him dance his way out of this one.'

Another episode took place in a school in Market Drayton. The story was that of Antigone and the dead bodies of the brothers were lying on the floor. The boys had covered themselves with their overcoats to indicate their burial. But this threw the King's guard into a state of confusion since the point of the situation is that Creon has refused them burial. I can recall vividly the anxiety on the boy's face as he said, 'What are you all lying there – not being unburied for?'

And yet another story concerns a youth group in Basingstoke who were giving an improvised performance of the fairy story The Frog Princess to an audience of Old Age Pensioners. When the princess who had been transformed into a frog was turned back into a princess, an old old lady in the audience said wistfully, 'I'd like to be a princess, one day.'

'And so you shall,' said the girl with astonishing quickness of mind, and taking the crown from her head, she placed it on that of the old lady.

It is this quality of facing reality, however apparently unpleasant, that is most impressive about the work of Dorothy Heathcote. Many teachers will have seen the films made of her work. In one she asks some very tough boys to consider the brutalities of life in a prison-camp. In another she takes as her theme political assassination. I have seen her handle other subjects of considerable social delicacy, but her attitude to those she is working with is always direct, honest, and totally unsqueamish. She produces a sincerity of response by the sheer strength of her challenge. 'The stuff of drama,' she says in one of her films, 'is man when he's in a mess' or words to that effect.

This ability to reorganize reality is an extraordinary phenomenon. E. H. Gombrich has provided some fascinating examples of how Constable was accustomed to reorganize the reality he saw before him, rearranging trees, houses, hedges, ponds to satisfy some inner sense of rightness.[76] Artists play around for years with sketches, tunes, ideas until they have found the satisfying artistic form, imponderable though this may be and often defying cricitism. The justification of art lies in this transformation of reality; and if standards of young people are less demanding than those of Constable and Beethoven, and the whole process is worked out on a simpler level, the difference is only one of degree. One cannot work in art form and pretend that it is something different.

It is a sign of our insecurity that the word therapy crops up constantly in any discussion or definition of dance and drama. We are concerned about the vulnerability of the species. We are more concerned with decision-making and personal develop-ment than with art, matters which are implicit in the act of creation but which are not its beginning or its end. For many years there was emphasis on the emotional aspects of drama and teachers looked on themselves as the great stirrer-uppers of excitement amid the dreary wastes of other disciplines. They would begin their lessons with limbering-up to emotional pop, often in a darkened studio with great pools of coloured light. They chose subjects of a highly emotional kind, Domesday, for example, and the four-minute warning of the end of the world. I remember my disgust, during the 1960s, at the number of improvisations I saw on those last four minutes of human existence – as often as not to a background of powerful sym-phonic music such as Mars from *The Planets* Suite with its insistent 5/4 rhythm which created an atmosphere of distur-bance in which the one thing that could not take place was organic creative work.

There is of course a very considerable difference between excitement, which is a stereotyped reaction to moments of alarm, fear or jubilation, and which motivates some immedi-ately adaptive activity, and emotion which is a deeper visceral response and a basic element in the creative act. I am sorry that more teachers have not read their Maeterlink.

It is exceedingly unfortunate that so many drama teachers should have identified their work uncompromisingly with the expression of emotion, partly because it is bad politics, but also because it shows a misunderstanding of the nature of emotion. Let us take the latter first.

While drama teachers need not become involved in the more

complex controversies of the neurologists and psychologists, it is nevertheless important that they should understand that recent research has tended to play down the ancient dichotomy between thought and emotion. They are both phenomena which in scientific terms are exceedingly difficult to define; but it is nevertheless apparent that the particular activity of the brain which we call intelligence and which involves the so-called power of thought, involves an element of those sensory experiences which we associate particularly with emotion. I have quoted both Coleridge and John Macmurray in support of the close identity of thought and emotion and I am aware that the whole problem can become an intensely philosphical one. The subject clearly preoccupied Plato and other Greek philosophers who between them brought both poetry and sterility to their discussions. But the lesson for drama teachers does not seem to me to be a difficult one. It is simply to repeat that however much art may have become associated with the expression of emotion, it is to misunderstand the process and to misuse the medium if we exclude the faculty of thought and subscribe, by implication, to the idea that thought and emotion are inimical to one another rather than complementary facets of the same neurological process.

I have already drawn attention to Susanne Langer's *Philosophy in a New Key*. In her invaluable discussion on music she establishes a direct relationship between emotion and its expression in musical form. But since music is usually considered, of all the arts, to be the one most clearly identified with an expression of emotion, one might wonder where the thinking comes in. Yet when one considers the prodigious amount of intellectual organization that goes into the scoring of a major symphonic work it is impossible to see the process of composition as anything but a prodigious intellectual feat, however emotional the nature of the music. Our difficulty in grappling with the idea derives, I think, from this false concept of thought to which I have already referred. When one ceases to think of it as a cerebral activity, isolated and independent, and sees it as a matter of association and perception, though of a most complex kind, one can begin to escape the dangerous dichotomy that puts scientists into the category of thinkers and artists into that of feelers.

The whole subject has been carefully investigated by Professor Liam Hudson in his books *Contrary Imaginations* and *Frames of Mind* wherein he discusses the now well-known categories of convergers and divergers.[77]

In his most recent book, *The Cult of the Fact*, he returns to the discussion.[78] The distinction remains valid; but what he now establishes is that the stereotyped methods of 'thinking' are established for the child who is going to be a scientist between the years of five and thirteen and for the artist in adolescence. The former is marked by a quality of emotional control, the latter by an interest in emotional self-expression, a distinction that becomes most evident in the response to dreams. While the diverger can accept irrational elements in his emotional functioning, the converger allows irrational impulses to suffuse his perceptions. What the teacher needs to know is to what extent he should watch for these tendencies in the growing child and counter them in the name of providing a balanced education.

I also said that I thought it politically maladroit for drama teachers to associate themselves with the idea that drama is excessively concerned with emotion. The reasons are clear. If drama is to husband its own integrity, it must establish its balance of interests between the cognitive and the affective. Of this interrelationship I have no doubt. In the rehearsal of a play one is moving freely between a variety of experiences. One is looking closely at the text, perhaps a single line, a word, or even a punctuation mark. One is puzzling to understand, to get the thinking right. Then we are on our feet trying to express that thought in voice, in movement, in gesture, in terms of human behaviour. One moves freely, though in no kind of rhythm, between the inner schema or understanding where intelligence and thought reside, and their outward embodiment. And the whole process takes place in an atmosphere that is charged with creative excitement, the excitement of trying to discover, select, organize, pin down, and shape the symbolic form in which the initial concept shall be finally expressed.

The important question of the 'control' of emotion has been the subject of a most interesting book by Robert Witkin called *The Intelligence of Feeling*. I described something of its origins in an earlier chapter. Malcolm Ross says[79] that 'the prime concern of the arts curriculum should be with the emotional development of the child through creative self-expression.' Readers will recognize that I accept this definition so far as it goes but realize the need to take it further. Mr Witkin helps us to do so.

The crux of his argument is that

*feeling impulse* expressed through an *expressive medium* yields feeling-form. Every artist . . . chooses a medium that he feels will adequately respond to his attempts to externalize, to embody his feelings. He engages in a reciprocating relationship with his medium, his consciousness oscillating between his own expressive impulse and the expressive response of the medium. The process results in a 'feeling form' that recalls his sensing and allows him 'to know his being'.

I am not sure that this takes us much beyond what Susanne Langer said many years earlier, but that does not invalidate it. The particular value of the book lies in Mr Witkin's submission of the arts – dance is unhappily not included – to the same five criteria.

The first is *self-expression and the individuality*, since he considers it to be generally agreed that the creative arts provide an opportunity for self-expression and the individual approach to a greater extent than do other parts of the curriculum and that they are about the individual and his personal relationship to the world rather than about facts.

The particular problem of drama, as I see it, is that the actor, in the words of the great Louis Jouvet,[80] is both instrument and instrumentalist. Mr Witkin found that drama teachers were intensely aware of the ease with which dramatic action can lead into a crisis situation which can only be channelled with the greatest difficulty into 'feeling-form'. The justification for a pupil experiencing a release of emotion lies in the opportunity it gives him to objectify that emotion, which is to channel it into some symbolic form. This is a subject which I think we have already adequately discussed.

The second of Mr Witkin's criteria is *control of the medium*. 'The creative act,' he says, 'has significance not only for one's own production of an expressive form but also from the point of view of an expressive form produced by others', which an individual can use in a variety of ways. This is a point which I have left to tackle until this moment for Mr Witkin puts the problem clearly.

> The vast body of rules, techniques, conventions and practices that constitute the heritage of expressive form are an immense threat to the expressive act itself . . . Images can be painted, sequences of dance steps enacted, music composed and performed without being self-expressive . . . The sensate impulse of the human being must be projected into the expressive medium, sustaining or reshaping it in a continuing creative process that enables the individual to make the continuous live adjustments in expressive behaviour required to realize feeling in the release of the impulse.

This is truly said and, as I have already confessed, it is one of the reasons for this book. For many teachers, dedicated to a concept of emotional self-expression in dramatic form, have viewed the constraining influence of technique with such abhorrence and constituting so grave a threat to the creative impulse that they have rejected any faint suggestion of such constraints. And the result has often been chaos, for it is in the nature of the impulse to seek coherent creative expression and form. The form that eventually emerges may have little evident relationship with the original impulse for it has undergone a profound process of assimilation that results in its transformation into eventual creative acts or acts of creation. What is really inescapable, and it is where many teachers need to be more assured in their methods, is that young people must be able to handle a medium with ease. Some will show more natural skill in dancing, painting, writing or acting than others. But because a teacher is helping them to express themselves confidently in these media it does not mean that he is imposing upon them a technique in any limiting sense, except in so far as an acceptance of a limitation is a crucial part of the whole process. For there is really no half-measure between unrealized emotion which is chaos and an attempt at channelling an emotion into expressive form which is clarity. No one will pretend that the process is easy. Artistic creation is associated with extremes of pain and pleasure. While I see no need for young people to be asked to experience the creative process in any way that induces personal anguish, nevertheless I think there is no escape from the fact that it is very hard work. A film of the early work of Martha Graham shows her dancers rehearsing in the studio. 'When you have worked like this for ten years', she says, 'you are free'. When you have worked less hard for less than ten years, you are less free (in your medium) but the initial impulse may have been correspondingly less demanding.[81] It is a similar thought to that of Noel Coward – 'I like complete spontaneity on the stage – after six weeks' intensive rehearsals.'

Mr Witkin's third heading is *the use of realized form*. He is referring to the relationship between an individual's own impulses and 'the expressive forms created by other forms that are already realized'. This is an exceedingly difficult problem, for while it is true, as Mr Witkin says, that a masterpiece may be appreciated on many levels, that it can absorb an infinity of different approaches and interpretations, many young people find it exceedingly difficult to come to terms with *Hamlet* and the Choral symphony. 'O' and 'A' level examination rooms are strewn with the ruins of rejected masterpieces.

The acceptance of inherited works of art is closely bound up with the question of the creation of a work of art, and that involves the role of the audience, spectator, viewer, teacher or listener. It is an exceedingly difficult question which I shall consider in detail in the next chapter. The walls of school corridors are lined with usually not very good reproductions of masterpieces of visual art; at the turn of a switch one can hear the musical masterpieces of the world superbly performed; the classics of literature are available in cheap paperback editions – yet we live in a society whose cultural values are abominable and getting worse. It is three thousand years since the Homeric poems were written, the Bible and the great Indian epics, six hundred years since Dante, four hundred since Shakespeare. What in the name of civilization are we about?

Fourthly, Mr Witkin writes about *personal development*, suggesting, rightly, that it is the whole *raison d'être* of the arts curricula as seen in many schools. Here is an example of what I mean. These few lines come from the review of a book called *Drama for Upper and Middle Schools* by Christopher Day, who is a well-known and most able drama adviser. The book is published by Batsford and the review, which is by a college of education lecturer, appears in the Summer 1976 number of *Speech and Drama*.

Mr Day, says the reviewer, defines drama as:

> a process of exploration rather than a preoccupation with acting. To him the usual priorities of movement and voice are secondary to the more inner attributes of problem-solving and decision-making, and his project work with his classes is structured to develop these maturing experiences. He is closely in tune with the Dorothy Heathcote approach in regarding drama as concerned with social and personal development first and with the aesthetic of acting second. Emphasis is on attitudes rather than characterization . . . .

The emphasis is moral – problem-solving and decision-making; social – personal development; abstract – attitudes. All this is of considerable educational importance; but para-sociological concepts can in no way be considered the main subject-matter of drama. The repeated emphasis on drama as 'learning by doing' is to devalue drama until it is virtually unrecognizable as an art.

I must refer once again to the work of Dorothy Heathcote. She has quite properly been much discussed, filmed, televised, and generally publicized since she encapsulates an approach to drama that commands respect while defying the accepted values. The first time I saw her working in a school – it was in Jarrow, I believe – she had taken marriage as her theme. It was immediately apparent that the extraordinary quality of her work lay in the direct and almost brutal manner in which she approached the children. 'All right', she said to the bride's parents, 'if your daughter said to you that she was going to get married, what would you say?' Obvious hestitation. 'Then let's take it farther back. What would you think about having a daughter youself?' Pause. 'Have you any sisters? are they married?' And so on. Gradually the answers came. They came as the children began to realize that this was not a 'con trick'. Their own individual views were really wanted. Told in these terms, there will be those who claim that this is an unwarrantable intrustion into the private lives of the children. That that is not the case is the result of the absolute integrity of the relationships that Mrs Heathcote establishes with the children she is teaching. Even so, there were a couple who could not face the challenge, and in those days, for I am speaking of ten years ago, Mrs Heathcote did not always know when to relax the pressure. She was not always aware of the power of her own considerable personality. But I have little sympathy with the criticism for if we are to help children to think and feel for themselves and to have confidence in what they think and feel, we must be prepared for heresies. There is really no other way. But Mrs Heathcote is not perturbed. 'Put those thoughts and feelings into words! Come on, now, I'm a local priest. Come and tell me why you want to get married.'

May I revert to the problem of the child who cannot face the challenge of this approach? It is a situation in which the greatest sensitivity of the teacher is called for. For in drama a child, every bit as much as an adult, is exposing himself more than in any other activity. The good teacher demands this exposure and often gets it. But he must know how to handle the inevitable embarrassment in a child: when to leave him alone; when to press; when to return. It is playing with the deepest sensibilities.

A second point is closely related to this. Dorothy Heathcote is a role-playing teacher. She frequently plays a part in the improvisation she is structuring. She has a very powerful personality. She is also very intelligent and combines these qualities with considerable moral integrity. She is also something of an actress. It is these qualities that enable her to get astonishing results from boys in an Approved School. She places herself in the middle of the group and creates through her warmth, her strength, and her north country accent, a great sense of security. If there is danger, she is sharing it. But there are children who cannot stand the physical proximity as well as the emotional challenge and who will try to retire behind their own defences.

By assuming a role a teacher places himself in a position of both strength and weakness. If the children accept his role, it enables him to move into a situation of shared experience. But if the children do not accept the role, he has placed himself in a position from which he has no freedom of manoeuvre for he can only comment from within the role in which he has placed himself. He has imposed on the children a reality which in certain circumstances they cannot, or will not accept. I have observed that some of Mrs Heathcote's most successful pupils, notably Tom Stabler whose work I have already described, use her direct and challenging approach but do not assume roles themselves.

Gavin Bolton's methods of work throw up other interesting points. With a sharp analytical mind and less moral fervour than Mrs Heathcote, he creates drama from the here and now; but he is quick to challenge the class on the significance of what they are doing. He is close to the Schools Council's team's emphasis on 'the negotiation of meaning'. Yet in this sense the phrase is perhaps a misleading one and I do not want to saddle Gavin Bolton with it. For the evident meaning of meaning is a rational one; while the meaning of the dramatic action, the poetic or literary symbol or the visual image, may contain both significance and meaning at many different levels. An actor at a certain point in the action may decide that he wants to light a cigarette. The meaning of this action may be that he enjoys smoking; or that he is nervous and wants a sedative; or bored and wants a distraction; or simply wants to put an action between himself and his feelings. The manner in which he lights his cigarette will indicate which of these meanings, or of others, is the relevant one. Whether he carries through the action deliberately, or clumsily, or slickly, or casually will each carry its meaning. So that when he leads a group into a new reality of its own contriving he will help the participants to see the significance, and in the broad sense, the meaning of what they are doing.

He gives the example[82] of a boy throwing a stick, which in due course he transforms into the concept of Robin Hood throwing a spear. This leads him to describe – guardedly he does not use the word 'define' – dramatic activity as 'the creation of meaning that is independant of the environment by using actions and objects present in the environment'.

This involves three criteria: a sense of time; a quality of meaning; a quality of feeling.

I have already used the word 'transformation'. A response to the environment is transformed into a symbol; and that response is one of feeling. It is emotional. Hence the quality of that emotion is crucial for the creative act. In the process of transformation we see the problem of the creation of the symbol. The symbol embodies a concept and involves a 'meaning'. But this symbol which in the first instance carries meaning for the creator of the symbol, the artist or the actor, has ultimately to carry meaning for the audience. So that one of the crucial problems facing drama in schools may be expressed like this: at what stage is it educationally desirable that a performer, of whatever age he may be, should shape the symbol so that it is not only expressive of the feeling he wants to express but clear in meaning to the audience? Teachers tend to minimize the importance of this latter process. My own view is that it is crucial; but that a child will not be ready to handle such abstract concepts until he has at least reached a mature stage of development.

It is unhappily not only in drama that the nature of the medium is side-stepped. In a recent paper,[83] aims for teaching dance, as expressed in a CSE Mode III syllabus, included the following:

to help children reach their creative potential ability;

to allow children to participate at their own level and gain personal satisfaction and achievement;

to provide for children to use their imagination and express their ideas through using their bodies;

to display an awareness of and a response to others;

to encourage the moral growth of children;

to use dance as a means of continuing to explore the nature of human beings and the quality of their relationships;

to externalize their inner states and feelings as a way of coming to terms with them.

O Justification, what monstrosities are committed in thy name!

Here is another example. A new syllabus for a Mode 1 CSE examination is being discussed. The draft begins with a statement of the 'four essential areas of learning through drama'. These are:

range of languages uses

to reflect upon particular themes and topics

to cooperate with the group in the way of drama work

to develop the pupils' critical appreciation and enjoyment of his own work and of drama in a wider context.

These may have a good deal to do with English teaching. I cannot see that they have much relevance to drama. I would as soon propose Transcendental Meditation or the celebration of the Mass.

Yet again, Richard Courtney, an Englishman who has worked in Canada for many years, analyses the three main goals in drama teaching as:

to enhance students' learning

to enhance students' lives

to enhance students' abilities in the dramatic art form of theatre.

The teaching of drama must be of a very high quality if these claims are to be substantiated.

So we find that the arts are being used for a wide range of personal, social, psychological, and educational purposes. I see no objection in this provided that no one assumes that various kinds of therapy are the main function of the arts. For in the whole process of the creation of the symbol there cannot avoid being great personal and even therapeutic advantages. My argument is that the art process does not deny any of this, but goes further, deeper, wider and that we are selling our children short when we limit drama to role-playing and the exploration of personal relationships.

Any kind of creative expression has its appropriate form. Yet the form of an idea is inseparable from the idea itself. An idea cannot exist as a form distinct from its own identity. The free-wheeling, open-ended improvisations of children at junior school cannot be described as formless because it is the timeless unselective quality of the improvisation that constitutes its form. It may not be a very evident form, but it is form nevertheless. A young person, having undergone various experiences, will articulate aspects of those experiences. It is part of his developing awareness and power of differentiation that he should wish to identify a concept with a certain form. But, let me repeat, we are not dealing with two separate experiences. The concept or idea is only fully realized in its appropriate form. Otherwise it is like the world before the Creation. That is why I believe that we must not let our passion for creativity blind us to the need to acquire technique.

Technique is different from skill. Skill is an ability, natural or acquired to cope with a certain activity. It is a kind of dexterity. Technique is the manner in which we master aspects of that skill. It is evident how frustrated a pianist or a dancer will be if his legs or his fingers will not perform what he requires of them. Acting requires far less technique than dancing because it is very close to patterns of behaviour we use in real life. But a certain control of voice and body are essential if the projection of the idea is to be clear and satisfying. A friend of mine who is particularly interested in the relationship between drama and language instanced the other day an improvisation based on the use of the passive tense. Under what circumstances does one speak in the passive? Who would speak in this way? Constrictive, yes; but what freedom in mastering the constrictions. The composer who, can construct an eight part fugue and a dancer who can do 32 fouettés on each leg has achieved an enviable creative freedom.

Richard Courtney, in the article from which I have already quoted,[84] begins with a rather alarming passage in which he makes clear that we are up to our eyes in psychology and sociology.

> Writers in the field approach drama education from different viewpoints. Literature in the field demonstrates basic differences in the underlying assumptions of the writers, as Scott has shown.
>
> Basic philosophies appear to differ. Winifred Ward's work, seminal in the United States, she herself acknowledged was based upon Dewey's pragmatic idealism; on the other hand, Slade has a romantic base in the style of Rousseau, while Burton and Way relate closely to modern forms of existentialism.
>
> Understandings of psychology can differ. Whereas Slade and Wethered assume the work of Jung, Witkin bases his work upon Piaget. Many of Heathcote's assumptions have similarities with those of Rogers and Maslow, while G. T. Jones has a basis in behavioural psychology.
>
> Social assumptions can differ from writer to writer. Adland, for example, tends towards group theory, Hunt towards Marxism, while Burton, Heathcote, and Way proclaim the dignity of the individual inter-acting with society.[85]

Well, it is not my intention to chase up all these references. The passage will be grist to anyone looking for a subject for his thesis. The British are notoriously disinterested in theory. But there comes a point when the most articulated theory can inhibit the stimulus to action. And that is the point we are just about to reach.

In the last section of Robert Witkin's book, he discusses examinations and assessment. The aspect of drama that we have so far discussed does not lend itself to examination in any way.

Assessment, perhaps. It is perfectly reasonable to expect a perceptive teacher who knows her class and has planned her lessons carefully to be able to assess the progress that her pupils have made. But I do not think that what is bound to be a somewhat subjective judgement can be adapted fairly to any public examination unless it is set and assessed internally. And then its point is probably lost. When the child is old enough to study the theatre arts – a subject that will be dealt with in Chapter 12 – examinations will be possible; for the young person can be set a clearly defined task and he can be assessed for his success in doing it; and this assessment will be no more subjective than that which is used for other arts subjects. But to hope to achieve more than a fairly rough and ready assessment of a drama lesson using the first five letters of the alphabet, when its purpose has been the development of the personality, group relationships, and an enhancement of life itself, is to formalize the very nature of an activity that is before all else informal and regenerative. Let us beware of imposing irrelevant examinations and inappropriate assessments on our children for the sake of achieving respectability for a subject that must be allowed to stand on the basis of its own integrity.

# 10 The Nature of Dramatic Art

Let us move on to the more disciplined aspects of our subject, though, goodness knows, discipline is required in plenty in any productive improvisation. First drama – performance, and the nature of a play; then acting and the other arts of the theatre.

If, speaking in very general terms, we consider a kind of extended improvisation as principally relevant to the pre-adolescent stage of child development and to young people in the first four years of a secondary school, so the present chapter might apply to adolescents and to the upper forms of secondary schools. But there is nothing hard and fast in these distinctions. Some years ago I came across a fascinating experiment in a Bristol comprehensive school when the drama teacher had contrived a complex and ambitious production that involved young people of all ages but with the roles most carefully related to the attainments of the performers. One of the most valuable results of the experiment was that pupils from both ends of the school came to work together and to know each other for the first time and so developed considerable mutual respect. In the same way some of the most impressive improvisations I have seen have been the work of young people in the sixth form; and my own students who include men and women in their thirties attach considerable importance to improvisation however great their devotion to Shakespeare and Chekhov.

I have used on a number of occasions the word 'performance', and am aware that some of my readers will have winced. I mean by performance the right of a young person to be helped to do whatever he wants to do to the very best of his ability, and this applies to work in primary as much as in secondary schools. When a child is making an aeroplane out of bits of old wood or a ship out of cereal packets he will often go to his teacher uncertain how to make it better. It will be for the teacher to decide what he means by 'better' and how to give him the help he wants. But if he brushes him aside and says 'it will do as it is', he is planting in the child the attitude of slap-dashery and of

113

anything-will-do and what-can-I-get-away with. In 1966 when the country was celebrating the 900th anniversary of the Norman Conquest I saw some quite magnificent reproductions, in all kinds of media, of the Bayeux tapestry. The opening of the Severn bridge was celebrated in many West-country schools with superb models; and when I am thinking of quality of work my mind reverts to the Kelmscott School where the children could do exquisite lino-cuts in the manner of William Morris and even cut original designs in rosewood. Has not the annual *Daily Mirror* exhibition of children's art demonstrated the exquisite achievements of which children and young people are capable? And collections of children's prose and poetry the quality of writing they can achieve?

I emphasize the point because there is a school of thought that considers 'performance' – and I use the word to imply achievement in any activity – as inimical to the growing creative process. The more questionable aspects of competitive athletics, as demonstrated particularly, for example, in the Olympic Games are justifiable perhaps as an excuse to denigrate all forms of competition and so to prevent the more gifted children from ever exerting themselves to the very limit of their strength. I have absolutely no doubt that children and young people want to test their skills – to discover how clever or strong or swift they may be and it is right that they should do so. There has been in the past a good deal of hostility to the teaching of ballet in schools, and I quite recognize that owing to its particularly demanding nature it is not an art that is appropriate for every young person. Yet I have been into schools where ballet is well taught and boys and girls of thirteen and fourteen will work at an exercise until ready to drop and then attempt the exercise again with renewed vigour. What is the reason for this but the very real need of a young person to discover the utmost of which he is capable. Much though I dislike the atmosphere in which competitive athletics are carried out I am impressed with the remark, constantly made by long distance runners, that the discipline of the mind is quite as important as the training of the body.

The denigration of performance and an attendant terror of technique seems to me to stem from two sources. One is a misunderstanding of the creative process. There is a belief that performance is in some ways inimical to the process itself, that it is imposing forms and structures when the young people should be evolving and experimenting. I think I have given my answer to this. A child when improvising is indeed in one respect exploring an area of experience; but he is doing so not only because it is fun but because he is trying to embody that feeling in form. This is what art (and life too) is all about. And the maturer he is, the more capable he will be of a full embodiment of his ideas in what Robert Witkin (and Susanne Langer) know as 'feeling-form'.[86]

I have seen Dorothy Heathcote push a group of tough boys to the very limit of their expressive and imaginative ability; but there was absolutely no question of them giving a performance in the conventional sense.

The other and more serious attack on performance comes from a widespread and slovenly concept of democratic values which is translated in educational terms into a sloppy egalitarianism. It is evident in our hesitance to encourage the brighter young people for fear that this may be at the expense of the not-so-bright. If only the gifted can do better why should anyone be allowed to do it? High performance by some pupils can only emphasize poor performance in others. Let us preserve everyone's self-respect by making us all as anonymous and equal as possible. *Animal Farm,* in which these attitudes are splendidly refuted, is deservedly a best seller.

This is why I am so critical of the limp slovenly improvisations I have so often seen in schools. It is work that is not only far from the best of which the young people are capable, but of a kind that implies any concept of 'performance' as a clarification or of bringing work to a satisfactory conclusion, to be outside the scope of that kind of improvisation.

I use the word 'performance' in the sense of achievement, not to imply an audience. Nevertheless the audience is an aspect of any performance, for it is a natural instinct that having discovered or demonstrated skill in a particular activity the 'performer' should look for a certain appreciation or even acclamation. While it is absolutely proper that drama teachers should resist the tendency as long as possible, they must recognize the close relationship that inevitably exists between achievement, communication, and emotional response. But the whole question of an audience in relation to performance is so crucial that perhaps we can look at it more closely.

It is a very normal instinct in a child, no less than an adult, that he should wish to show something that he has made or done to his friends. The instinct for communication is not a subject that I have pressed strongly in this book but it is nevertheless a powerful aspect of the will to make contact and to share experience. When a child has climbed to the top of a tree he cries triumphantly 'Look at me!'. When he has painted a picture he will show it to his teacher who may suggest he takes it to the headteacher. This is proper encouragement. But even this kind of shared experience marks a development in his social consciousness. At the egocentred stage he is oscillating between an anxiety to see and be seen, unable to differentiate conflicting emotions; nor does he speak to his friends unless he has something positive to communicate, although he may be talking to himself almost constantly. First stages in communication are closely related to whoever it is with whom the child wants to communicate, as well as the nature of the experience he wishes to share. Certain acts of communication are acts of assimilation. It is the sharing of the experience as well as the experience itself that he has to master. This is why quality of relationships between teacher and children is so important. Nobody wants to communicate or share an experience with anyone for whom he has little regard.

The nature of the experience that is to be shared is another complex matter. A child can paint a picture and pin it to the wall and it may or may not impinge greatly on the other children. But directly a teacher stops a dance or movement class, for example, to ask everyone to watch how Johnny does the exercise, we have moved into a new area of shared experience. It is the same thing if teacher invites Johnny to read his poem or to play the piece of music he has composed. The attention is not on the artefact that Johnny has created but on the personal ability of Johnny, his skill in reading or in manipulating his limbs or acting a part. Now it is possible that this is exactly the kind of encouragement that Johnny needs; but it may also be the kind of encouragement he does not need.

Let us look at the experience from Johnny's point of view. He is doing something perhaps quite unselfconsciously as a member of a group. Suddenly thirty pairs of eyes are all turned upon him. If this is a new experience various results may ensue. He will be overcome with selfconsciousness and cringe; or he will suddenly realize that this is his moment and exploit the situation by extending his performance in a manner that he thinks is likely further to impress his 'audience'; or he may be able to repeat the performance exactly as he did before, a feat that requires a good deal of emotional stability and control.

Now let us look at all this in terms of drama. When drama is play there is no question of an audience, though I would like to record that no role is more difficult than that of being a visitor in a school, particularly a good infant school. For the play of the children, as I have been at pains to stress, depends on an atmosphere of intimacy that has been created in the classroom by the teacher in her relationship with the children. One quickly discovers that there are qualities of observation and that children can detect whether they are being observed critically or with the same regard that their teacher has for them. Any stranger in a classroom creates an experience for the children and an element that in certain circumstances can throw the work out of joint. Whether he likes it or not he is an audience of one.

But there is a stage which I have carefully described when drama begins to lose the element of play and to be recognizable as drama. One will assume that the whole class is involved. The only observer is the teacher whose relationship with the class is accepted, particular, and privileged. There may arise an occasion, however, when a group of children in a class do something of particular interest. Teacher may ask the other children to watch. It is an extension of the moment when she asked the class to look at Johnny's cartwheels. I am not suggesting that any harm may arise from this; but it may mark a new stage in the development of children. Their work, instead of being turned inwards among themselves, is now by a kind of magnetism pulled outward by the observers. If these observers are other children in the class the magnetic pull may not be very strong; but if the head or another teacher or even another class of children are invited, it may become considerable.

This is why I think that suddenly to place a crowd of infants in front of two or three hundred adults to give a performance requiring a variety of skills, far more complex than anything they have yet learnt to handle, is educationally inadmissable. And if anyone should think that in the whole of this discussion I am being over-sensitive, I would point out that in the drama school of which for some six years I was principal, we exercised the most scrupulous control over the exposure of students to audiences. Even the student actors go through two years of playing in front of small audiences, at first of staff only, then of other students, before they appear in front of the general public. But it is never an easy problem. The whole subject of sharing, showing, observing, and performing to an audience, what, which, who, and how big, throws up some unexpectedly troublesome questions.

Before moving on to my next subject, however, there is one further point I would like to make about audiences although logically it should be placed later in the discussion. The relationship between an actor and his audience goes far deeper than observation of one by the other. The unique aspect of the performing arts is that they only come properly to life in front of an audience. There is an extraordinary difference in quality between a dress rehearsal, however smooth, to an empty house and a performance to an audience. In the latter the performance 'lives' and this is because the whole production has been conceived and executed in terms that presuppose the presence of this audience. I repeat – it is not a matter of 'showing-off' but of creating a shared experience. This is why so much thought is being given in contemporary theatre design to the spacial relationships between actors and audience. There is something of the same quality in the work of all artists. Very few of them genuinely and profoundly 'don't give a damn what the public think'. Every artist in struggling to find the best way in which to present his material is not only seeking personal satisfaction but a way of making his work accessible to the public. There is a most subtle relationship between the two processes. Excessive emphasis on the personal vision leads to the obscurity that bedevils so much contemporary art; emphasis on the public presentation, and the work lacks human vision and personal integrity. But the duality is present in every work of art. And it is the very mixture of subtlety of concept with complexity of technical execution that explains why it is not until they are relatively mature that young people will be able to combine this dual approach, the private vision expressed in communicable terms. That is why so much school drama is rightly cherished as a private intimate process – as it is for two years among our professional acting students. But there comes a time when young people are ready to experience a full act of communication. I only hope it is not too full, with not too large an audience, before not too many mayors and governors. An important education experience must not be confused with a window display for the school's prestige.

What is this dramatic experience of which we talk so much? I have given examples of the dangers of definition and I shall not attempt one myself. But I think that it is worth having a look at what the first dramatic critic whose works have survived had to say on the subject of drama.

The name of Aristotle does not thrill everyone that hears it; but this is not Aristotle's fault. *The Poetics* is for the most part highly readable and presents us with no considerable problems of meaning. The trouble has come from former critics who with their monumentally pedantic commentaries transformed a few lecture notes, or a draft for a book, into a kind of Holy Writ.

I do not, for a start, care greatly for the title *The Poetics*. Aristotle's title is the perfectly straightforward expression *Peri poetikes, About poetry*, which is far more comprehensible.

First of all, however, I would like to make it clear that by discussing Aristotle I am not forgetful of the subject of this book. My object is simply to suggest, contrary to what some enthusiasts believe, that drama in schools is basically and essentially no different from drama anywhere else.

Much of what Aristotle says is really quite simple. He begins by describing the arts of poetry, music, dancing, painting, and sculpture as acts of imitation. His word is *mimesis*. It is quite clear that he does not mean imitation in the sense of mimicry but as Piaget uses it, as an act of recreation. He gives a clue to this when he says that music is the most imitative of all the arts. Music is the least mimetic, but the one that involves the greatest transformation of reality.

Where is drama? In his third chapter he explains that poetry may be narrative, lyric or dramatic. I sometimes think that if English and drama teachers would both take this concept of poetic unity a little more seriously, the tendentious relationships between the two subjects would be largely avoided.

In his fourth chapter he discusses the origins and development of poetry. Man, he says, has an instinct for imitation, harmony, and rhythm. In the sense in which we have discussed 'natural processes' of behaviour, I do not think that many would disagree. Tragedy and comedy, he says in a much disputed passage, developed from improvisation. Historically this is a very complex issue; but if I am right in suggesting that there is bound to be a quality of improvisation in the developing creative process, it would be surprising if somewhere in its dim origins there were not a tradition of improvisation in the composition of both tragedy and comedy as well as other kinds of poetry, particularly epic. In any case it is apparent that since the great Greek epics were composed long before the days of print or even of written manuscripts, they must have been the product of some inspired poetic improvisation by the Ionian poets.

It is interesting to note that rather by what he does not say than in any positive statement, Aristotle betrays an uncertainty – or could it be lack of interest – in the nature of comedy. In his sixth chapter he gives his celebrated definition of tragedy.

'Tragedy,' he says, 'is an action.' In this respect it is to be distinguished from narrative.

'It is an action that is complete.' He develops this point in his seventh chapter by adding that 'it is an action of a certain magnitude having a beginning, a middle, and end.'

In the sixth chapter he continues with the sentence which has probably caused more critical controversy than any other statement in literary history: 'Tragedy, then, is an imitation of an action . . . through pity and fear affecting the proper purgation (catharsis) of these emotions.'

He completes the chapter with a final analysis of the tragic action. It must contain, in this order of importance, plot, character, thought, diction, song, and spectacle. Plot is the manner of the action, character, diction, and thought are the objects of the action, and spectacle and song are the media. Spectacle includes the visual side of a performance, including the physical, the dancing, which he seems to take for granted. He includes music since the particular quality of classical tragedy derives from the fact that the dramatists wrote their text in linguistic and musical terms as a single operation. There was no question whatsoever of them writing a text and setting it to music. They heard the sound, the music of the words, as they composed them, and they taught the manner of speaking or singing the lines to their actors.

To analyse what Aristotle means by catharsis is extremely difficult, and especially so if we take the word in isolation. Aristotle is analysing tragedy and tragedy, as he makes very clear, is the enactment of a myth; and a myth, as we now know, is not merely a story, although it may contain elements of narrative, but a prodigious archetypal symbol that seems to sum up in a very simple concept some huge area of human experience. The great figures of Greek myth – Apollo, Dionysos, Prometheus, Circe, Medusa, even the characters in Homer, encapsulate human qualities that relate to our condition on many different levels. The concept of purgation or cleansing through a process of identification with the suffering of these heroic figures – the pity and terror their sufferings arouse in us – is one that we have learnt to accept through familiarity with the idea. But our attitude towards Greek tragedy remains on the whole equivocal, and our attitude towards the theory of catharsis non-committal.

Unhappily Aristotle has been as badly served by his supporters as many other original thinkers have been, and I exclude neither Jesus nor Lenin, in this somewhat sweeping statement. Dramatists have gullibly accepted the dogma of authoritarian critics who, purporting to expound the words of the master, have turned them into dogma. I am thinking particularly of Italian and French critics of the Renaissance, many of whom were so-called humanists, who cooked up Aristotle's quite modest discussion about the need for there to be an organic connection between the episodes in a tragedy into a great structure of dramatic form requiring unity of time, place, and action. This formed a basis for the concept of seventeenth-century French classical tragedy and the nineteenth-century ideal of the well-made play which under the designation of Sardoodledom was the butt of some of Bernard Shaw's wittiest critical sallies.[87]

Nevertheless in its simplest form Aristotle's analysis is useful. A play is an action of a dramatic kind consisting of a reconstruction of reality. When he says that it is an action of a certain length one thinks of children with a capacity for improvisation who have no idea of what constitutes appropriate length or proportion between different parts. When he says that a play must have a beginning, a middle, and an end he is making a point that is easy to concede and hard to realize. Even an improvisation must begin somewhere; it must have a middle that must develop from the beginning; it must have an end, because it must stop some point at which the significance of that particular action and its consequences are completed. Aristotle's proposals for a certain organic unity of action and time – he never mentions place – have provided the basis for some of the world's finest drama – one thinks particularly of Racine and Ibsen; but what we might call the epic tradition, which had its fullest expression in the medieval drama and in Shakespeare, is just as valid. It is all a matter of the dramatist's artistic tastes and judgements and how he relates the structure of his play to what he wants to say. An interesting exercise on these lines would be to consider how Ibsen might have constructed *Hamlet*. We can certainly take as an example John Dryden's reconstruction of *Anthony and Cleopatra* as *All for Love*.[88]

While we are on this subject let me say an additional word about form. The traditional view is that form is shaped by content. This is a statement which I hope will be recognized as only partially true. I would not in fact discuss the issue were it not for the necessity of emphasizing that in improvised drama a sense of form will derive wholly from what the people involved want to express. And I am inclined to think that this is probably the main role of the teacher, to press the participants to clarify their attitude to their material and help them to see whether they are in fact expressing what they want to express. Young people with a particular interest in these matters will want to see how other people have written plays. At the time of the assassination of President Kennedy I saw a number of improvisations on political assassination; and it was by no means infrequent to find a school where the pupils were fascinated to see how Shakespeare had handled the subject in *Julius Caesar*. This is where improvisation begins to mesh with inherited form.

Inevitably we revert constantly to this subject. We cherish a love–hate relationship with traditional form. Any talk of introducing children to the great heritage of European culture is inclined to turn one's stomach. Yet one is aware that in the works of the masters we have embodied the highest visions and sensibilities of humanity. Yet every artist, every individual, is obliged to climb the slopes of Parnassus for himself; and the uniquely individual artist will choose his own mountain. As a young man he looks around him and sees the arts in a certain condition. He may accept this condition or he may want to reject it. T. S. Eliot, though a poet of astonishing originality, insisted, when he turned his attention seriously to writing plays, on using the insisted dramatic convention of drawing-room comedy. This was against the advice of some of his closest friends, but it seems to have given him a certain sense of security. On the other hand we know that some artists have had to destroy inherited form. Stravinsky describes how before he could write *Le Sacre du Printemps* he had to destroy Brahms. He could not hear his own sounds while those of the German composer were occupying his mind.[89] And we also know that Brahms in turn was inhibited in writing his first symphony by the sense that Beethoven was leaning over his shoulder. Aristotle attaches considerable importance to plot because plot for him was a myth and he uses this very word, *muthos*. I don't think there can be very much doubt that the Greek dramatist began to write a play by choosing a myth. It might have been a myth that provided him with opportunity to make a particular political or metaphysical point as Aeschylus does in the *Oresteia* or Euripides in *The Trojan Women*; but he did not begin by taking a character he had met in the market-place and developing a series of imagined circumstances to reveal some concept or meaning as a dramatist might well do today. The Attic dramatists, for all their astounding originality, worked within a structure which they and society accepted, a structure founded on ancient ritualistic origins, a society that was enjoying a brief spell of equilibrium.

It is an entirely theoretical point whether we place plot or character first in importance. Classic expositions on the art of the dramatist such as William Archer's *Play making* discuss at length whether plot should motivate character or character the plot. If Aristotle gives pride of place to plot it is because it was as a ritual exposition of the *muthos* or myth that drama originated and developed. But he realized the importance of character because what fascinates him about the story of Oedipus is the changing fortunes of the king and how these events purify an audience by imbuing them with feelings of pity and terror. It may well be in terms of plot or situation that a subject first strikes a dramatist; but the consequences of that initial situation will be shaped and motivated by the emotional response of the characters involved. No two characters respond to a situation in the same manner.

The classical concept of drama, fully discussed by William Archer,[90] is that it is a matter of conflict. It was many years ago that I first questioned this and developed a concept of drama as a growing process in the course of which we see an individual, or a group of individuals, not being tested with unimaginable hazards, (the romantic view), or at odds with society, (the nineteenth-century view), or with his fellow men (the Brechtian), but in a state of constant assimilation, drawing within himself the wealth of experience the environment has to offer, adapting his own intellectual schema and emotional attitudes accordingly, and then responding in a new way to new experiences and new circumstances. This is a dialectic process of a Hegelian rather than a Marxist kind and in this sense it may be a semantic quarrel to argue that there is no element of conflict. Indeed it may well be that what I am proposing is a more subtle and truthful approach to the manner in which we grow through conflict. The romantic concept likes to turn every issue into black and white, goodies and baddies. But the germinating quality of society must lie in the innate inconsistency of a human being. Who of us is not subject to inadequacies of character? In which of us are the seven deadly sins not rampant? Our very ability to keep them under constraint requires an effort of that moral will which lies at the heart of so much drama. Drama is not the battle of the hero to master his enemies, but himself. And if this presents us with problems of finding the appropriate dramatic image or symbol, that is all the more reason why drama in schools must begin with the marvellous proposal of a teacher to his class – 'Let us place ourselves in the situation of . . .' It may well be in terms of plot or situation that a subject first strikes a dramatist; but the consequences of that initial situation will be shaped and motivated by the emotional response of the characters involved. No two characters respond to the same circumstances in the same manner.

Who knows in what form the subject of Macbeth first occurred to Shakespeare? Some critics say that he decided to write a play set in Scotland with a theme (myth, story, or plot) involving witches as a double compliment to James I. He then seems to have turned to Holinshed to find a suitable story. But the development of the plot following upon Macbeth's first confrontation with the witches is entirely shaped by the particular characteristics with which Shakespeare has imbued his tragic hero. If Macbeth, having given rein to his ambition and murdered the king, had been a man like Cassius, a brutal political manipulator, instead of a poet, a dreamer, a visionary, the plot would have developed on wholly different lines.

With character Aristotle relates the word (lexis) and thought. Again it could be argued that the plot of *Macbeth* would have developed on different lines if Shakespeare had not been a master of poetry and the poetic image. A modern naturalistic dramatist would not have been able to put into the mouth of Macbeth those tumultuous images which lead to his spiritual destruction. It is quite a different matter to create a character who talks about being subject to visions to creating one who is shown to be so. Neither Macbeth himself nor anyone else in the play refers to him as a visionary, or a poetic, yet the tragedy derives from Macbeth's inability to cope with the results of his own ill-conceived course of action. This is not the place to expatiate upon the poetic drama except to say that since language and its attendant thought or imagery are a part of the very concept of a drama a poetic play will cover different areas of human experience from a naturalistic play. Moreover poetry provides a different set of symbols from prose. Shakespeare could not have achieved anything like the simultaneous number of levels and meanings we find in a play like *The Tempest* if he had written in prose. There is a certain symbolic poetry in Ibsen but neither he nor Chekhov, another of the most sensitive dramatists to have written in prose, are in this respect comparable with Shakespeare.

It is quite proper that these aspects of drama should be pointed out to young people in the upper school. There is virtually no poetic drama being written at the moment, although there is a good deal of poetry. The reason for this must constitute a separate study. But the door must be kept open; for I see no reason why if after the war we could have had a body of poetic plays from T. S. Eliot, Christopher Fry, Anne Ridler, Norman Nicholson, Ronald Duncan, and a number of others, we could not have a renewed renaissance of poetic drama today.

People will say the conditions are not right. What was more right about 1950 than 1970?

There are a number of sensibilities of which young people stand in need if they are to develop their interest in drama. First in importance I would say is an interest in society, in living ideas, in human behaviour, in thought, in passion, in the conservative and the rebel. I have always had a sympathy for the propagandist in the theatre, for propaganda springs from passion for an idea. Virginia Woolf must have detested propagandists; yet she describes the highbrow as 'the man or woman of thoroughbred intelligence who rides his mind at a gallop across country in pursuit of an idea'. And to complete the picture she describes a lowbrow as 'a man or woman of thoroughbred vitality who rides his body in pursuit of a living at a gallop across life'.[91] And it is surely at the age of sixteen and upwards that young people will pursue ideas with the greatest passion, at a reckless gallop, in pursuit of a thousand ideas and ideals.

Yet this passionate involvement in one's subject does not give anyone the right to compose bad plays. And if I were asked to define a bad play I would say it is an unactable play. One result of practising improvised drama throughout our time at school should have been to establish in us a feeling for what is actable and what is not. For what is actable is quite simply a scene or a situation that can be brought to life by an actor in terms of understanding, of vocal and physical expression; and what is unactable is what remains lifeless when it is spoken and moved. Actable poetry is not necessarily better than unactable poetry; it is different. A poor play, like a poor novel, is a failure on the part of the writer in his transformation of reality.

The second necessary sensibility is for the rhythms of human speech. This is not to preclude the poetic drama, for Dyland Thomas even more than Christopher Fry has left us some vibrant examples of how the vernacular can be translated into poetic terms. But it is perhaps with ordinary prose dialogue that we should principally concern ourselves. Anyone who would improvise successfully, let alone write speakable and actable dialogue, must have an ear for the nuances of speech, the linguistic registers of different people playing different roles.

And then there is a sensibility that is very difficult to describe. I would probably not have been aware of it but for having worked with Michel St Denis who inherited a kind of Gallic tradition for mime that had its origins in the Italian comedy and was translated into French by Molière. It is a sense of the

physical expressiveness of drama. It comes down to a view of
the stage as two boards and a passion – a celebrated remark of
obscure provenance. In the acting area, the 'green', the stage,
the actor can reveal a world about himself without the aid of
words. It is Barrault's concept of total theatre – the revelation of
dramatic situation through the total expressive capabilities of
the actor. Louis Jouvet, a marvellously physical actor himself,
wrote vividly of the physical basis of Molière's plays, most of
which can be adequately performed with a couple of chairs and
a fan. This concept of the stage as a playing space for the
physically expressive actor lay at the heart of Copeau's demand
for a bare stage, un tréteau nu, and of William Poel's concept of
the great open Elizabethan stage.

It is not a quality that is in evidence today when the emphasis
in playwriting is on a kind of verbal psychology against a
socially conscious background; though what I have said about
a physical or mimetic basis for drama does not preclude a
psychological or sociological content. What it does preclude is
naturalistic scenery; and what it requires is language rich
enough to create its own world and its own environment. Thus
we find that the bare stage, and concepts of both poetic theatre
and physically expressive acting, have a kind of relationship,
though it is not one in which contemporary dramatists seem to
be very interested.

This emphasizes my enthusiasm for Aristotle as an apologist.
He begins his book by saying that drama is an action. Plot and
character show the development of the initial action and its
consequences. But drama, which is action, is something that is
done, not something that is thought, and this provides us with a
splendidly secure base for further theorizing.

We are, however, to a certain extent, victims of our society.
Intellectual and artistic fashions are as prevalent and contagious
as epidemics. Playwrights now assume a kind of socially conscious naturalism. The dramatists of the so-called 'fringe', more
prolific in England than elsewhere in Europe, are largely concerned with the projection of a kind of social reality, rather than
with theatrical images in which this reality is embedded. Thus
we are far from a poetic theatre. But the fact that directors
hanker for the theatrical image leads many of them to prefer the
classic to the contemporary play. In directing Shakespeare they
tend to twist the text to extort his contemporary relevance.[92]
This is why it is so important that the current concept of drama
in schools should not be limited to classroom improvisations,
the purpose of which is simply to learn some social or historical

concept. Drama must be related, and so children must be exposed to poetry, music, and the visual arts so that the theatrical image (or presentation) can be realistic (rich in expressive form) and not merely naturalistic (and so limited in texture however socially truthful). I am sure that the present popularity of Brecht throughout Europe is the result of his profound concern with political and social reality coupled with his ability to express these 'truths' in richly varied and imaginative theatrical forms.[93]

# 11 The Nature of Theatrical Art

The school play, which is the occasion when the theatre arts are traditionally most fully realized, has been the subject of particular vilification, and often not without justice. This, however, has not deterred teachers from putting on plays or headmasters from encouraging them to do so; but it has tended to drive a wedge between more traditional forms of theatrical activity and the work of the new wave of specialists with their enthusiasm for all those aspects of drama which distinguish it from theatre.

I have a good deal of sympathy with the criticisms. My own experience of schools plays at Aldenham gave me little understanding of theatrical art as a creative process. Acting was treated as a skill you happened to possess or not; and most of the innumerable school plays I have seen as parent, friend or official guest confirm the rather formal quality that has encouraged detractors to apply the word creative to other aspects of drama that tend to be more imaginative, exhilarating or inventive.

Some of my colleagues have suggested over the years that the evil provenance of the school play was the Nativity play in the infant school. This is usually the first occasion when children are required to go through the formal procedures of performing in front of an audience. The occasion usually involves a fairly large number of children, dressing-up, lines learnt, scenery shakily erected, and as large an audience as the hall will hold. In performance we have inaudibility, lack of involvement, angel's eyes searching for Nan in the audience and friendly smiles when contact is made – every kind of distraction that destroys the very nature of the performance that is being offered. But is anything else to be expected? I have described the stages of child development and how they relate to the whole expressive process in order to establish the reason why traditional methods of acting plays are rarely viable in primary schools. A performance of a play is, and can only be, a highly disciplined and carefully organized experience in group communication involving a whole set of skills that children of primary-school age do not and should not be expected to possess.

All the embarrassment I have suffered at such performances is emphasized by delight I have had in children's own plays. I have described the Bristol Nativity. I think of a small school in Northumberland where one class was acting the Nativity story in the school hall without costumes, scenery or properties. At one moment, when Joseph and Mary were moving around little groups of children lying on the floor, as if in the inns of Bethlehem, they knocked at a certain door. The innkeeper opened, there was a short altercation, and then a sleepy voice from the back said, 'Shut that door' – in a rich Northumberland accent that stretched 'door' into I don't know how many rising phonemes. Immediately one felt the wind blowing through that draughty inn and was aware of a moment of complete artistic truth.

Another of the stumbling blocks to the formal presentation of plays is the learning of lines. If children can read and speak with reasonable fluency they do not find it particularly difficult to learn lines. Whether it is desirable that they should do so is another matter. Contemporary opinion seems on the whole not to favour the practice but I think that very often contemporary opinion is being a little mealy-mouthed. To learn the lines of a play is like learning the lines of a poem or a song: it is to come into sharp contact with inherited form. The extent to which this is desirable is a matter of relationship with the child's own creative work. It is very difficult for a child to bring his own vitality to a highly concentrated and selective form of expression that has been created by somebody else, and I am not very sure that in a primary school it is ever desirable. Of the impropriety of learning anything parrot-fashion there can be no question. But there may be a case for learning by heart as part of the process of coming into close contact with work of undoubted excellence. Nevertheless I have no confidence in arguing the case strongly.

I remember that as a boy I was particularly obsessed by Milton and learned chunks of his poetry by heart. But my own poetry, which I wrote in great quantities and with enormous enthusiasm, became so impossibly Miltonic that I spent forty years in search of a spare, laconic, and near conversational style.

With children of secondary-school age one's reservations are much less serious. I do not think there is very much to be said in favour of learning lines, to use an infelicitous expression, as a mental discipline. But to learn lines in order to act a play is an acceptable activity provided that the teacher can find a way of helping the young people to make those lines, as we say, their own, to integrate them with the character they are creating. This is not a natural process and it is clearly not an easy one. A most interesting example of an attempt to solve the difficulty occurred some years ago at a school in South London. The children and young people performed the *Chester Deluge* and André Obey's *Noah*. The teacher-producer had achieved a remarkable balance between original text and improvisation. The cast moved from one to the other with considerable ease. While it is not a technique I would strongly advocate, I remember clearly the vitality with which the players elaborated, commented, and improvised upon the passages they had learnt by heart.

When all is said and done the learning of lines is only an element, though an essential one, in acting a role and that is the next aspect of theatrical art we must consider.

Acting consists in the recreation of a character. At the time of the Russian Revolution the Soviet director Meyerhold tried to turn actors into acrobats but his experiments found no general favour, least of all with the Soviet authorities, and one can say that on the whole the concept of acting as the creation or recreation of a character is one that has never seriously been challenged. Yet it is a result of the identification of theatre with acting and acting with dressing-up and pretending to be someone else that there has long existed a kind of puritanical suspicion, if not positive opposition to the art as anything socially acceptable.[94] The change of attitude that has taken place in the present century is revolutionary.

Interest in drama is widespread. I have spent some little time in discussing Aristotle's theories on drama in order to suggest that basically there is little difference between a dramatic action that is a simple improvisation by a child in a primary school and Laurence Olivier in *Othello*. It is commonly observed that people behave differently at work and at home, when talking to one person rather than another. Sometimes this change of role is conscious, usually unconscious; and I fancy that there are few professions offering such opportunities for the assumption of a variety of roles as teaching. And I wonder – is it an instinct? Is it anything different from the way in which a very young child will don her mother's skirt or boa or high-heeled shoes? Or small boys will go around in cowboy's hat or a policeman's helmet? This is not acting but a gesture of identity with a certain character, be it a stereotype like a cowboy or a desirable ideal like the sophisticated appearance of mother. Yet it is the stuff of which acting is made, concern with our image, our persona.

This identification with another character is partly an assimilation of that character, partly a kind of challenge to the child's own identity. There is something within himself that makes him unsure of himself. But he is less unsure when he is wearing a helmet, as the business man is when he dons his bowler hat. We have given our unstable personality a secure and socially recognizable identity.

So dressing up, even if it only involves the wearing of a single garment, is not an act of identification but an assertion of the self-image, the kind of image we want to present to the world; and this image is so often at odds with the image of ourself we think the world will accept that we establish a compromise within the bounds of certain social and professional conventions. We reveal a lot about ourselves in our choice of clothes.

This is the function of the dressing-up box; children can be given opportunities to externalize the assimilative and imitative aspects of their play by assuming the exterior symbols of the character they are playing – by dressing-up.

I am disposed to emphasize the importance of the relationship between self-image and the personality because of the claim most commonly made for drama, and one that I find most difficulty in understanding, that it develops the personality. Reference to textbooks of psychology reveal that the personality is an exceedingly abstract concept and one on which no one can expatiate with great conviction. It can be best measured or assessed in terms of a person's relationship to other people. If, therefore, it means anything at all, it must involve some kind of concept of the self-image and the way in which we project our behaviour in social situations. Yet for all its abstract qualities it is perhaps the aspect of ourselves that we treasure most wholly. That a certain experience affected our personality is one of the most powerful comments we can make, and we resist aggressive approaches to our personality as we do people who would change our way of speaking. Some of our human characteristics may be poor and inadequate but they are our own; and if the doctor cures us of our weaknesses we may feel in better health but spiritually bereft.

I think that the validity of the practice of meditation lies in this attempt to reach the thin small centre of our being and it is horrifying to find that the more we cast aside our attitudes and prejudices, the less is left. We are like the button-moulder's cynical metaphor of the onion in *Peer Gynt*. But we rise in the

morning and don our working clothes and put a bold front on
the world and what we can't substantiate we act.

It was only after this book was almost finished that I came
across the works of the Canadian Professor, Erwin Goffman,
who has analysed in most entertaining fashion the roles we
sustain both individually and in groups throughout our life. He
argues, in fact, that role-playing constitutes so important an
element in natural life that many people find stage-acting
surprisingly easy.[95]

As we get older and pass through the phases of development
I have described, we get better at acting. We control our
instincts for identification since the process of assimilation has
now been superseded by one of recreation as we learn to adjust
with ever increasing adroitness to the curious personalities we
meet in daily life; and the close study of personality in a
subjective or sensory-motor manner becomes the material of
acting. We move from identification with a character to full
characterization. The process is slow and gradual. When we
watch young people acting, improvising perhaps, it is not their
capacity for characterization that usually strikes us as being the
outstanding quality of their work. They may be increasingly
skilful linguistically and in the physical expressiveness of their
bodies; they may be adept at mimicry; but we do not look for
that total transformation of the personality that we find in the
greatest adult acting. Nevertheless the process has begun. The
teacher bids his young ones to use their eyes, their ears. 'What
kind of a man do you imagine this Roman Emperor to have
been? What kind of a woman was Lady Macbeth to incite her
husband to kill the king? Have you ever seen anything like these
people in real life? Can you imagine from what you have seen or
heard how they may have looked? behaved? spoken?'

George Devine, when he was a teacher at the London Theatre
Studio and the Old Vic Theatre School, used to begin an
improvisation class by sending the students into the streets to
watch the passers-by.

So the young actor will do what the teacher bids him do, open
his eyes and ears, look about him, and imitate. At first why not?
Has not Piaget assured us that a large part of our behaviour is
based on imitation, either immediate or deferred? And we know
that many children can be excellent mimics. How is teacher
going to explain that mimicry is not acting, or at best only a part
of acting? I think by two courses of action: not encouraging the
mimic too enthusiastically, and by quietly suggesting aspects of
character that can only be fully encompassed by a deeper and

more imaginative approach. I do not decry an element of mimicry in acting but I suggest that mimicry will not get us far either in investigating some aspect of role-playing or in acting Hamlet. Mimicry is a superficial skill, very useful to an actor, but only as an aid to complete characterization.

The imitative aspect of characterization is not immediate but deferred. The teacher tells the children to use their imaginations. They are not quite sure what this means. In time they realize that imaginative creation is the result of selecting from all their memories and deferred imitations those aspects of human behaviour they can piece together to create the character they want. Piaget says that deferred imitations are incorporated into our mental schema and so condition the kind of person we are and the way we see other people. Stanislavsky says that memories are the material on which an actor draws for his creative work. Acting then begins with imitation in Piaget's sense and ends with imitation in Aristotle's. Imitation is a learning process; it involves the assimilation of new observations and experiences; but if we simply copy, instead of assimilating, making our own, adapting the model to our own mental schema, the experience will be unproductive. Piaget says that there must be a stable equilibrium between assimilation and imitation and what is true for the growing child is true of the actor who is growing into a new personality. Acting makes the whole process a particularly creative one since it is performed under the stress of a powerful creative drive, it is sometimes difficult to understand why its educational value cannot be quickly and readily understood.

Thus we find that in acting, more than in any other art, the spectator is looking for a sense of reality, of truth. If we consider the art of painting for a moment we realize that we can accept every kind of visual representation from that which is photographically naturalistic to wholly abstract. I know that there are plenty of people who enjoy scoffing at non-representational art: there is nothing similar in acting. In literature too there is scope for a very wide range of expressive styles, with complaints similar to those raised by abstract painting if the reader cannot follow what it's all about. Dancing is very close to music in this respect. It is a highly mimetic form and if the movement pleases us we do not worry greatly if we cannot follow the story or determine the identity of the characters. But that is an aesthetic problem I do not wish to pursue at the moment.

Acting then is an art in which the relationship to truth and reality must be apparent. If we don't believe in the reality of a performance there is very little more to be said. These days we do not accept a rhetorical or declamatory style, however impressive of its kind, as an alternative to this sense of truth. And this is where Stanislavsky comes into the picture. In *My Life in Art* he describes how he and his friend Nemirovich-Danchenko found in the contemporary Russian theatre very little of this sense of truth and a great deal of falsity. They were not being entirely visionary. They had been led to envisage new possibilities in theatrical art by performances of the Italian actor, Salvini, and those given by the German company of the Duke of Saxe-Meiningen, and they wished to bring this new concept of theatrical truth to the Russian theatre. The two men thereupon created what came to be called the Moscow Art Theatre and Stanislavsky devoted the remainder of his life not only to acting and directing plays with the kind of reality which made his work the core of the naturalistic style but in working out a method of training that others could follow. He describes this method in a number of books[96] but they have not on the whole been very well translated[97] and they are badly in need of thorough editorial revision. Nevertheless they contain a treasury of splendid material.

Here is an attempt to summarize the essence of Stanislavsky's theories by David Magarshack. It is from the introduction to Stanislavsky's book *On the Art of the Stage*[98] a series of lectures that the author gave to singers from the Bolshoi Opera. The book provides an admirable summary of the master's ideas.

> The main task of the creative actor, therefore, is not only to represent the life of his part in external manifestations, but above all to recreate on the stage the inner life of the character he represents, adapting his own human feelings to this unfamiliar life and devoting to it all the organic elements of his own soul. It is the inner nature of his part, that is to say, its inner life, brought into being with the help of the process of entering into the feelings of his part, that is the main purpose of the actor's work on the stage.

The various exercises that Stanislavsky describes in his book and that David Magarshack clearly summarizes, are a means of helping the actor to reveal his own 'true' feelings about a certain character in a certain situation, and adapting them to this fictional situation. Put like this – and I cannot think of a way of expressing the process more simply – it sounds most difficult. In many ways it is. But it has many points of contact with ordinary human behaviour. The difference between role-playing in real life and acting on the stage is largely that in the former activity we create our own role, and except in cases of extreme abnormality, we make the identification intuitively, whereas in stage-acting we adapt ourselves to the role 'created' by the dramatist.

Nevertheless it is a highly psychological process and if certain safeguards are ignored we find that this so-called 'method' can lead to a very introspective and inexpressive kind of acting, with the players giving so much attention to their own inner feelings that they fail to project them in performances which are acceptable to an audience. Consequently there have been some severe critics of the so-called 'method', notably the German, Bertholt Brecht[99] but there is danger of confusing Stanislavsky's methods as a style of acting or an approach to acting with the kind of naturalistic presentation with which it is usually associated. It is one thing to create a sense of real conviction when acting the play of a writer who uses the naturalistic convention; but it is a more difficult process to identify one's own sense of truth, one's own inner feelings with those of a character who thinks very differently from us and expresses himself in, say, iambic pentameters[100]. This is simply to say that it is easier to apply the Stanislavsky method to Wesker than to Shakespeare, although, paradoxically, many actors find Shakespeare easier to act than modern plays, probably because the thought and emotion are so embedded in the structure and imagery of the verse that psychological analysis is pointless. Shakespeare provides us with a perfect example of the fusion of content and form.

It is all a question of feeling and that is why some consider the art of acting to be suspect. They are suspicious that an overindulgence in artificial feeling cannot be good for a young person; so I will make one or two reassuring remarks.

Firstly, an ability to shed real tears has little to do with deep feeling. I once knew a lady who shed illimitable tears while watching sentimental films. It was embarrassing to go to the cinema with her. She was aware of the stupidity of her reactions, but she was incapable of controlling them. Some people can cry almost at will. It is simply a matter of sensitive lachrymal glands.

If on the other hand an actress does readily shed uncontrollable tears it may well be a sign of some emotional instability and she should be given emotional roles only with great circumspection and possibly in the light of medical advice.

Actors rarely live their parts. It is fortunate that this is so for a real identity of feeling involves a lack of control and an assumption of the actor's real feelings by stage or fictional feelings. Sometimes in rehearsals professional actors do tend to 'go over the top', to experience moments when their emotions are momentarily out of control but this usually occurs when they are making a supreme effort to arouse their emotions in some highly affective scene. In this case the director would be standing by to help them through the crisis, and in any case one assumes that a professional actor has acquired the necessary control.

I call it a crisis for this reason: an actor summons his own emotions and then by a process of intense imagination he adapts them to those of a fictional character. The curious part of the process is that he learns to think and feel in a certain way and these thoughts and feelings, which to those watching are of a fictional character, he learns to express in a certain tone of voice, with certain gestures. The function of the director – the man who used to be called the producer – or the teacher in the school play – is to help the actor through this crisis, partly by creating an atmosphere in which he can do creative work, partly by letting him know when his tone of voice and his gestures are convincing and have an element of truth, first in terms of the actor's own thoughts and feelings, and then in those of the character he is creating, which may not be the same thing.

The striking part of the process is that when in future rehearsals he has achieved this identification of his own feelings with those of the stage character, in repeated performances he can fairly easily recall his original feelings by assuming the tone of voice and physical disposition he has created in rehearsals. This is not to say that a certain creative effort is not required at every performance. One is highly critical of the actor who rushes into the theatre five minutes before his first entry, smears on his make-up and goes on stage with next to no psychic preparation. At the same time it is a well-known fact that an actor can move an audience to tears with his mind on his income tax. I am not saying that this is a desirable or even a frequent occurrence but it has been known to happen and it shows the power of the symbol (the actor's performance) in embodying emotion. This process was first discussed by Denis Diderot in a celebrated essay called *The Paradox of the Actor*;[101] a splendid and fascinating book but strictly for theorists.

In applying this complex process to children and young people I think the only helpful thing one can say is that the teacher must use a sense of discretion. I have suggested that young children do not characterize but identify. The process of characterization comes slowly. It is clearly related to and explained by stages in personal development, especially where affective qualities are concerned. This again is why I have been at some pains to emphasize the importance of young people not being excluded from emotional experience or activities that provide opportunities for the embodiment of emotions, the forms in which they are expressed. Emotion is not an isolated visceral activity: it is a nervous response to experience that results in or calls for action; and in terms of art, that means a creative act that embodies or canalizes the emotion. But it is an act that is closely related to acquired social behaviour. This is why it often comes so readily.[102]

In fact the process I have been describing is supported by neurologists and psychologists who have been investigating in recent years the various centres of the brain. Their experiments have tended to support Stanislavsky's main contention that emotions arising from the recall of emotion and from a creative and energetic use of the imagination acquire much of the force and the authenticity of original emotions. The reverse is also true, that a kind of mimicry of emotional expression has no real creative force and does not touch any of the centres of emotion in the brain. I mention this because one still meets the occasional drama teacher who invites students to assume facial expressions expressive of various emotions such as joy, terror, anxiety or pity; and indeed one can associate the tragic voice of the old actor, the style that Stanislavsky was trying to supplant, with this attempt to signal by outward form an inner feeling. But it is no more than a signal, when what we want is an original, deeply felt, and newly created symbol.

So we find that a considered and deliberate approach to an emotional condition can arouse a genuinely emotional response. This explanation of the process is of course to simplify the language almost to the extent of perverting the process; but the truth, I think, is clear, that an emotion of a fictional kind, aroused by imaginative consideration of a fictional idea, takes place in and involves the same centres of the brain as a genuine or spontaneous emotion, or an emotion aroused by contemplation of the circumstances that gave rise to that emotion. This shows that one can create a genuine fictional emotion by proceeding from exterior circumstances as validly as by fishing about in one's subconscious in an introspective manner. With young people this may be the safer approach. But it does mean that the work must be serious, imaginative, and energetically undertaken.

What exactly does all this imply? That a gesture, if it is made with a sensory quality, will arouse a certain emotion. But if it does not involve a sensory quality it will be nothing more than an imitation, and without meaning. If an actor, young or old, is playing the role of someone who is angry, it is not enough for him merely to tense his muscles in imitation of an angry person: he must respond to the sensory and so the emotional activity that is aroused by a tensing of the muscles. The relationship between muscular expression and emotional motivation must be made apparent by sensory, or even sensual, awareness.

In my early twenties I was a member of the Group Theatre. We were trained, taught, and directed by Rupert Doone, a dancer and choreographer of original talent. The great lesson he taught us was never to make a gesture or a movement, even in a limbering-up session, without sensory awareness. It is a lesson that could well be learnt by many teachers in what they call their 'classes in technique'.

In this way it is possible to mark various stages in the creation of a character. There is the identification of young children. There is an imitative phase which in some cases can stop short at mimicry. There is deferred imitation when the imagination can make use of memories both emotional and of characters that have been observed. There is a phase of role-playing when the young actor can enter into some of the cognitive life of the character he is portraying; and there is a growing ability to transform the role with emotional and imaginative adhesions until something approaching a complete transformation of the personality has been achieved.

I want at this stage once more and for the last time to revert to the subject of emotion since it is the most crucial and by far the least understood aspect of the whole process, providing the most important justification of acting as an educational activity.

John Macmurray has been quoted in support of the contention that in educational circles there is an urgent need for a proper training of emotions, a point he makes repeatedly. 'Emotional education should be, therefore, a considered effort to teach children to feel for themselves . . .' and 'we should really recognize that one's emotional life does need educating.' Why?

'The training of emotions', he says, 'is primarily a training in the capacity of sensitiveness to an object . . . maintaining and increasing our sensitiveness to the world outside, irrespective of whether it gives us pleasure or pain . . . I mean being open to *reality*.' Again – 'objective emotion is not a mere reaction to a stimulus. It is an immediate appreciation of the value and significance of real things . . . The senses are the gateways of our awareness . . . Without the sensuous awareness of the world, no consciousness and no knowledge of any kind is possible . . . .'

In a long passage he discusses the tradition which would persuade us that the capacity for sensuality is undesirable. I am reminded of the dismay of my father when as a young man he caught me reading John Cowper Powys's splendid *In Defence of Sensuality*.[103] The tradition suggests that sensuality is harmful, destructive, uncontrollable. The world, he says, has degenerated in its application to the extent that 'the degeneration is itself strong evidence of a persistent attitude to the organic and sensuous aspect of our experience which makes the development of the emotional life impossible.'

Most splendid of all is the manner in which the professor relates emotion to reason . . . 'reason is primarily an affair of emotion and the rationality of thought is a derivative and secondary one. For if reason is the capacity to *act* in terms of the nature of the object, it is emotion which stands directly behind activity, determining its substance and direction, while thought is related to action indirectly and through emotion, determining only its form, and that only partially.'

I need hardly add that it is art which he sees as the most potent expression of emotion and the actual means by which we provide a balanced humanistic education in thought and emotion for our children. It is strengthening to find such resolute support in this difficult subject. Further arguments in favour of the need to educate our feelings can be found in books by R. G. Collingwood and Robert Witkin.

Let us now return to the subject of the school play. An encouraging point for those whose task it is to choose the school play is that it is far easier to act a good play than a poor one. It is, for example, far easier to make a success of *Hamlet* than *Henry VIII*. The reason for this is that a play is termed good because, to cover the elements required by Aristotle, it has acceptable plot, convincing characterization, lively and well-written dialogue, a thoughtful content, and a well-structured theatrical form. Some of these epithets may not apply equally to both *Hamlet* and *The Importance of Being Earnest*, but the similarity in these respects is nevertheless striking. To find the common characteristics is a game that could profitably be played in any sixth form and I hope that this would include an analysis of exactly what are the qualities that make a play come to life when it is acted. The fact is that a well-written play gives the actor all he needs to act: the poorly-written play requires a considerable contribution from the actor. If you speak the lines of any good play intelligibly and don't fall over your own feet, you have made a start.

Yet what more can one say about the school play except that its choice is a kind of crystallization of the school's attitude towards drama. To produce a classic is to make a considerable gesture towards inherited form. Fine, if you know why you are doing it. The gesture is less extreme if the teacher chooses a contemporary play. To handle contemporary themes in theatrical form is to flirt with the spirit of the age which some will consider to be a more profitable activity than to flirt with times past. What I hope is not excluded from the reckoning is the possibility of an original play – perhaps by one of the pupils.

I wonder whether we encourage original playwriting sufficiently? I don't recall ever having seen an original play in a school, a written play as opposed to an improvisation. Is the art then so difficult? Or is it that it is not encouraged? One reads original poetry galore, less fiction, no drama. Or is there something inherently difficult about the art? There is clearly a far greater number of reasonably readable novels published every year than actable or viewable plays. I suspect the reason lies in the sheer technical complexity of the form. A work of fiction or of literature is a direct statement by the writer onto the page. He can use almost any form of words that suits him. But this curious hybrid, a work of dramatic literature, a play, has to be written in terms of what people can say and what actors can speak, it has to be stageable and viewable; there are requirements as to its length, and the whole production is subject to the contribution of a daunting number of specialists. It is their contribution that we shall consider in the next chapter.

Yet I wonder whether the somewhat debilitated state in which drama finds itself in the latter half of the twentieth century may not be at least in part the result of the instability of our culture and of the individuals that compose our society. Drama seems to demand both individual and collective techniques and this opposition of interests is clearly evident throughout the western world. Drama is often popular with the young, particularly with those who are seeking a new collective organization of society; and they press their ideals in the face of a society that poses the illusion of individual freedom while failing to create the conditions in which such freedom is possible. Contemporary drama is thus an affirmation of certain ideals of our society, a reflection of the disintegration of others, and sometimes a weapon in the hands of those who would further change. No wonder that some of us are confused.

# 12 Some Particular Aspects of Theatrical Art

It has long been argued that among the merits of theatrical art is the number of subjects, disciplines, techniques, and specialisms it involves. As a young man I held this view of the theatre as a passionate conviction. Now I am no so sure. A rather more puritanical strain has possessed my tastes and prejudices. We will examine this concept of 'total' theatre, but only after we have examined the parts that add up to this totality. I will begin with design.

Design in the theatre requires the disposition and organization of three-dimensional space. The first task of the designer is to decide how he is going to use his stage or his playing space, and this is a matter of close collaboration with the director–teacher. If the production is to take place on a stage they have to work out together what kind of scenery is to be constructed, whether steps or rostra are to be used; and if it is a naturalistic play, where the entrances, windows, and any other requirements demanded by the action are to be placed. If there is to be furniture, its position on the stage is of great importance since this will largely dictate the movements of the actors. This is why in the professional theatre there is a certain opposition to the employment of what designers call easel-painters since they claim, quite correctly, that theatrical design is basically the working-out of a ground-plan, not painting a picture which may require another specialist to translate it into terms the stage carpenter will understand, someone we might call a scenic artist.

It is the custom now in many theatres and theatre schools to give productions in a studio as well as in a theatre. The advantage of the former is that it provides considerable opportunities for variety in choice of playing space – whether it shall be round, square, rectangular, and how the ninety or so chairs shall be arranged. This is all a matter of design even though the director may have as much or more to say than the designer.

Distinction is sometimes made between the designer of scenery and costumes. Whether this is advisable or not is really a matter of convenience rather than of principle, provided that if two or more people are involved they work as a team. Somewhat different skills are required. Designing and making scenery involves many unusual technical problems, but clothes are within many people's competence. Nevertheless I wish that a collection of garments and fabrics was more in evidence in schools, both primary and secondary. I have said a good deal already about the pleasure that children take in dressing-up and the interest shown by many adults. Yet I do not recall having visited a single school, primary or secondary, where lively and interesting work in improvisation was extended by any significant use of costume. George Devine, a brilliant teacher of improvisation, when working at the London Theatre Studio before the war, and the Old Vic Theatre School after, made considerable use of hats, scarves, capes, skirts, any available garment in fact that was characteristic, together with carefully modelled stomachs, bosoms, bottoms and shoulders which, with the use of masks, could suggest a world of caricature.

Dressing-up in infant and primary schools is part of the process of creativity. In secondary schools, where most activities are more specified, choice of costume is made more carefully and deliberately. In an improvisation class it might initiate quite as often as substantiate and extend dramatic ideas. It is when we begin to deal with the theatre arts that we must consider the designing and making of costumes and this becomes a far more creative process if young people have acquired a feeling for costume from childhood and parents have helped them to develop a dress-sense.

Visual standards in school plays are not usually very impressive. There is far too much dependance on the hiring of costumes from theatrical costumiers. These are often splendid in themselves, but far too 'heavy', sitting upon the wearers like robes on a dummy in a shop-window. And that is the crux of the matter. Clothes are a most individual expression of character; and that is a lesson for life that can be profitably learnt at school.

Art on the whole is extremely well taught in secondary schools, both two- and three-dimensional, and often that goes for craft as well – a distinction, incidentally, which I find unacceptable. I am not suggesting that schools should find time to establish courses in theatrical design, for the demands on their timetable are already excessive; but I believe that art teachers, in collaboration with drama teachers, might do something to introduce young people to the principles of line, colour, texture, and decoration, all of which are closely related in a manner which can be clearly exemplified in the school play.

The problem of constructing scenery is far too complex to consider in a book of this kind. I have said something about the principles involved: if the art department can find time to help anyone interested to investigate the subject, so much the better.

I would say this, however: in no aspect of art is the element of transformation so crucial. To design stage scenery is to conceive a three-dimensional environment which must fulfil at least three requirements: it must be honest to its own visual style; it must be responsive to the conceptual intentions of author and director; and it must provide an acceptable environment for the actors in both practical and imaginative terms.

It is the art of visual transformation in its most advanced and sophisticated form; for it is a well-known fact that genuine materials have a way of looking exceedingly ungenuine and unreal on the stage. I would suggest that before all else a stage designer must be interested in fabric and material, both constructional as well as ornamental. It is no accident that perhaps the greatest British stage designer of all time, Inigo Jones, combined the qualities of architect and engineer. I believe that design is not wholly a matter of an inner vision expressed in two-dimensional pictures, but a visual concept created out of the practicalities of the play, the actors, and the materials available.

The element most responsible for this apparent transformation of the stage-scene is lighting. This is a relatively new subject in schools since it is only in recent years that it has come to be considered an art in its own right. At the same time a far greater range of equipment in the form of both lanterns and control-boards has become available; but although the boards are increasingly flexible in use and compact in design, they are becoming extremely expensive and far too complex for ordinary maintenance. Nevertheless a large number of schools are now provided with drama studios usually equipped with lighting that offers considerable opportunities for imaginative use.

Lighting has become an important aspect of theatrical art. Its status is marked by the emergence of a new specialist who is often billed in type no smaller than that accorded to the scenery and costume designer – that is the lighting designer.

Light is a very powerful ingredient in visual experience. To the painter this is a truism, to the architect a truth. To the housewife the lighting of a room is often a consideration of which she is acutely aware. Great variety in the design of lampshades suggests the truth of this. Light is not only a convenience, something that is necessary in order that we might see, but an emotional experience in its own right. A bright and flatly lighted room provides one kind of experience, a darkly lighted room another; a room with well-balanced and carefully arranged lighting can provide an atmosphere of great ease and contentment.

Drama teachers with access to a well-equipped studio have tended to be somewhat unscrupulous in their use of light, exploiting its emotional resources in rather the same way that they have tended to exploit the power of emotional music. In a darkened studio they are fond of creating pools of brightly coloured light in and out of which, to the accompaniment of highly rhythmical music, the young people are asked to move in expressive and creative fashion. I find this practice akin to a kind of emotional masturbation with no quality of genuine creativity about it whatsoever. But that stage lighting can contribute powerfully to the visual effect of the scene cannot be questioned.

One of the most notable changes in attitude towards stage lighting over the last forty years has been the positioning of the lighting control panel so that the operator can see the stage. This is of particular importance in any production involving young people. For to light a play or a dance can be a highly creative undertaking provided that the designer-operator can see what he is doing, and so control, in collaboration with the director, the colour, intensity, positioning, and direction of the lanterns.

It is often specifically claimed that lighting falls within the responsibility of the physics department. I do not know how many physics teachers are interested in stage lighting, or for that matter in light at all; but I have rarely visited a school where any serious investigation was being made into the effect of different coloured light on differently coloured fabrics or textures. Yet a simple lighting set provides an ideal opportunity for experiments on these lines. If we accept, as we surely must, the importance of line, colour, and texture in stage costumes, it is logical to light these costumes, not to mention the scenery, in a manner that will extend and not kill the visual values that are required. And it is important that these decisions and responsibilities should be given to young people as part of their emotional and aesthetic, as well as scientific education and not hogged by teachers who are frustrated directors and require little of their pupils but to do what they are told.

The next subject to consider is sound and music. Recent developments of the tape-recorder have transformed possibilities of controlling one's sources. Making a tape is a technique that offers almost limitless opportunities for manipulating sound and music and it is one that has been fully exploited by contemporary composers such as Karl Heinz Stockhausen; and it is enormously enjoyed by young people.

Before developing the subject more fully I should explain why I use the term sound and music. A sensibility towards the qualities of sound I take to be the beginning of musical experience. Music is a manipulation of sound to create a certain emotional effect. One can have sound without music but not music without sound. One of the basic elements of music is rhythm or beat and this can be established by clapping hands or stamping on the floor or tapping on a variety of surfaces. When we add to this the expressive qualities of the voice, we find that a wide variety of sound–music is possible without recourse to a single musical instrument. The use of sound–music aided by the voice and subject to the technical manipulation that is made possible by ingenious use of the tape-recorder is being increasingly used for sound effects in the theatre. I have no wish to put a lot of worthy enthusiasts out of business but I am as anxious that young people – and why stop at the young? – should make their own background music rather than rely on dollops of classical recordings as I am that they should make their own costumes, however simple, rather than rely on skip-loads of fustian from theatrical costumiers.

So much for the designing of scenery and costumes, lighting, sound and music, which in the theatre are all related to the arts of the dramatist and the actor. How well do they mix, the arts, how effectively can they be combined to create a single art, that of the theatre? The question involves a discussion on the relationship between drama and music (opera), drama and dance (dance–drama), and music and dance.

Artists have been obsessed with theories about the possible relationship between the arts since Renaissance humanists put their skills together to produce what seemed to them to be ideal theatrical form, the one form that combined into an organic unity the arts of poetry, music, and dancing, and that was Greek tragedy. In Italy these experiments led to the creation of that hybrid but captivating form – grand opera; in France to that similarly esoteric but fascinating art – classical ballet; in England to the most bizarre of all hybrid theatrical concoctions, the court masque. The same kind of idealist concept lay at the heart of

Wagner's *gesamtkunstwerk* (together/art/work), an unholy amalgam of music, poetry, and drama. And there are still rumblings among the so-called progressive companies in favour of various kinds of inter-disciplinary forms of theatrical art.

The limitations of Wagner's ideal of 'the art work of the future' are obvious and no one has tried to repeat the experiment on a similar scale. Operas continue to be written and performed but composers no longer make such lofty claims as Wagner. In fact we have begun to discover that it is exceedingly difficult to combine any two arts in an easy equilibrium. How often in Lieder singing, let alone in opera, do we ever hear the words? How often can we really listen to Stravinsky's incomparable score for *Le Sacre du Printemps* while giving equal attention to whoever's marvellous choreography is being danced on the stage? The integration of the performing arts is a splendid but questionable ideal.

That most wise though whimsical man of the theatre, Jean-Louis Barrault, has defined total theatre in a manner that makes far more sense both for the artist and the teacher. By this term he means 'the total utilization of all the means of expression at the disposal of a human being'. It involves the full use of all parts of man's anatomy, an ideal to which I think many of us whole subscribe.[104]

Theories of integration are being strongly advanced in contemporary education and there are powerful arguments in favour. There has been far too much isolationism and specialization among the arts and it is high time we helped children to take a more panoptic view. But in practical terms the arguments for integration are even stronger for when we look at the arts closely we find that there are remarkably clear areas of overlap. Let us begin, since it is the subject of this book, with drama.

And how difficult it is to establish the integrity of drama! Remove the elements of which it is composed, voice, movement, characterization, and give them to English, music, dance, and literature, where they can find a ready home, and what remains? But of course the reverse is also true: what other art can offer a home to so many other arts? But is that enough to establish its integrity? I myself turn gratefully to Aristotle's definition of drama as an action – from which much follows.

Let us nevertheless see what we can do. Drama requires an expressive body. This is the sensory-motor part of creativity. The body is capable of almost as many registers of expression as speech and these are plentiful. But we are less perceptive in understanding intuitive involuntary gestures than the deliberate volitional code of language. But this is largely a matter of social education. The deliberate, volitional total bodily gesture is dance.

The pathway from expressive bodily movement to dance is by way of rhythm, or metre as for quite practical reasons I prefer to call it. Walking is metrical. If we walk unmetrically, we are probably stumbling which suggests an abnormality either in ourselves or the terrain. It is possible to walk in many different ways expressive of an emotional attitude. If the emotion becomes very strong, we run or skip; or if the emotion is of a depressing kind we drag our feet. This whole subject has been thoroughly investigated in a manner far more penetrating than any recent research by Emile Jacques-Dalcroze in a fascinating book.[105] Some of the antiquated educational methods he advocates and the rather whimsical atmosphere surrounding the practice of eurhythmics must not be allowed to obscure his profoundly original views on the way in which musical sensibility is built into the very neurology and musculature of the body.

There is another art in which a metrical element plays a very important part and that is music. Rhythm, tempo, metre, the time-signature are the basic elements of music, and to this extent and in this respect they are conjoined. Rhythm (or metre etc.) is expressed equally in dance and in music. And, we can add, it is an essentially physical–muscular–motor quality. I would also add that experiments have shown that what most people judge to be a 'normal' rhythm is in fact the speed at which we normally walk; and that this sense of what is normal is also related to the tempo of the beating heart.[106]

Another marriage: a supreme element of music is singing, and this involves, like instrumental music, pitch, tempo, and dynamics. What we usually sing are words or sounds, but words bring us into the area of speech and language. Speech uses rhythm, pitch, dynamics, and tempo to express meaning quite as much as the meaning of the words it employs. So we find that music and speech are closely related, and speech in so far as it makes use of language is English (or whatever is the home language). The difference between words sung and words spoken is largely an emotional one, but that is a matter for further colloquies.

Thus we find a profound interpenetration between dance, music, and human speech, and since we know that drama is compounded of these very elements we can see that there is a fusion between the performing arts and that it is unrealistic to study them in isolation. There is a particular virtue in pursuing these profound relationships with children even more than with young people since children, as we have seen, do not break up their experiences into subjects and disciplines but tend to see the various elements of life as aspects of undifferentiated human experience.

Our view is supported by a celebrated passage by Ezra Pound who says that

> . . . music begins to atrophy when it moves too far from dance; that poetry begins to atrophy when it gets too far from music; but this must not be taken as implying that all good music is dance music or all poetry lyric. Bach and Mozart are never too far from physical movement.[107]

In its context, this passage needs no comment.

There is, however, a danger. In terms of the subject of this book the relationship that is most often met is that between drama and dance. We have seen that drama in its concern with physical expressiveness moves readily towards dance. Dance, on the other hand, moves towards drama when its emotional tension falls and it becomes involved with narrative. The great classical ballets such as *Giselle* are extraordinary phenomena. There is a kind of story which is told in sporadic bouts of formal mime which act as links between and excuse for long passages of dance which on the whole do very little to advance the narrative. This is understandable since dance is concerned not with narrative but with the physical expression of emotion in high profile, with total bodily gesture. A story like *Giselle* or *Petrushka* with a little less dancing and a little more mime or story-telling could easily fall into a genre accurately described as dance–drama, and that is exactly what has developed in recent years. It is not a genre that has been taken up by the professional theatre since actors prefer to act and dancers to dance. But in education teachers have found a genre that in some cases uses the best of the two worlds of dance and drama, though I am bound to add, in some cases the worst.

I do not know what to think of dance–drama. The best I have seen was at a school in Northumberland where the teacher concerned on one occasion directed a masterly piece on the Theseus story. In the scene in the arena there were some splendid bulls taken by the heavier children. When Theseus and his young companions ran towards them preparatory to doing a double somersault over their backs, as we are told took place in Cretan bull-fighting ceremonies, there was a stunning moment of near impact when the bulls neatly stepped aside and the acrobats did a cartwheel or a double somersault. Yet it was all done with such speed that the effect was astonishingly convincing.

One of the most impressive of the bulls turned out to be a waitress in the hotel where I was staying. She had left school quite recently. I commented to the Manager that he had a gifted actress on his staff. He replied that he had a gifted so-and-so. Alas, she was another failure. Where do we go so badly wrong?

As to poor examples of the genre I will say nothing. The danger of this kind of synthesis is a mutual loss of integrity. Drama that has been generalized by a more or less irrelevant background of music and movements that are neither dramatic nor lyric; dance that has been reduced to inexpressive movement and a generalized dramatic content, these two degenerate forms do not make scintillating bed companions.[108]

When drama is combined with music it produces opera. I do not wish to discuss the musical aspect of this collaboration any more than I did in the case of dance since both music and dance have their own problems to contend with in establishing their integrity. The reason for the somewhat uphill battle that both arts face in many secondary schools lies in the degraded position of both dancing and singing in our society. Who dances? And who sings? However popular ballroom dancing among adults may be, it has no relevance to young people in the creative sense. However popular the 'pop' singing of the stars may be, it is not a symptom of an endemic national passion for singing as existed throughout the country in Elizabethan times. Children and young people go to school without any tradition for dancing and singing in their blood and their bones and teachers are faced with a difficult problem in making these activities interesting and relevant. Of real and immediate interest to young people are those subjects that have some kind of obvious relevance to the outside world, the world of which they are looking forward to becoming active members.

I have yet to mention the visual arts. They do not have the same dynamic relationship towards the performing arts which the latter have towards each other. If one pursues the kind of analysis we have been making it becomes clear that the visual arts lack that dimension of time which is physically embodied in dance, music, and drama. What they possess which is lacking in the other arts is a dimension of space. When we move we do so in a certain rhythm which is experienced or expressed physically. But we can only move spatially; so that although we can sense the space in which we move in physical terms, we also assimilate it visually. We develop spatial concepts by moving in space until the perceptual powers of the brain take over from the sensory-motor. This is confusing only if we regard space in terms of an area to be decorated. If we consider the area itself and its relationship to adjacent areas we begin to understand the visual nature of space.

This explains why theatrical design requires a relationship between the director who judges the physical requirements of the environment that is to be created, and the designer who can judge the visual relationships.

Decoration is another part of the process. One can see that this is so in a great deal of contemporary architecture most of which is wholly without decoration. The success of many of the great concrete surfaces we see in new buildings depends very largely on their spatial relationship to each other. The eye, undistracted by any imposed decoration, becomes the more sensitive to texture and proportion.

I suspect that our denial of decoration is as much due to incompetence in the art as in the need for economy. The nineteenth century saw an excess of imposed decoration. What is in fashion today is clarity of line and surface texture. There is absolutely no tradition in decoration. The two places where our own inadequacies have been brought home to me are the churches in Ravenna and the Alhambra palace in Granada. Here we find artists with an almost unbelievable fertility in design and I take this to be the result of a most sensitive response to natural objects which the artist has reduced to formal shapes placed in varied relationships to each other.

One has only to go to outstanding productions of the classics to realize the truth of this analysis. It is in productions we consider to be almost laughably old-fashioned that we see painted scenery or backcloths. The emphasis today is on spatial relationships and texture. Tactile experience has now become an important element in the visual experience and it is important that this sense of touch should be included in the visual education of young people.

So we find that the visual arts are more closely related to the dynamics of the performing arts than we might have expected. I have considered the arts that are principally concerned in theatrical production separately since in the divisive curriculum of most secondary schools this is the way in which they are usually studied. But in response to current fashion in inter-disciplinary activities I have discussed in detail their relation-ship. In fact, however, this common element hardly needs emphasizing since we are concerned with sensory-motor experience which has its own decoding centre in the brain. The faculties of intelligence and imagination consist in the ability to make an almost limitless variety of associations and relationships, and so to create those concepts which in the first instance were perceived by direct sensory-motor involvement. If on the one hand there are artistic difficulties involved in relating the arts to one another, there are very powerful educational ones to explain why the effort should be made.

This book is not about contemporary aesthetics. Young people who acquire a particular interest in the arts will observe for themselves the direction in which they are moving and note how artists use inter-disciplinary techniques to escape various predicaments or extend the imaginative range of their work.

It was only in the course of writing this chapter that I came across a new book by Elizabeth and John Paynter called *The Dance and the Drum*.[109] John Paynter is a musician and a teacher whom I hold in the highest regard and to whose work I have already referred. I was therefore fascinated to find that in the introduction to his book he advocates *gesamtkunstwerk* which in breadth of conception puts Wagner in the shade. I quote:

> What is music–theatre? It is, quite simply, the total integration of all those elements of human expression which we call art. That is: words, movement, music and the two- and three-dimensional visual arts. . . . Music–theatre is an art form in itself. In fact, it is probably the oldest 'art-form' of all, and its revival today . . . has particular significance when it is seen side-by-side with those developments in modern education that aim to release the creative artistic potential in all the children we teach – not merely the 'artistic' or 'musical' ones.

Need I say more?

# 13 Space for Drama

It was in the 1960s that the Department of Education and local authority architects turned their attention to the provision of drama studios and workshops in schools and colleges. The development was a response to necessity, and followed the growth of drama as an educational activity. Schools of the 1930s and 1940s had usually been provided with immense rectangular halls in order to provide for the clause in the Education Act requiring that every day – not necessarily first thing though this is how it was usually interpreted – there must be an act of communal worship. This was usually taken to mean that the whole school must be brought together for a single morning assembly and this required provision of an immense flat hall that would accommodate up to 2,000 pupils – sometimes more. But for what other purpose could one use such a white elephant of a place? The two most obvious uses were school dinners and dramatic performances. So the architects, who for many years could not be persuaded to consult the people who were going to use this specialist provision, made a rectangular hole in one wall and built behind it a stage. This served to elevate the headmaster at assembly and the Governing Body on Speech Day while providing a large area where drama and dance classes could take place. At the other end of the hall they placed the kitchen so that dance lessons could enjoy the accompaniment of the clatter of plates and the chatter of the cooks and dinner ladies except between the hours of twelve and two when tables and benches were set up for the school meal.

In the 1950s and 1960s when attention was turning away from the school play and towards new concepts of drama, teachers began to use the floor of the hall for performances and set the audience on the stage. In the early 1960s two of the Department's most brilliant architects produced a book on space for drama and music in which they reproduced designs of some of the purpose-built drama studios that were beginning to emerge and descriptions of the more imaginative ways in which school

152

halls were being used.[110] The rapid growth of drama in schools during the 1960s – a period of considerable education expansion – led to the widespread provision of drama studios in secondary schools and colleges of education. Here was yet another occasion when there was vigorous interaction not only between the private and public sectors but between the educationalists and the professional and amateur theatre. The 1950s saw the beginning of a new wave of regional theatres, the Belgrade Theatre, Coventry, being among the first. But the first theatre to be built at that time with genuine experimental possibilities was the Questors Theatre, Ealing. This enterprising amateur company was then led by Alfred Emmett and he and his committee set about investigating the form that a new theatre in the 1950s should take. They formed an advisory committee and over the space of about two years plied us with questions about our views on actor–audience relationships, size of audiences, shape of stage – in-the-round, thrust, or proscenium – and so on. What emerged was the need for an almost infinitely flexible set of relationships and this the architect, Norman Bransome, tried to provide in his fine new theatre.

This experiment set the theatre-world thinking about these problems and the results can be seen in a number of theatres such as, notably, Chichester, The National Theatre complex, and the new Royal Shakespeare Theatre in the Barbican.

In educational circles the interest lay not so much in theatres as in studios and workshops. Among the prototypes was the studio of St Mary's College of Education, Strawberry Hill, another design by Norman Bransome. This was copied, modified, and discussed until the basic requirements began to emerge. The studio should be rectangular, with a floor-space of something between 1,500 and a little over 2,000 square feet, depending on its use – the bigger area being preferable if the studio was to be used very much for dancing – about 15 feet high and provided with a limited number of dressing rooms, toilets, and storage. A large number of variations on the basic design were produced. The more sophisticated studios had a gallery running round on two, three or four sides which provided a useful attachment for lanterns and a viewing place for observers. The finest point of design in such studios is the roof. A grid for lanterns and plenty of electrical outlets is crucial but access is not an easy problem. A moveable tower was found to be cheap but cumbersome; cat-walks the most convenient but expensive; for these required the grid to be strengthened and the roof heightened.

One of the most interesting of the more sophisticated studios is the Inner London Education Authority's Cockpit Theatre, designed by Edward Mendelssohn, and this should be visited by anyone interested in the general principles involved.[111]

Drama studios in turn fostered work in-the-round for they provided conditions wholly different from those pertaining in the proscenium theatre which tended to be associated with the less attractive aspects of the school play. Nevertheless it is interesting to note that few of the regional and public theatres that have been built during the last ten years or so have a conventional proscenium. The whole subject of actor–audience relationships has become a subject of detailed investigation.

This architectural reflection of artistic and educational trends establishes a most interesting point, that the nature of drama does and must take its form from the space and the environment in which it is happening. Children in infant and primary schools discover this for themselves. The old-fashioned Wendy house or play corner is usually an arrangement of screens in the corner of the classroom that provides the intimacy required by very young children for their dramatic play. The more secure children can play openly in the classroom or even in the passages and cloakrooms. It is the disregard of this highly sensitive and important relationship that makes nonsense of so many nativity plays.

It is an interesting fact that as children's confidence in their acting increases – and this means their ability to handle words and to use their bodies expressively – so they are able to use space with greater confidence. It is sometimes forgotten that use of space is one of the elements of drama – even more so of dance – that has to be mastered in all dramatic work.

It is the nature of this relationship between the actor and the space in which he is performing that underlines the problem of the school play in a large hall. That the floor of the hall is usually flat with the stage at one end only increases the difficulties. For in these circumstances the actors must not only organize to the full the stage-space they are using but project their performance to the back of the hall. This is a feat of immense technical difficulty requiring not only a highly trained voice but skill in a kind of projection of the personality.

Many years ago when I was a member of the Old Vic Company and we played in both the Old Vic and Sadlers Wells, it was fascinating to watch how the more experienced actors would subtly enlarge their performance when we moved from the Waterloo Road to the greater spaciousness of Sadlers Wells.

During the 1950s, when those developments were in the wind, it was agreed that the furthest distance that even a professional actor should be required to project himself is 60 feet. If one uses the centre of the stage as a focal point and disposes the audience around the stage one can design a theatre with a far larger capacity than if the audience is sitting in straight rows facing the stage, and with a far greater possibility of 'contact' between actor and audience. This is another interesting example of changing theatrical fashions. In the eighteenth and nineteenth centuries, when many theatres held audiences of two and three thousand, actors were trained, as my great-grandmother said, 'to plaster their voices on the back wall of the circle'. We now look for more intimate and sensitive relationships. Smaller and more intimate theatres do not require the magnificent voices of the great actor–managers; smaller and more naturalistic plays and styles of playing require more intimate theatres. There is constant reciprocity between architectural styles and aesthetic tastes in drama.

But the whole question of the audience, as I emphasized in the chapter on the school play, follows from the ability of a young actor to use his space confidently. Spatial awareness is one thing; projection to an audience another, though the two faculties are related.

A word of warning. Educational administrators are much concerned with the expression – cost-effectiveness. What this means is that a room, like any piece of equipment, must justify its cost by the amount it is used. They tend to argue that a drama studio, which is an expensive piece of equipment, should be conceived as a multi-purpose studio, even though the requirements of the different potential users are often in conflict.

Drama is not unduly jealous of space. Excessive space, as I have already suggested, can be nearly as great a limitation as too little.

Movement and dance, with adequate space for running and leaping, require a bigger studio than is necessary for drama alone; and the floor will have to be rather more resiliant.

Music requires a more lively acoustic than is needed for drama.

Art requires workshops adjacent to the studio and considerable storage space.

All the teachers involved must decide how often the studio is to be used for public performances for this affects the design and provision of entrances, exits, cloakrooms and toilets, and in particular where and how the audience is to be seated.

This is one of the most difficult problems, for if it is accepted that not more than about two rows of chairs should be on the floor, one has to consider how to raise the remainder of the audience. Any kind of permanent provision of 'bleachers' tends to limit the flexible use of the hall, and temporary rostra raise problems of storage. In any case, if the studio is to be used for the public performances, the fire regulations impose intractable conditions of design.

Experience has shown that in the design of a studio or theatre, the greater the compromise and the more uses the hall is designed to meet, the less satisfactory it will be for any single purpose. If this is a limitation imposed by inescapable economic demands it should be understood from the beginning that compromises will be inevitable and the architect will have to balance the requirements of one user against another. And this of course is another problem that advocates of multi-media or interdisciplinary activities must face.

As a kind of coda to this chapter I should like to add an explanation of my insistence on children and young people acquiring a sensibility in the use of space. I first became aware of this unique area of experience many years ago when as a BBC producer I was involved in the music and movement programmes. I would go to schools where a class of so-called 'A' stream children were taking the broadcast to find that their work was hopelessly inhibited through lack of any sense of spatial awareness. They bunched, straggled, and fell over each other. On subsequent visits to schools I found that children who had been working with teachers possessing some knowledge of the art of movement were far more confident and sensitive in their use of space, an element that emerged very clearly when one was doing improvisations with teachers themselves. Even professional actors show a varying ability to sort out intuitively their relations with others and the size of the stage on which they are working. A supermarket is an admirable scene to observe the curious spatial clumsiness of many adults.

These empirical observations were reinforced theoretically when I read Jean Piaget's A Child's Concept of Space.[112] In this book M. Piaget expresses his views on the sensory-motor process with such clarity as to explain aspects of child development and the acquisition of perception in a far wider context than the title of the book suggests. The whole process by which muscular activities become internalized – thought taking over from imagery – and the whole external world reproduced in terms of symbols and imaginative concepts, seems to lie at the very heart of our adequacy as a human being.

# 14 Drama in Further and Higher Education

So much for schools.

This book is largely about drama as an aspect of the school curriculum. It is not realistic, as I have explained, to claim that all the arts should have a place on the school timetable for all the pupils all the time; but I would hope that no child leaves school without a certain familiarity with all the arts and having enjoyed the opportunity to specialize in any of them in which he has discovered interest or talent.

When a young person leaves school, there are certain choices open to him. He can finish with the arts altogether, even to celebrating the occasion like boys jumping on their Kennedy Latin primers on completion of 'O' level classics, and singing joyfully, 'No more Latin, no more Greek!' (O tempora! O mores!) Poor Horace! It is difficult to go through life without bumping into the arts in one way or another but most people need not go out of their way to meet them if they do not feel so disposed.

Or our young person can continue to take a mild interest in the arts when they are thrust under his nose in the form of television programmes. If he is so rash as to marry a creative or artistic partner he may be required to admire a picture the other wishes to hang on the wall of the bedroom, or appreciate a new garment. Most people assume the role of reader viewer, listener, spectator or member of audience or congregation of one time or another.

His third choice is to practise one or more of the arts as a hobby. In a world of increasing leisure this is to be encouraged. Or he may decide that his passion and talent justify him trying to take up one of the arts professionally. It is with these two eventualities that I shall concern myself in this chapter; but not sociologically. That is a different subject.

On the whole there are reasonable opportunities for people to pursue the arts of their preference as amateurs, and I mean absolutely no disparagement by this expression. One can write

at home and even though paper is expensive it is not pro-
hibitively so. Painting can also be done at home at very little
more cost. And there are classes in creative writing and in
painting at many evening institutes. Sculpture is less available
for the same reasons that limit it in schools – space and cost of
materials. You can play musical instruments at home – if your
neighbours are complacent, and teachers, though expensive,
are not hard to find. As for acting, the country is liberally
supplied with amateur dramatic and operatic societies and
amateur dance and ballet groups are becoming plentiful. To say
that provision for the practice of the arts through the youth
services and in the field of adult education is adequate will be
challenged. By and large the local authorities have accepted a
modest responsibility for adult education and the establishment
of Regional Arts Associations is proceeding slowly but steadily.
But there is a long way to go. The Russell Report on Adult
Education[113] was greeted with thunderous silence and teachers
in the field consider it to be weakest area in the public sector.
Adequate provision for the amateur practice of the arts requires
deeper thought than even Lord Russell's committee gave the
subject and a government courageous enough to have conviction and act on it.

In further and higher education, however, the situation is far
more complex. Let us consider in the first place my fourth
category, that of opportunities open to young people who want
to make a professional career of practising a certain art.

If they think they have sufficient talent there is nothing to
stop them writing a book and trying to get it published, painting
a picture and trying to sell it, or writing to the director of a theatre
for a job in his company. Until the period following the Second
World War this was the acceptable way of going about things. If
one had trouble with one's voice or one's body, one went to a
private teacher for a few lessons, and then continued to hang
around the agents and read *The Stage*. There were, of course,
art, drama, and music schools, but there was no system of
grants for training and one had to solve one's own professional
problems as one went along.

Art has been well provided for in further education ever since
the Great Exhibition of 1851 when it became clear that to
preserve our lead in industrial technology the country must
equip itself with courses in industrial design. These were made
the responsibility of local school boards and formed the basis of
what developed into a very large number of schools of art.

Dance was badly provided for until Ninette de Valois' epic

achievement at Sadlers Wells put the whole training of dancers in this country on a new footing.

Drama has been in a strange position since with certain natural gifts of voice and body and a certain familiarity with acting at school or in amateur groups, one can or could make one's way into the professional world altogether without training.

What caused the establishment of a number of independent drama schools in the 1950s? The increasing practice of drama in schools would suggest to many young people the possibility of a career in the theatre. The Education Act of 1944 made it possible for local authorities to offer grants for vocational further education or training; and the Arts Council of Great Britain was providing for a considerable revival of the whole regional theatre; and these theatres needed the services of intelligent and well-trained actors.

In this atmosphere there has been a predictable development of drama courses in other establishments of further and higher education, especially the universities. For some years after the war, Bristol offered the only university course in drama, but now there are courses at the universities of Glasgow, Exeter, Birmingham, Hull, Manchester, and Aberystwyth. London University is beginning to teach drama.[114] Cambridge has a professor of drama, and few universities are without some kind of dramatic activity on their campus.

Perhaps the most striking development of all was the increase in the opportunities to study drama in colleges of education. During the 1960s these courses increased in number from some half-a-dozen to around 100; but the decimation of teacher training has now closed a number of colleges and put paid to what promised to be an exciting development.

There is, however, a rather strange aspect of university and college of education courses which it is dangerous to take for granted. University entrance is rigidly controlled by entry qualifications; but once a student has been accepted his fees are paid by mandatory grant from his local education authority while his maintenance is subject to a parental means test. In the same way the whole of the cost of teacher training is borne by the Exchequer, again with the same parental means test for maintenance.

Thus in their separate ways, students of universities and colleges of education find much of their training paid for by various state provisions. In which case both the local education authorities with their mandatary grants and the Department of Education and Science are involved.

But this state patronage of higher education operates far less generously in the case of training for the arts. Local authority grants for a student who wants to be trained as an actor, or dancer, are discretionary on their own regulations. Thus a student who studies drama at Bristol University without any vocational outcome in view is in a far more privileged position financially than the student who studies drama at the Bristol Old Vic Theatre School with the clear intention of becoming an actor.

The musicians have escaped this dilemma by having long since established degree and degree equivalents in the performance of music.

All this suggests some exceedingly erratic thinking on the part of our politicans and administrators, and one is faced with some inescapable conclusions. The main one is that teachers are financially privileged because the state has need of teachers; but actors and dancers are not because the civil servants and the politicians consider that the state has less need of them. Graduates are privileged because, presumably, a degree·is a guarantee of a trained mind, whereas a vocational qualification is the guarantee of artistic ability and so, apparently, of less value to society. Where Plato sowed, the Department of Education reaps!

It is only now that ever increasing economic pressure has forced certain governments in the western world to relate numbers of students in training to opportunities of employment, not only in teacher training, but throughout the university faculties.

The whole situation is exacerbated when we consider the status of the establishments concerned. The position of universities is assured through the University Grants Commission and of polytechnics and colleges of education through the local education authorities and the DES.

The only security for dance and drama schools lies in winning some kind of support from the local authorities. The whole precarious edifice has been analysed in *Going on the Stage*,[115] a report of an enquiry into professional training conducted by the Gulbenkian Foundation.

The upshot of this erratic situation is understandably bizarre since the government has created a complex dialectic in which there is neither sense, justice, nor consistency.

The philosophy of a university course is that it is a course of liberal study unrelated to any vocational considerations. But it is impossible to study drama out of its vocational context. Drama does not consist in the critical analysis of plays or a study of theatre history: it is, as we have seen, acting and writing and design, and to study it in any other way makes little sense. English universities, long under pressure from their American counterparts who are more realistic in these matters, have moved in a practical direction and turned the attention of their students towards the professional theatre for employment. Recent statistics make this trend absolutely clear.

The converse of this is equally interesting. Some years ago the schools of art which, as I have said, were the first and most considerable group of schools in the field of art to be publicly supported, obtained recognition of their qualification as the equivalent of a university degree. The organization responsible for awarding degree equivalents in art amalgamated with a newly formed organization, the Council for National Academic Awards, with the result that the degree equivalent, the Diploma in Art and Design, was transformed into a straight BA degree. This established the precedent of degrees being awarded in professional artistic subjects with a minimum of subscription to academic and liberal studies, although this was only an extension of the facilities that had long existed in the colleges of music.

It is intriguing to consider the basis on which BA degrees are awarded, for example, in abstract painting; but this is not to knock an admirable development, for it is far better that credit should be given for living creative work rather than, as happens in universities, for commentaries on the work of dead artists.[116]

The CNAA then let it be known that it would not be averse to validating professional degrees in the other arts. The drama schools pricked up their ears. Strange though at first it might appear to take a degree in professional acting, it is no more strange than to take a degree that largely involves playing the piano. Such a degree could be sustained without serious mutation to existing courses and in a form that would not perjure the respect of managements and union; the benefits would include mandatory, that is compulsory, grants for the students, and a far higher degree of general respectability in the eyes of the local authorities upon whom the support of the drama schools must ultimately rest.

The national schools of drama are hesitant to offer degrees but two or three of them are moving in that direction.[117] Thus we have the curious and rather disturbing situation of higher education moving towards the professional and vocational field, and the professional vocational schools moving into the field of higher education.

Why disturbing? In some respects the whole movement is producing an enlargement of frontiers. The theatre is to receive better educated workers and those students who do not go into the theatre will have a clearer and fuller experience of the nature of the theatre arts. Anxiety rests about the nature of each discipline. Is breadth and intelligence of training to be won at the risk of lower physical and vocal standards, the latter being none too high as it is? Is intellectualism and a thorough theoretical understanding of the theatre to take the place of the sheer ability to act? Moreover the union is particularly alarmed that at the very moment when it has received assurance from the drama schools that the number of students they are producing, which is not excessive for the requirements of the profession, is not likely to be increased, very large numbers of young people from training establishments other than the drama schools may be seeking to enter an already overcrowded profession.

Unfortunately this is not the end of the problem. It is well known that the government, acting on predictions from its computers which foretell a considerable fall in the school population in the 1980s, are in the process of decimating teacher training. This will leave the very large colleges of education, which went through a vigorous period of expansion in the 1960s, with their reduced numbers of teacher students rattling round in corridors of empty study-bedrooms. The order of the day is therefore 'diversification': the colleges are being urged to offer a variety of non-vocational courses to fill up the vacancies left by non-existant teachers. In the general enthusiasm for drama and with CNAA ready to validate more courses, drama is a natural contender; and one has only to follow the theatrical and educational press to note the number of degree courses (BA) that are being offered in drama and the performing arts. I am very happy to note there is so much interest in drama; but at the same time I am concerned to know what the hundreds of young people equipped with BAs in drama, art, and music are going to do for a living. CNAA makes a paper distinction between a professional vocational degree and a so-called 'performance' liberal arts degree with a good deal of practical content. But the qualified graduates will not be interested in this distinction. The anxieties of the union seem to me to be very well justified.

This is to adopt, of course, a rather pragmatic attitude to the situation. There will be those who feel that whatever the immediate problems that have to be faced by the profession there is cause for rejoicing in the general status that is being given to drama by its widespread acceptance as a valid discipline in higher education. I find it difficult at the moment to hang out flags in celebration of any of these developments. I am deeply concerned about the educational and artistic problems that have been thrown up and some of these I would like to mention since they have repercussions on work in schools and our whole attitude towards drama and theatrical art.

The first and most important point is the intellectual hierarchy that places vocational work at the bottom of the scale and intellectual work at the top. This was emphasized for me the other day by a distinguished academic who said that an MA was different from a BA by virtue of its totally abstract and theoretical content. Who does not admire intensely the man with the fine mind? But who does not also admire the fine craftsman? It is arguable that the anonymous craftsmen responsible for the windows of Chartres or the iconography of Autun have made as big a contribution to European culture as the scholars who sat in their cloisters and produced critical exegeses on ancient texts. (These days there would be more people to design the windows than to make them.) In the labour market each will find his level of payment. But in intellectual circles there is a hierarchy that awards the goodies to the intellectual and not the craftsmen. In the supermarket it may be different.

I find it very strange that the cognitive qualities of a human being should be regarded so much more highly than the conceptual, the intellectual than the artistic, especially when we learn from the psychologists how closely the two faculties are related.

For in this division we have omitted the artist. The intellectual, whose status is based on the Platonic tradition, has always been suspicious of the artist by reason of the latter's involvement in the expression of emotion which tends to be unruly, uncontrollable, and wholly imprecise.

There was a time in medieval Europe when the craftsman was valued highly. He went through a period of apprenticeship for a prescribed period, usually seven years, and then on presentation of his masterpiece, was accepted as a master; and as a master-craftsman he held a recognized position in society. In medieval Europe the scholar was not held in very much higher regard than the master-craftsman is today.

But this particular social structure was broken when the master-craftsman became an artist and assumed a position of almost celestial authority. This was the work of the artists we associate with the High Renaissance. Former artists, Cimabue, Giotto, Simone Martini, Pietro Lorenzetti, Masacchio and scores of others working in Florence and the hill towns of Northern Italy learnt their trade in the workshops of the masters who organized their craft like any other. It was Michelangelo and his kind who laid claim to qualities that put the artist onto an altogether different level of achievement from the craftsman.[118]

The guild structure broke down, the apprenticeship scheme collapsed, and the artist of even moderate competence was able to sustain the unwarrantable claims of Michelangelo. This led rapidly to the exploitation of works of art by patrons and dealers. The attitude was emphasized in the eighteenth century when art critics dubbed painting and sculpture as 'fine arts' (*beaux arts*) to distinguish them from the more useful arts of architecture and woodwork. This has given painting today a total supremacy over the other arts and the arts in general supremacy over craft.

But does this hierarchy reflect the reality of the situation? Every form of expression involves what we have called the ability to handle a certain medium. This is what we mean by craft. Now this handling of a medium, whether it is clay, wood, paint, a musical instrument or one's own body involves a very great range of sensual and sensory sensibilities. These sensibilities are in turn very closely related to emotional responses. To handle a piece of wood, or even more to shape a piece of wood with a chisel, is to produce the very strong emotional reaction, be it simply of pleasure, or satisfaction, that results from almost any creative activity. One is moved – and the action implied in the word is a proper aspect of its meaning – to do something about the surface of the wood to reveal its texture; or to fashion it into a shape that responds, as we say, to some creative urge or inner necessity.

May I reiterate that I do not distinguish the early response of a craftsman to a piece of wood as markedly different from the way a child plays with a ball or a girl dons her mother's dress. One can watch the small boy bouncing the ball, seeing how far he can control it, kick it, get it past someone else who would like to take it from him. Creative but not artistic impulses. The artist takes over from the player by virtue of his determination to create some artefact which will combine aesthetic satisfaction in its shape, colour, texture – with perhaps some practical use. And I would not attach much importance to the question of use since different objects are useful to different people. It is not everybody who needs a teapot for making tea: in the navy we used to make it in the kettle.

We refer to the process of transforming a lump of wood into an artefact as a conceptualizing process. The mind produces an image or concept of what it wants the fingers to achieve. The fingers are motivated by emotion; but it is wholly unrealistic to suggest, as society has tended to do, that a very strong cognitive element is not also involved. It is perfectly true that emotion, uncontrolled by thought or any other means, is unruly and imprecise; but I think it even more unrealistic to suggest that art is the expression of emotion that is not subject to the very severe restrictions of control of the medium and conceptual discipline. The expression, coined by Robert Witkin as the title of his book, *The Intelligence of Feeling*, is a most useful one. Feeling is indeed intelligent; but we do not always know how to interpret our feelings. Mr Witkin's book is not an analysis of the psychology of feeling but an argument that it is through the processes we know as art that we come to resolve certain emotions and by that means to understand more clearly what that emotion means for us. And all this is very much in line with the philosphical approach of both Susanne Langer and John Mac-murray.

I am not therefore arguing the priority of art over the physical sciences or intellectual disciplines; only that art should not be undervalued in the educational hierarchy any more than artists should undervalue the importance of craftsmanship.

And this is the point at which I would like to consider in rather more detail opportunities for a professional training in the arts.

I am also aware that in the course of these various arguments I have been somewhat cavalier about the nature of intelligence. I repeat, to ensure I am not misunderstood, that I do not for one moment underrate its importance. My concern is that it should not be considered alien from other human functions, notably the creative power of emotion, capacity for association, the imagination, and the ability to which Arthur Koestler quotes many scientists as admitting,[119] to 'think' (conceive?) visually. I am wading through deep waters: my complaint is that far too many people look on them as shallows, take off shoes and stockings, and are well content with a paddle.

# 15 Education for the Arts

This chapter is concerned with provision for those who want to make a professional career in the arts. Its subject is virtually preparation for performance.

Whatever degree of unity we may be able to establish between the arts we find very different requirements in training. In fact the very word is in question; for whereas it might be said that a child trains to be a dancer, we would not usually talk about training to be a writer. The word training suggests the acquisition of techniques of a rather limited and perhaps esoteric kind. There are some educationalists who hate the word training and keep it well separated in their vocabulary from education.

Very well, education or training, there may be important concepts hidden by these semantic distinctions.

We will begin with music since this is a talent which can reveal itself at a very eary age. It is a talent of so unique a kind that I believe it to be based in some modular structure within the brain rather in the way that some psycho-linguists claim speech to be. And speech and music, after all, in their dependence on the interpretation of sound, are very closely related. The child who is born of musical parents, or who is brought up in home or school where music is practised, will reveal this talent, whether it be for composing or playing an instrument. But when I consider a society such as ours, in which music is held in no regard at all by the bulk of society, I wonder how much talent is lost, buried, undiscovered.

I do not accept the glib truism that 'talent will out'. Well, I suppose that if it is on the level of genius, a positive unquestioning talent, it will assert itself; but I suspect that there are many cases where those electric nodes that think in sound flicker a little fitfully and require encouragement and opportunity to develop their full potential.

The teaching of music in school suffers from two considerable constraints. One is the debased condition of music in our society; the other is the very limited attitude towards musical education that generally prevails. A friend of mine, now unhappily dead, who for a time was Staff Inspector of music in the Department of Education, used to say that music education was constricted by excessive use of the piano, a limited concept of instrumental teaching, and an attitude towards notation that enclosed potential musicians behind the five-barred stave like sheep behind a five-barred gate. A powerful talent will jump over the gate, or knock it down, or even open it and walk through; but a less assertive talent, and all the many young people who are capable of enjoying musical experiences as amateur instrumentalists, singers, and concert-goers require help in striking a balance between creative aspirations and the limited acquisition of techniques that make possible their realization.

The problems affecting dance education are not dissimilar. A powerful talent for dance will only reveal itself if the children are given opportunity for dancing. Expressive movement based on the principles of Rudolf Laban is widespread in English primary schools; but admirable though these activities might be as first steps in movement education – physical education is something different – they do not often develop into forms of dance; and I doubt the ability of many primary-school teachers to detect the particular quality of dance in the undemanding cavortings of natural movement.[120]

A rather unfortunate situation has arisen as a result of this faint-heartedness on the part of the public sector of education. Specialist teachers of dance have recognized that the training of a ballet-dancer – and I will comment on this emphasis on ballet as opposed to other forms of dance shortly – must begin somewhere around the age of ten or eleven, for physical reasons. Many teachers, in league with ambitious mothers who like to see their pretty daughters wearing tutus and turning out their feet, grab the children from as young as five and impose upon them a training that is usually as limited and technically orientated as the educationalists rightly fear. These are the 'brass-plate' schools, private and independent, claiming that they offer a training, for which there is considerable demand, which local authorities do not supply.

The public sector has for long taken an ostrich-like attitude to the whole thing and claimed on the one hand that there is no need for children to receive a specialist training from as young as ten, and that if parents cherish these fads, they must be ready to pay for them – which many are ready to do. But for most of the time the administrators claim that the problem does not exist, or that if it does it is none of their business. One can therefore welcome as indicating a slight change of heart the recent decision of the DES to support the Royal Ballet Junior School – as well, incidentally, as Yehudi Menuhin's school for talented young musicians at Stoke d'Abernon.

Serious professional training for young musicians and dancers is still largely provided by the private sector of education, that is to say by teachers who give classes outside schools and school hours. This is the brass-plate syndrome. There is a small number of schools where a thorough training in dance is offered as part of a general education, and in strictly professional terms there is no need for more so long as opportunities for employment of professional dancers are as limited as they are at present. The problem facing these schools is not one of numbers but of finance, for they are expensive to run and dependent for survival, like the public schools, on a supply of parents ready, willing, and able to pay fees, by 1978 standards, of well over £1,000 a year. Local authorities offer a few places to a few schools but this only touches the fringe of the problem.

I fear, however, that short-sightedness is not only a weakness of the bureaucrats. Some of the dance and music schools do cherish, as I have already suggested, an excessively narrow concept of professional training and have subjected themselves to the control of a number of examining bodies offering grades and models. Of the standards required and the scrupulous methods of examining there can be no question. What is dangerous is that these examinable techniques may have almost no relationship whatsoever either to the creative, individual, and artistic aspirations of the young people who are subject to these tests, or to the choreographers who are likely to employ them. They are welcomed by the schools for they provide a syllabus, national standards, and a generally accepted developmental technique. A school that had the courage to break away from this system might find difficulty in getting its own standards accepted but at the same time it might well release a creativity in the young people of an entirely new kind. I believe in fact that the lamentable shortage of choreographers, who are the creative people in dance, is largely due to intensive technical and limited artistic training that young dancers receive in their secondary schools.

Let me emphasize that the blame is by no means wholly with the schools. They must cut their cloth according to the measure. And they are subject to measurements on every side. The educationalists want a high standard of teaching and impressive examination results. So do the vocational teachers. They compete against each other for time, and very often the latter win because they can point to the immensely high standards demanded by the professions; and nothing impresses parents more than a good record of employment.

Music, as I have already mentioned – and in this respect we can couple it with dance – has been particularly subject to traditional forms. The music industry has covered the western world with performances of an extraordinarily high technical level but reaching so narrow a public and offering so traditional a repertory that one cannot equate them in any way with the real musical life of the country. It is very much the same with dance. Classical ballet on a grand scale is still a best-seller even though the basic repertory consists of barely a dozen works. Other styles stemming largely from America are enlarging horizons but as with music they have no close relationship with society as a whole.[121] Teachers of music and dance have therefore had an excuse to base their training on traditional lines. And this limited concept can be supported by an equally limited concept of job opportunities. To get into one of the major ballet companies one needs an unequivocal classical technique. To get into the Graham company a dancer needs to have mastered a largely though not wholly different style. It is the same with jazz dancing – classical ballet plus plus plus.

The innovators have got nowhere by tinkering with traditional forms: they have had to be iconoclastic to get anywhere at all. I have seen extraordinary experiments in music education being conducted at various schools and I am sure that in educational terms they will induce a new musical sensibility in young people. But in terms of professional performance the future is gloomy, for while the great British public will pay many pounds for a seat at Covent Garden to see *The Rhinegold*, they will grudge a few pence to hear the latest off-beat experimental non-traditional composition.[122]

And the same with dance. There seem to be nearly as many 'fringe' dance groups as there are theatre groups. But in their efforts to escape traditional forms of dance, they have elected for a style of performance that sometimes can hardly be credited as dance at all. There follows a typical over-reaction on both sides. The traditionalists become more traditional and the opposition becomes increasingly inchoate.

I do not pretend that this is a situation to which there are any easy answers; but I do suggest that if throws considerable responsibility on everybody who claims to have any interest in or responsibility for training young people in these arts. But I must emphasize that the constraining factor is as much fear as economics. If we do not train dancers as we have recently trained them, the dance companies will not be able to maintain their present standards and if standards fall, audiences will fall and we shall be in the grip of a spiral that will end in the collapse of English national prestige in the world of dance. And we must ask ourselves frankly, 'Does that matter?', are there not compensating advantages? When one suggests that artistic standards may be a sacred cow, and an expensive one at that, half the dance world has an ulcer.

Yet the time may come when the young people consider that classical ballet is a form that has had its day; and when they become adults they may want to begin teaching dance with other styles and other values than those that pertained when they were being trained. For the creative process operates as forcibly in terms of dance as of drama and it may well be that the impetus for acts of choreographic creation in the form of classical ballet may weaken and the tradition wither. But if it is to be replaced by a dance that is expressive of the creative impulse of young people, responding to the dynamics and the values of contemporary society, the credit in terms of sheer cultural vitality may well more than balance any loss there may be.

This is why those who control the present public sector of education are maintaining a perilously dangerous attitude by enforcing this divisive policy that leaves vocational training to the private sector while offering in the public sector so flabby an attitude towards art education that only work of the most superficial kind can result. I am not going back on what I said earlier about claims on timetables. I was then speaking of general secondary schools. I am now thinking of the need for schools in the public sector which will offer opportunity for the specialist study of music and dance by young people who are considered to be temperamentally and physically suited to make a career in that art.

Drama along with art comes in a rather different category since drama teachers, as I have already remarked, are far less interested in traditional forms. It is arguable that they have taken their iconoclastic attitudes too far. It has been for them a far easier problem since even on its most professional level drama has not been associated with traditional forms of anything like the kind pertaining in music and dance. They have had very little to destroy to find their freedom. Contemporary dramatists and directors have done their work for them. In the same way the enormous number of artistic schools, movements, and cults over the last century have freed art teachers from the responsibility of teaching formal and inherited techniques. There are virtually none to teach.

The extent of this freedom from traditional form varies of course according to the nature of each art. One cannot express oneself adequately in dance or music without a reasonable technique. But one can act and draw with very little mastery of the subject. The actor may not be audible and the artist may not be able to draw a likeness but the actor may well answer by saying that audibility is not his intention – he is acting for his own pleasure and not for that of others, while the artist may claim that there is no artistic dogma that insists on representational veracity. I believe that these may be spurious arguments, but they have a superficial relationship to current thinking.

Whatever the validity of the arguments they have resulted in drama winning for itself a somewhat stronger position in secondary schools than music. Music maintains its position out of traditional respect for the subject; drama has been winning its position through the vitality of its contribution to education. If this is to falsify the true state of affairs, I shall be the first to rejoice. No art enjoys educational hegemony; all are of profound importance for young people, music as much if not more than any.

I have said a good deal about the visual arts in secondary education. Visual experience has played a most important part in the development of the human species, so much so that Coleridge wrote penetratingly about the dangerous 'despotism of the eye'.[123] Art is well established and although children are still required to study such technical trickery as perspective, most will have had opportunity for what the jargon now calls 'creative self-expression'. Talent in the visual arts has, on the whole, plenty of opportunities to reveal itself.

The same is probably true of English. Generalizations may be wide of the mark, but I guess that there are quite enough teachers of English aware of the need to provide opportunities for creative writing to ensure that young people discover whatever talent they may have within them. While there is much difference of opinion about the importance of spelling, grammar, sentence construction, and even general presentation and handwriting, most English teachers recognize the importance of touching whatever creative ability their pupils may have. Attitudes to traditional literature have become increasingly liberal; and more contemporary literature is now read and studied in schools than classical. If there has to be an emphasis, it is preferably in this direction. Many contemporary poets, novelists, and playwrights have pinned down aspects of contemporary society on paper; but it is not easy to put up a strong argument in favour of the Romantics. It must, of course, be done. But their eternal verities do not always seem to be eternal or even verifiable in the brutal world of the 1970s. My point is simply that teachers of English are not on the whole letting traditional studies stand in the way of original creative work.

In the case of musicians and dancers we are dealing with minority groups. There are a few schools that offer traditional training of a high professional level but fewer still that offer training with a genuinely original and creative education. The trouble is that we are dealing with artistic and educational concepts that none of us fully understand or know how to realize.

I have said enough about drama. Many young people are likely to have had some drama at school and many will have acted in one or more school plays. A curious feature of drama is that talent both for acting and for playwriting tends to reveal itself very much later than in the case of the other arts. Indeed the Principals of some drama schools prefer to delay a concentrated training until the students are well into their twenties. This seems to suggest some rather interesting implications about the genetic and neurological structure of the various arts.

So generally speaking we can claim that reasonable opportunities are offered in secondary school to young people who are interested in some preliminary experience in one or other of the arts. If anyone attempted a breakdown of the capital involved, both in terms of teachers and equipment, he would find, I suspect, that the figure would run into many millions of pounds. Perhaps the country is not so entirely philistine as we sometimes fear.

This fairly considerable outlay must be held to support the view that educationalists in general consider that the arts can make a significant contribution to the education of young people. In fact I don't think that this is a view that stems from any collective thinking on the part of educationalists or politicians; but rather a process of infiltration made possible by the decentralized nature of English education and a large number of highly articulate apologists to many of whom I have already paid my respects.

But when we move from schools to further and higher

education we find a number of issues hopelessly confused. Tertiary education in general offers a variety of non-vocational qualifications in the form of degrees as well as degrees and diplomas of a highly vocational and professional nature. The schools are the first level of a three-tier structure: schools, further education or training, and the professions. The confusion to which I have referred results from the partial involvement of the government at many stages in this complex process. The situation is neither one of total *laissez-faire* nor of total government control. At the moment we are getting something of the worst of both.

If the public sector of education has enabled a young person to discover a talent it is for the public sector to help him develop that talent. The young (visual) artist is not in too bad a plight. Schools of art have not on the whole been dismembered like colleges of education although so many have been absorbed into polytechnics and establishments of higher education that it is difficult to locate the existence of courses. Nevertheless many still exist and offer degrees in a wide range of artistic subjects.

The situation is somewhat less promising for the young musician. He can count the number of reputable music colleges of national standing on the fingers of one hand. Hazards of admission are far more serious than the payment of fees, for competition is considerable and standards of entry are high; but the colleges are subsidized and offer a variety of degrees.

And the dancer? For obvious reasons degrees in dance are slow to emerge and therefore there are no mandatory grants. There are some half-dozen reputable schools of dance in the country but they are expensive and not always generously supported by local authorities. While ballet is paramount at the Royal Ballet School, some of the other schools offer training in a variety of styles. The Arts Educational Schools go even further; for they represent a visionary attempt by their founders to provide a secondary education in which the arts should be strongly represented and closely integrated with the academic subjects. To a modest extent the vision has been realized although the integration of vocational and educational subjects is sometimes difficult. The profession demands high standards of performance and the educationalists see the need to provide the young people with a proper clutch of 'O's and 'A's. Principals have to show tact and understanding to establish a balance between the two.

Yet this very conflict is a clear result of basic misunderstanding as to what we are about. One becomes a good dancer by dancing and a good writer by writing. But there is more to dancing and writing than a well-trained body and a gift for words. Nor is the answer simply that we must give the young people something to dance or write about. It is what I have been arguing throughout this book, that we create as the result of a stimulus, but of a stimulus that may be visual, auditory, tactile or of unrecognizable provenance. The stimulus creates – what can we call it? – a concept? And we transform this concept into whatever medium the concept has been conceived in, which will probably be that artistic discipline in which we are most gifted and in which we have been most fully trained. But it is clear enough that before we consign a student to the absolute technical demands of a profession we do our best to introduce him, while he is at school, to all the various forms, disciplines, and arts into which this creative transformation may be made. And this is the difference between education, with which we begin our life, and training that may come later. But I do not think the latter ever wholly supersedes the former.

It is significant, I am sure, how well a ballerina painted when she was at school. I have observed that the standard of painting in schools of dance is very high. Is there a relationship between kinetic experience and the visual image? I have observed that the standard of music is often rather poor. There are, clearly, different reasons for this. For one thing it is often poorly taught. Beryl Grey once said to me, 'English dancers enter on their points, Russians dancers on the cellos.' Time and expense can be produced as explanations but I believe that the subject of vocational training across the whole field of the arts requires disinterested study.

Dancing might be thought to involve an element of drama.

I once saw an exquisite *A Midsummer Night's Dream* at the Royal Ballet School. It was played on a summer evening in the open air in Richmond Park. But drama was not pursued because in the main it was thought to be a diversion from the demands of dance and one for which time could not legitimately be spared. In another school I found drama being taken with the dancers by a brilliant and most unorthodox young teacher-director. He formed the opinion that dancers are so disproportionately occupied with mastering a most demanding technique that they gave little attention to projection or communicating with an audience. He also felt that they enjoyed little opportunity for fun which in his meaning of the word constituted a kind of play which in turn he considered to be a method of stimulating the visceral creative juices. He thereupon devised a series of exercises that culminated in street games in a London park. These shennanigans were not favoured by the management and quickly terminated. I mention the episode not for its historical importance but because it underlines a weakness that can be inherent in the performing aspects of music and dance when an excessive emphasis upon performance technique can lead to technically excellent performers but creatively limited artists.

Drama schools tend to be more favoured than dance schools, less so than art. Drama, however, can be, and has been a source of fascination to many different artists. The reason seems to be that it provides a human context. It is concerned with the here and now of the human predicament. The interest of many composers in opera seems to suggest some such argument, and Renaissance artists, though undoubtedly well paid for their work, were rarely hesitant to design decor for all manner of princely and popular festivals, diversions, and entertainments.[124]

As a result of the diversified nature of theatrical art, the curriculum of most drama schools is fairly wide and this is possibly why their students are often found in a wide variety of professions. They offer a range of work on the voice – speech, language, and singing; on physical movement, which may include various forms of dancing, acrobatics, fencing, or, what is more likely these days, stage-fighting. And the practical study of plays involves a familiarity with a great range of linguistic styles, social mores, and historical references.

There is little need be said about the young person who wants to be a writer except this: he needs sympathetic guidance. I hope that he is given the right kind of encouragement and criticism while he is still at school. I hope that he will have been encouraged to try his hand at a variety of writing – fiction, poetry, drama, essays, reporting events, descriptions of situations, and decent letter-writing.

Writing is not an act of immediate communication like the performing arts. One can write at home in seclusion and privacy and one's relationship with one's publisher is direct and intimate. One dances, acts, and sings in the very fullness of an emotion, in the very process of making an act of communication. This is another reason why it is much easier to establish a degree in English than in drama. The literary product is coolly assessable. The dramatic action is transitory and evanescent. This is why it is grossly unjust that degree courses which are awarded to subjects, not which are academic but which are assessable, should be supported by mandatory grants, and the performing arts, which require no less intelligence, but which are not so readily assessed or examined, dismissed with discretionary awards. It is also arguable that critical skill is being rated more highly than creative and the contemplative more generously than the active.

Professionalism involves considerable dedication to the art or discipline concerned. This dedication involves a willingness to take endless pains 'to get the thing right' which means, in drama, what may be a protracted struggle for the dramatist to project his concept into dramatic form, and for the actor to arouse in himself the appropriate emotions for the character he is playing and then find form for their expression. This process may involve long hours of work requiring a strong constitution and immense emotional control. But one of the curious and rewarding paradoxes is that this tremendous expenditure of psychic energy is at the same time a creator of energy which explains, I think, the Herculean achievements of some of the world's great artists.

This is to take a somewhat traditional attitude towards professional stage training and the principles that apply generally to the other arts. Yet one is bound to wonder whether one is justified in preserving so intractable a concept of training for a profession the aesthetic standards of which are changing rapidly and radically even though perhaps not more so than in the other arts. In the report of the Gulbenkian enquiry it is pointed out that students have to be trained for possible employment in television, radio, films, repertory theatres, West End productions, theatre-in-the-round, theatre in pubs, in the street, in clubs, Theatre-in-Education, with roles embracing the classics, contemporary drama, the theatre of cruelty, of the absurd, of alienation, mime, and improvisation. Every Principal will be balancing standards of traditional training against contemporary pressures. What is one to think of training for the classical ballet with its marvellous *Swan Lakes* and *Giselles* and its prodigious government subsidies, an aristocratic form of art that was highly suitable for the court of Louis XIV but sits oddly in the midst of our democratic and egalitarian world? Is the concert pianist an anachronism? Or are we right at almost any cost to preserve traditional values, our patrimony and cultural inheritance?

There has been a recent development in the theatre that crystallizes some of this dilemma. I am referring to the emergence of what are now known as Theatre-in-Education groups, usually referred to as T.I.E. I use the word 'dilemma' not to signifiy any uncertainty in the actors concerned, for most of them turn to work in T.I.E. with considerable confidence, but to suggest that this is an area of work that is inevitably, and in its very nature, a compromise or, should one say, a fusion between the wholly independant, thought in some ways related, disciplines.

Unfortunately, it is easier, in a superficial way, to establish educational practices than artistic principles; so the documentary type of play is the stock-in-trade of the T.I.E. group. This may be of value to children and young people but of less interest to the new adult audiences for whom the groups are increasingly giving performances.

I have said that their existence is symptomatic of a contemporary dilemma. Actors accept certain traditional concepts of their art: they must be audible, convincing, expressive – they are as much as ever 'servants of the public'. Yet the stages of the National Theatre are no longer where they all want to perform, any more than all young pianists want to play in the Royal Festival Hall or dancers join the Royal Ballet. Rarely have there been periods in history when what excites the artist in society is society itself. He is no longer on a separate level from his audience: he wants to be one of them; he even wants to explain to them how he works. And it is understandable that he should want to begin with children, to establish an artistic empathy with young audiences and to share with them an exploration of social phenomena. Hence their emphasis on 'documentary' plays rather than plays of more overt entertainment which are increasingly the province of children's theatre. Those who want to know more about this fascinating subject will turn to Mr Parnaby's book, *Actors in Schools*,[125] but it is clear, nevertheless, that the whole European phenomenon of cultural democracy, to which reference was made early in this book, is both a cause and a result of upheavals in which artistic and social pressures can be seen to be playing upon and so re-shaping each other before our very eyes. Like many a European at the present time I look to the emergence of a new theatre or of new relationships within the existing theatre.

The whole provision of training for the arts is based on short-term objectives and lacks a basic and well construed body of theory which will lead to coherent policies. I have written about the need for there to be a far more consistent policy between art education in schools, and in further and higher education, including, of course, vocational training.

There was a time when the Arts Council began to interest itself in professional training but the Department of Education has let it be known that it does not favour this involvement; and the Arts Council has not thrust forward its case with any great conviction. Nevertheless something has got to be done to smooth out the contradictions to which I have drawn attention and to ensure that there is a proper deployment of public resources for training in the whole field of the arts. At present the general provision is confused and this leads to frustration and poor quality work.

Politicians and administrators may rest assured that I am not asking for one penny more public money to be spent. But I am anxious to trouble their rest about policy. The general provision of training for the arts must be followed by a rethinking of degrees and qualifications in general and their relationship to the acqusition of a union card in these professions where the unions occupy a controlling position. There may be a case for the creation of a National Training Council for the Arts; but the qualities that Hercules had to call on in cleaning out the Augean stables will be nothing to those required by the director of a venture which will involve rigorous practical negotiations with the universities and a formidable group of well-established and deeply entrenched organizations. But I have never underrated the ability of our young people and I hope that future generations will be quick to clear up the mess that my own has left.

# 16 Some Final Thoughts

Writing this book has compelled me to think constantly not only about education and the arts in education, but also about the arts in society at large. It is a truism that we live in a world of increasingly rapid change: what impresses me as I take a panoptic view of society is the erosion of barriers, particularly in education and the arts. Mr Ivan Illich is quietly derided, when he is not being ignored, for his views on de-schooling.[126] Yet I am aware of a rapidly spreading disenchantment with conventional education. Here and there we hear of a free school where methods are being practised which leave those of the traditional progressive teacher far behind. Teachers and educationalists talk enthusiastically about their convictions and although they do not often say so, they constantly imply that the kind of work they advocate would not be possible in the curriculum structure of the typical comprehensive. There is considerable attention being given to under-privileged children, and expressions about their vulnerability and their being 'at risk' are commonly used, with the implication that there is little the country's maintained schools can provide that really touches their needs.

I consider the arts and I find the most extraordinary practices being advocated. The Professor of Visual Arts at the Open University expresses his complete lack of interest in the art object, and says that the only valid aspect of art lies in process.[127] A recent article in *The Guardian* describes the enormous sums of money being made by a distinguished Italian artist by selling bottles of human excreta, and John Weightman has given other vivid examples of anti-art.[128] The musicians are concerning themselves with instant music which may consist of any kind of manifestation involving the making of sound that can be practised by any number of people at the same time and which does not involve the need for one jot of skill, taste, talent, or preparation. Similar examples could be given from all the arts. The progressive movement is iconoclastic to the very last degree. De-schooling is supported by non-art and the anti-hero.

179

At the same time one may be justified, even in the most traditional terms, in not associating the final expression of art with a product or an object. Not only would this concept exclude the performing arts, but it is one that can be very easily disintegrated by philosophical arguments. That is why I lay a certain stress on the creation not of a work of art, but of the symbol, because the term provides a concept of considerable scope that includes both the process as well as the creation of an artefact while allowing scope for an initial reflex-stimulus that demands creative action.

I have nowhere in this book made much play of the relationship between the teaching of drama or art and the artistic values of our times. I believe that the teacher must work on certain traditional lines, such as those I have indicated, and then help young people, when they are interested in such things, to make the necessary correspondence. For it is not as if the artistic values of our times were assessable. The breakdown of traditional values is profound. Five hundred years of culture are being deliberately overthrown. And if the Marxists are correct in their analysis, it is a symptom of the collapse of our present society.

If this progressive movement is at least in part an over-reaction to the formality of traditional methods, the traditionalists and the academics have on their side over-reacted to the apparent anarchy of the progressives. Their attachment to assessment by examinations, to entry qualifications, to standards of achievement, to the end-product and the artefact becomes the greater as their position is undermined. As the progressives nurture the very slightest sign of creative achievement from the child, almost incomprehensibly written though it may be, the traditionalists emphasize the importance of spelling. As the progressives reject the relevance of middle-class culture for the inner-city child, the traditionalist insists on the purity of the text and adherence to the rules. As the one insists that the child should be able to speak, the other insists that this cannot excuse his inability to write. As one insists on the essential stability of society, another will accept, and even encourage, the opportunity for change.

I do not say any of this with a tear in my eye or anger in my heart; the emotion under which I write is one of profound anxiety. One of my reasons for writing this book has been to analyse my resentment at the indulgent self-expression that often goes by the name of creative or improvised drama. I have tried to argue that process is a part of creativity, but that it is in the nature of a human being to want to find the appropriate action for a certain stimulus. This action in art is a mode of behaviour that may take the form of the creation of an artefact. If we cut short the process at the stage of process we are saying that there is no biological or emotional necessity for action or behaviour, and therefore that there is no purpose to guide our process. We are not processing with an object, we are not like Odysseus seeking each his own Ithaca; we are moving like a knight in chess, forward and to the side and in any direction.

I have argued, honestly I hope, that there is a most subtle yet difficult relationship in all artistic creation between finding one's own voice and accepting or rejecting or accepting again traditional forms. The world is more likely to offer a living to the girl who can dance like Fonteyn than to the boy who tries to realize a vision in some almost inevitably underdeveloped experiment in inter-disciplinary activity. The world will pay for achievement, performance, skill: it is not interested in the process of self-discovery. But there are those for whom the challenge of society is as imperative as the acquisition of a skill.

So how does the teacher face this difficult situation? Dorothy Heathcote is persistently vocal about drama as education. And by education she means the necessity of helping a young person to face the truth about himself and about society, however tough, hard or unpleasant that may be. A noble ideal; and it enables her with justification to put drama at the top of her educational priorities. And it also enables her to remove drama, by implication, from the curriculum and even from the school. Her arguments, in her own context, are unassailable; and they go for many other teachers who look for the personal salvation of the child as the first responsibility of education and one that cannot be satisfactorily achieved in the structure of contemporary schooling. Yet this is to avoid the issue, the real problem, which is that we have to learn behaviour, we have to learn the meaning of creative activity, we have to learn what it is to use symbolic form, even if we don't employ so useful but perhaps pretentious an expression. In a world where 'anything goes', there is a danger that nothing will go satisfactorily.

I can hardly argue more strongly than I have already done by my belief in the importance of creativity and, to take the process further, where appropriate, the act of creation. But this is the moment where we stick; for however fiercely we argue about the importance of a young person finding his own dramatic language, the very process of embodying his feeling in some kind of dramatic action is an acceptance of inherited form, a gesture backwards to Aristotle. The problem, therefore, of the drama teacher is really the problem of every teacher and every artist, to use the symbolic forms that he has inherited, and that he has no option but to inherit, in as individual a way as possible. It is no imposition to consider the manner in which Aristotle has defined drama: it is a security, because it gives us a structure within which we can construct our own reality. Total freedom in any sense, spatial as much as political, is a will-o'-the-wisp, a delusion, partly because it is unattainable, partly because if it could be achieved we would not know how to behave. Total freedom in an abstract or even a philosophical sense is a vacuum, a nothing, a romantic fantasy. The teenager who is at risk is in need of help not because he has too little freedom but too much. He is in a sense like a newborn child who senses five times over a kaleidoscopic world of impressions that threaten and make no sense. So we give him drama as education to help him understand the nature of this threatening social reality; and we give him drama in education in order to ensure that he becomes familiar with the other symbolic forms, those of music, dancing, literature and language, and the visual arts.

The traditional teacher lets down the child by separating form of expression from the emotion it embodies. The progressive teacher lets down the child by failing to convince him of the excitement of embodying an emotion in an expressive form. We must make life easy for him, is the underlying attitude, we must make education acceptable. But life is not easy, the acquisition of any skill is a sweat, and education if it is worth anything at all means an effort. But there is a widespread assumption that children collapse under effort when the fact of the matter is that they have the right to skills they need for life. I have never in may life seen a single class of children being stretched too hard; but I have seen hundreds who were unhappily wasting their time through not being stretched at all.

It is the symbols of life that provide man with his greatest security. Yes, he needs a home, a roof over his head, clothing, and food. If he has them, fine; if he hasn't, he must play the world at its own game and set about acquiring them. Society is not opposed to other people earning a living even though it does not always seem to make much effort to help the weak. But a roof over one's head and a stomach full of food is of little help if one's own private inner self and personality are threadbare. What is encouraging is that one does not nourish the parched and starving personality by the acquisition of expensive goods but by helping him to face the reality with which we are surrounded. And that reality, through our sensual response, compels us to action, to behaviour; and action and behaviour in turn produce a reaction. The very form of that action and reaction can transform our fears, our sense of inadequacy, the belief in our spiritual poverty, into those strengthening and life-giving symbols of which I have been speaking and of which some of the most potent are recognizable as works of art. That is why I have argued in this book for a basic seminal approach to art as a part of all education. It must be for another book to expand the importance of art in society at large. For education, like Piaget's sensory-motor process, is not a chore that imposes itself on life between the ages of five and sixteen, but a part of the very fabric of living. If this is dismissed as the pious platitude of an enthusiast I would reply that it is the de-mythology of contemporary society that largely accounts for its poverty, as it is the de-emotionalizing of education that accounts for its irrelevance. For relevance in education is not what you teach or learn, but the way you teach or learn it. There is no subject on earth, as Jerome Bruner says, that cannot be made relevant to children; but this relevance depends on the emotional-intellectual quality that is embodied in that subject and the manner in which it is taught.

The reason why the performance of a Greek tragedy often gives us a feeling of such completion and satisfaction that we see no need for anyone ever to write another play is because the texture of its myth provides us with opportunities to intermesh on many different levels. This I believe to be the meaning of Aristotle's catharsis. Our emotional response is profound; but it does not finally preclude our own creative act. The suggestion that children should not be allowed or encouraged to come into contact with the work of the masters seems to me an outrage and quite as serious a deprivation as to prevent their contact with other aspects of contemporary culture. Homer, Aeschylus, Dante, and Shakespeare are not idols we must worship but the purveyors of the greatest and most life-giving symbols, and we deny or reject them at the possible loss of our own vitality. Life is not a matter of keeping alive. That is not difficult these days. What is essential is to keep alive fully. And that is becoming increasingly difficult. But it is by acting and dancing and painting and writing, and enjoying what others have acted and danced and painted and written that we can help ourselves and the children we teach to do so. I said at the beginning of this book that theory, theoria, the contemplation of the subject, plays a large part. And that is the justification of theory, to lay a basis for action.

# Bibliography and Notes

1. Analyses of the commercial theatre are to be found in Richard Findlater, *The Unholy Trade*, Gollancz, 1952 (critical). Ronald Hayman, *The Set-up*, Methuen, 1973 (descriptive).
2. Constantin Stanislavsky, *My Life in Art*, Bles, 1924.
3. R. W. Emerson, *Essays*. I have been unable to trace the context of this quotation although it has stuck in my mind for 40 years.
4. Tyrone Guthrie, 'A modern producer and the plays' in *The Living Shakespeare* ed. Robert Gittings, Heinemann, 1960.
5. Rudolf Bing, *5000 Nights at the Opera*, Hamish Hamilton, 1972.
6. The death of Caryl Jenner in 1973 was an irreparable loss to the children's theatre movement. She combined determination with total dedication.
7. The committee's recommendations were published in a small green booklet that has for long been out of print.
8. Gordon Vallins is one of the few people I have known with a streak of genuine originality.
9. Philip A. Coggin, *Theatre and Education*, Thames and Hudson, 1956. Still the only book to attempt a historical conspectus of the whole subject.
10. Notably by Allardyce Nicoll in *World Theatre*, Harrap, 1949.
11. Cauldwell Cook, *The Play Way*, Heinemann, 1914.
12. Mr Peckett, to whom renewed thanks, sent me his recollections for publication in a privately-printed periodical.
13. The Mummery and its recent use have been described by Christopher Parry, a former teacher at the Perse school, in *English through Drama*, Cambridge University Press, 1972.
14. Peter Slade, *Child Drama*, University of London Press, 1954. This book is of considerable historical interest but its subject-matter is clearly treated in the much shorter *An Introduction to Child Drama*, University of London Press, 1969.

15. A leading role in this development was played by Mr Leo Baker.
16. *Education: a Framework for Expansion*, HMSO, 1972. One of the most ironically entitled books of all time.
17. *Education Survey No. 2 – Drama*, HMSO, 1968.
18. Malcom Ross, *Arts and the Adolescent*, Eyre/Methuen, 1975.
19. Lynn McGregor, Maggie Tate, Ken Robinson, *Learning through Drama*, Heinemann, 1977.
20. As a result of merger (or amalgamation) the ATCDE has now become part of the National Association of Teachers in Further and Higher Education (NATFHE).
21. The quotation is from J. Stuart McClure (ed.), *Educational Documents*, Methuen, 1973.
22. Elizabeth Lawrence, *The Origins and Growth of Modern Education*, Pelican, 1970 provides an admirable survey.
23. Mr Schiller – I never heard him referred to or called by his Christian name – gathered round him a brilliant group of colleagues in the Inspectorate.
24. *Children and their Primary Schools* (The Plowden Report), HMSO, 1967.
25. James Boswell, *The Life of Samuel Johnson*, Everyman.
26. W. A. C. Steward and W. P. McCann, *The Educational Innovators*, Macmillan, 1967.
27. Black Papers, eds. C. B. Cox and R. E. Dyson, have appeared in 1969, 1970, 1975, and 1977 under various publishers. These were collections of essays attacking various aspects of 'progressive' education.
28. Neville Bennett, *Teaching Styles and Pupil Progress*, Open Books, 1976.
29. To be a member of Robin Tanner's club it was necessary to drink beer by the pint, wear hush puppy shoes and write in Italic script.
30. Neil Postman and Charles Weingartner, *Teaching as a Subversive Activity*, Penguin, 1969.
31. Sylvia Ashton-Warner, *Teacher*, Penguin, 1966.
32. Leila Berg, *Reading and Loving*, Routledge and Kegan Paul, 1977.
33. Ernst Cassirer, *An Essay on Man*, Yale University Press, 1970.
34. Jean Piaget, *Play, Dreams and Imitation*, Routledge and Kegan Paul, 1962. The book's original title, *La formation du symbole*, besides being less clumsy, gives a gloss on its real content. M. Piaget's books are not always easy to read, or even to understand, but they are of seminal importance in

the field of child psychology.

Nevertheless it is not what he has to say on the subject of the symbol that I find of primary importance, but his theory of sensory-motor perception, which seems to me to lie at the basis of the whole histrionic process.

For a summary of his complete work, see his own *The Psychology of the Child*, Routledge and Kegan Paul, 1966.

35. Charles Darwin, *The Expression of Emotion in Man and Animals* – many editions.
36. I refer, of course, to the works of Nahum Chomsky.
37. Richard Wilson, *The Miraculous Birth of Language*, Dent, 1937. I cannot overpraise the insights of this remarkable book.
38. Jean Piaget, *The Language and Thought of a Child*, Routledge and Kegan Paul, 1959.
39. L. S. Vygotsky, *Thought and Language*, M.I.T. Press, 1962.
40. S. T. Coleridge, *Biographia literaria* – many editions.
41. Jerome Bruner, *The Process of Education*, Oxford University Press, 1963.
42. Ernest Cassirer, *The Philosphy of Symbolic Form*, Yale University Press, 1970. Especially Volume 1. Susanne Langer reads like a love mag. after this tremendous ur-work.
43. Susanne Langer, *Philosophy in a New Key*, Harvard University Press, 1957. There is a vitality about this book which is missing from her later and fuller *Feeling and Form*, Routledge and Kegan Paul, 1963. Her more recent paperback, *Philosophical Sketches*, Mentor, 1964, is most readable.
44. John Macmurray, *Reason and Emotion*, Faber, 1935.
45. Plato, *Phaedo*. I must admit to blowing hot and cold about the Platonic dialogues, as questionable in their influence as Descartes, but also as the basis for the whole European philosophical tradition that runs through Boethius, Aquinas, Locke, Hume, Hegel, Marx, and Macmurray.
45. Bertrand Russell, *A History of Western Philosophy*, Allen and Unwin, 1946.
47. E. H. Gombrich, *Meditations on a Hobby-Horse*, Phaidon, 1963.
48. For many years John Huizinga's *Homo ludens*, Routledge and Kegan Paul, 1949, held the field; but its extravagant theories are not supportable. Far more acceptable is Susanna Miller, *The Psychology of Play*, Pelican, 1968.
49. Jerome Bruner (ed.), *Play*, Pelican, 1968.
50. Iona and Peter Opie, *Children's Games in Street and Playground*, Oxford University Press, 1969.

51. D. W. Winnicott, *Playing and Reality*, Tavistock, 1971.
52. C. R. Rogers, 'Towards a theory of creativity' in *Creativity*, ed. P. E. Vernon, Penguin Educational, 1970.
53. I saw this being done in an Oxfordshire school. It took four children three weeks. By the end there was nothing they did not know about the church.
54. Michael Tippett, *Moving into Aquarius*, Paladin, 1974.
55. John Paynter and Peter Aston, *Sound and Silence*, Cambridge University Press, 1970.
56. The Gulbenkian-sponsored enquiry into dance education, under the chairmanship of Peter Brinson, has revealed the difficulties of theorizing about dance.
57. This is discussed, along with definitions of drama, on pages 72–3.
58. R. G. Collingwood, *The Principles of Art*, Oxford University Press, 1960. This book has considerably influenced my thinking.
59. A. R. (Peter) Stone was headmaster of a Birmingham inner-city school immediately after the war and described what could be achieved by means of the arts in education in his far too little known *The Story of a School*, HMSO, 1950. In the same category might be mentioned Sybil Marshall, *An Experiment in Education*, Cambridge University Press, 1963, a book that was widely noticed on publication.
60. Ruth Foster was staff inspector for movement in the DES for many years and a leading member of the Schiller-Tanner group.
61. Tom Stabler has been responsible for the School Council's Drama 5–11 project.
62. *A Language for Life* (The Bullock report), HMSO, 1974.
63. *Half our Future* (The Newsom Report), HMSO, 1963.
64. Though making the timetable is an unenviable burden for the headmaster we are mercifully spared, in this country, the horror of the transatlantic professional curriculum manufacturer.
65. *Music in Schools*, Education pamphlet No. 22, HMSO, 1969.
66. Robert Witkin, *The Intelligence of Feeling*, Heinemann, 1974.
67. This thought is most movingly expressed by C. P. Cavafy, 'Ithaka' in *Four Greek Poets*, Penguin, 1966.
68. Aristotle, *About poetry* (The poetics). I do not favour any particular translation. The many commentaries are to be chosen, like food and clothes, according to taste. I note that John Dryden follows my own inclination in using a direct translation of Aristotle's title, *Peri poetikes*, about poetry.

69. Maurice Maeterlink – This essay is to be found in his collection *The Treasure of the Humble*, George Allen, 1907.

70. This is akin to the ritualization of aggression, a subject that has been discussed by Konrad Lorenz in *On Aggression*, Methuen, 1965.

71 Violet Spolin, *Improvisation for the Theatre*, Northwestern University Press, 1963.

72. Clive Barker, *Theatre Games*, Methuen, 1977.

73. John Hodgson and Ernest Richards, *Improvisation*, Eyre Methuen (2nd edition), 1974.

74. Brian Way, *Development Through Drama*, Longman, 1967.

75. E. M. Forster, from an essay 'The raison d'être of criticism in the arts' in *Two Cheers for Democracy*, Penguin, 1974.

76. E. H. Gombrich, *Art and Illusion*, Phaidon, 1972.

77. Liam Hudson, *Contrary Imaginations*, Penguin, 1967 and *Frames of Mind*, Penguin, 1970.

78. Liam Hudson, *The Cult of the Fact*, Cape, 1972.

79. Malcolm Ross, *Arts and the Adolescent*, Evans/Methuen, 1975.

80. Louis Jouvet, 'Avant-propos sur le métier de comédien' in *Réflexions du comédien*, Nouvelle Revue Critique, Paris, 1938. 'Le comédien est un instrumentaliste qui est son propre instrument'.

81. Or words to this effect spoken by Martha Graham in her commentary to her film *A Dancer's World*.

82. Gavin Bolton, 'Creative Drama as an Art Form' in *London Drama*, ILEA, Spring, 1977.

83. Jean Williams, 'Dance in Secondary Schools', 1976. Unpublished paper to the Gulbenkian Committee enquiring into Dance in Education.

84. Richard Courtney 'Goals in drama teaching' in *Drama Contact*, Ontario Institute for Studies in Education, 1977.

85. The books he refers to are Audrey Wethered, *Drama and Movement in Therapy*, Macdonald and Evans, 1973; Robert Witkin (66); Peter Slade (14); E. J. Burton, *Teaching English through Self-expression*, Evans, 1948; G. T. Jones, *Simulation and Business Decision*, Penguin, 1972; David Adland, *Group Drama*, Longman, 1964; Albert Hunt, *Hopes for Great Happenings*, Methuen, 1976.

86. See also Louis Arnaud Reid, *Meaning in the Arts*, Allen and Unwin, 1969. An important book deserving to be better known.

87. G. Bernard Shaw, *Our Theatre in the Nineties*, Constable, 1948.

88. This subject can be pursued in John Dryden's *Essay on*

*Dramatic Poesy* (1668) reprinted in *Dramatic Poesy*, Everyman, 1950.

89. Igor Stravinsky, *Conversations with Robert Craft*, Penguin, 1968.

90. William Archer, *Playmaking*, Chapman and Hall, 1930.

91. Virginia Woolf, from 'The Middlebrow' in *The Death of the Moth*, Hogarth Press, 1942.

92. For example, staging *Julius Caesar* in terms of Nazi Germany.

93. Young directors throughout Europe fear that the cult of social naturalism, which is not remarkably different from Soviet socialist realism, though artistically justified, may lead to a very grey theatre and so alienate potential audiences.

94. For example, the amateur theatricals in *Mansfield Park*, 'Impersonalization leads to the negation of self, thence to the weakening of the social fabric' – see Lionel Trilling, *Sincerity and Authenticity*, Oxford University Press, 1972.

95. Erwin Goffman, *Stigma*, Pelican, 1968. *The Presentation of Self in Everyday Life*, Pelican, 1972. *Relations in Public*, Pelican, 1972.

96. Constantin Stanislavsky, *An Actor Prepares*, Bles, 1936; *Building a Character*, Reinhardt and Evans, 1950.

97. A suggestion that derived from my friend Herbert Marshall in the course of working on an anthology of the actor's art.

98. Constantin Stanislavsky, *On the Art of the Stage*, trans. David Margarshack, Faber, 1967. Other useful books on acting in the Stanislavsky tradition are: Michael Chekhov, *To the Actor*, Harper, New York, 1952; Richard Boleslavsky, *Acting: the First Six Lessons*, Dobson, 1962.

99. The most accessible collection of Brecht's considerable writings on the theatre in John Willett's *Brecht on Theatre*, Methuen, 1964.

100. The whole subject is treated fully in *The Nature of Emotion* ed. Magda B. Arnold, Penguin, 1968.

101. Often quoted, difficult to find complete – and in English. For readers of French I recommend Diderot's *Writings on the Theatre*, edited by F. C. Green, Cambridge University Press, 1936.

102. May I again refer to Professor Goffman's books (95).

103. John Cowper Powys, *In Defence of Sensuality*, Gollancz, 1930.

104. Jean-Louis Barrault, *Theatre of Jean-Louis Barrault*, Barrie and Rockliff, 1961, includes an admirable essay on 'total theatre'. See also *Reflections on the Theatre*, Rockliff, 1951.

105. Emile Jacques-Dalcroze, *Rhythm, Music and Education*, Chatto and Windus, 1921.
106. Terence McLoughlin, *Music and Communication*, Faber, 1970. Particularly interesting on synaesthesia.
107. Ezra Pound, *The ABC of Reading*, Faber, 1961.
108. Education has been more to blame than the professional theatre for pressing the relationship.
109. Elizabeth and John Paynter, *The Dance and the Drum*, Universal Edition (London) Ltd, 1974.
110. *Drama and Music*, Building Bulletin no. 30, HMSO, 1963. The work of two brilliant architects, Mary and David Medd.
111. Gateforth Street, Marylebone.
112. Jean Piaget, *A Child's Concept of Space*, Routledge and Kegan Paul, 1956.
113. Lord Russell, *Adult education: a plan for development*, HMSO, 1973.
114. At Westfield and, shortly, Royal Holloway Colleges, in collaboration with the Central School of Speech and Drama.
115. *Going on the Stage*, published by the Gulbenkain Foundation, 98 Portland Place, London, W.1 in 1975.
116. The proliferation of degrees in drama, even if ostensibly academically based, is not without anxieties for an already overcrowded profession.
117. Natural hesitancy is due to the difficulty of striking a balance between the practical work required by the profession and the academic study that is prerequisite to a degree.
118. Jean Gimpel, *The Cult of Art*, Weidenfeld and Nicholson, 1969.
119. Arthur Koestler, *Act of Creation*, Hutchinson, 1964.
120. Two standard works on this important subject are: Laban, *The Mastery of Movement*, Macdonald and Evans, 1960; *Modern Educational Dance*, Macdonald and Evans, 1963.
121. For example, the Contemporary Ballet Trust which runs the London School of Contemporary Dance where the teaching, though based on the work of Martha Graham, is finding its own language.
122. The domination of the classics in the musical repertoire is curious and unusual. There is no such emphasis in the theatre.
123. I have been unable to trace the origin of this striking phrase in Coleridge's considerable works but it is quoted by

William Walsh in at least two of his essays on the poet.
124. See Arnold Hauser, *The Social History of Art*, Routledge and Kegan Paul, 1962, Volume 2.
125. *Actors in Schools*, HMSO, 1977.
126. Ivan Illich, *De-schooling Society*, Penguin, 1971.
127. Simon Nicholson, 'Art is not Yesterday' in *New Destinations*, Greater London Arts Association, 1976.
128. John Weightman, *The Concept of the Avant-Garde*, Alcove Press, 1973.
129. The LEA in turn claims a percentage of Mandatory grants from the DES.

# Index

192